LABOUR'S REVIVAL

LABOUR'S REVIVAL

THE MODERNISERS' MANIFESTO

PAUL RICHARDS

First published in Great Britain in 2010 by
Biteback Publishing Ltd
Westminster Tower
3 Albert Embankment
London
SE1 7SP

ISBN 978-1-84954-024-7

10 9 8 7 6 5 4 3 2 1

A CIP catalogue record for this book is available from the British Library.

Set in Constantia
Printed and bound in Great Britain by CPI Cox & Wyman, Reading, RG1 8EX

For Oliver and Alexander

'To appeal for more fraternity and less fratricide within the Labour movement needs a thick skin as well as a clear head. The Labour movement used to be proud of exhibiting within itself the very fraternity it wished to create in society as a whole, but of late brother seems more eager to revile brother, and sister sister, than to argue with opponents and to seek to persuade the vast majority of the unconvinced.'

Bernard Crick, *Political Quarterly* (1976)

'To my mind, there have always been two fundamental cleavages in socialist thought – the cleavage between revolutionaries and reformists, and the cleavage between centralisers and federalists.'

G. D. H. Cole

Contents

Acknowledgements

There are so many people who have shaped my outlook on politics over the years, through their speeches, articles, books and most importantly deeds, that to name any individuals would be invidious. I would like to thank Iain Dale, my publisher, for continuing to allow me to appear in print, and Jonathan Wadman and all the team at Biteback Publishing for their hard work. Thanks too to Sarah and my family for their forbearance. All the mistakes herein are my fault alone.

Preface: Climbing out of the wreckage

This is not a book about policy; it is too soon after Labour's defeat for one of those. It is a book about the values and approaches that must inform Labour's revival. Looking back over the period since the 2005 election, at the wasted opportunities and botched initiatives since 2007, and at the calamitous result of the 2010 generation election when a million people turned away from Labour, it is a book written more in sorrow than anger.

It is too early in Labour's current period of opposition to be dreaming up clever policy wheezes. If the Conservative-led government elected in 2010 survives for a full fixed term, Labour will not need an election manifesto until early 2015. In the coming half-decade, who knows how the world will have changed, what Conservative ministers and their Lib Dem allies will have done to our economy and public services. One way to understand the potential for change over the next five years is to remind ourselves that in 2005, five years before the publication of this book, Tony Blair had just won a significant election victory for Labour, few had even heard of Barack Obama, and Twitter was what budgerigars, not people, did.

The centrepiece of the Conservative-led government's programme is a reduction in public spending, which will have a far-reaching and almost certainly negative impact on the fabric of the nation. Once the fat has been cut from little-known quangos and pointless government programmes, the carving knife hits bone pretty fast. One of the first acts of the government was to abolish the child trust fund, which encourages the poorest families to create assets for their children. A recent act has been to abolish Building Schools for the Future, an initiative which would have refurbished 700 school buildings. It is hard to see where deficit reduction ends, and ideological cuts to the size of the state begin.

Public arguments about the size of the state, the limitations of government and the role of public expenditure will rage, just as they did in the 1980s. It is vital that the Labour Party, in formulating its response to the Tory and Lib Dem programmes of cuts, does not fall into the trap of resisting every reduction, as though public expenditure was a 'social good' in itself. In opposition, Labour must look like a government-in-waiting, not a placard-waving permanent protest.

Labour has yet to come to terms with the severity of its defeat in 2010, or the reasons for it. It will be easy to blame it on Gordon Brown's inability to present Labour's message in a compelling way, and his absence of appeal to swing voters, especially in the southern parts of England. Deborah Mattinson, a long-term pollster for the Labour Party and latterly polling adviser to Brown, told the audience at the launch of her book *Talking to a Brick Wall* in July 2010 that Labour would have won if it had replaced him with another leader before the election.

To blame Brown, his temper tantrums, violent behaviour and misjudgements over the 10p tax band, residency rights for Gurkhas, the expenses scandal, or Gillian Duffy's worries about eastern Europeans misses the point. It's just too easy to point the finger at the former PM. To do so avoids the deeper, more difficult questions. Without a proper audit of defeat, Labour cannot avoid making the same mistakes. Labour's leadership election in the summer of 2010 allowed some debate about past mistakes to take place. But the kind of debate in a leadership contest is inevitably coloured by candidates' desire to get elected, not the overall best interests of the Labour Party or the country. A new leader has the opportunity to conduct an audit of defeat. He or she has a mandate to make bold moves and big symbols, as Tony Blair did in 1994 with his decision to rewrite the Labour Party's aims and values contained in Clause IV, Part IV. The moment for radical repositioning doesn't last long.

History will probably judge Gordon Brown's leadership during the banking crisis favourably, or at least kindlier than the electorate. It is clear that Britain came very close to a collapse in its banking system, with the prospect of cash machines being taken out of service, people's savings and pensions vanishing, and actual money disappearing from the economy. Andrew Rawnsley reports a conversation with a broker who bought a flock of sheep from a local farmer, for fear of being unable to feed his family.[1] Social and economic chaos was narrowly averted, and Gordon Brown should take the lion's share of the credit. Most of us never knew how close we came to living through a kind of Weimar Republic-style meltdown.

The public don't use general elections as the opportunity to say 'thank you', especially if the thing for which they're being expected to show gratitude is something that didn't happen. Since the 1970s, avoiding an economic crisis is the *de minimus* public expectation from a British government. People expect to get paid at the end of the week, for there to be food in the shops and petrol in the pumps, for the lights to work at night, and for the bus to turn up in the morning. You can't win an election on the slogan 'We stopped it being much, much worse' (something the Liberal Democrats will soon learn).

The underlying fault was the Labour government's failure to be the agent of real change. In its dying months, Labour became conservative. It was the lack of a coherent, radical programme that cost Labour the election, not the personal failings of the leader. Labour didn't fail to get onto the 'front foot' because of the bombs, floods, and economic turmoil which bedevilled it. It was because it didn't have a front foot to get onto.

That does not mean that Labour lost because it wasn't 'socialist' enough, the traditional cry of Labour's left wing following defeat. People don't vote Conservative because the Labour Party is too right-wing. That was the response in 1979. A coalition of left-wing factions and pressure groups argued that the reason tens of thousands of skilled workers in the Midlands and south of England, living in council houses, voted for Margaret Thatcher's Conservatives was because the Labour Party had failed to nationalise more industries and abolish the House of Lords. These factions and currents won the party conference over to that point of view, elected a left-wing leader, and presented a manifesto to the public in 1983 which cost the Labour Party even more seats. There is no sign that today's Labour Party is going to 'lurch to the left' in the same manner, but every step away from the centre ground is a step further into opposition.

It does mean that in defeat we need to analyse how and why the government's reforming instincts were stifled, and the zeal to be the party of change, not the establishment, was snuffed out. Labour's ministers became tame and timid. They obsessed about their individual legacies, not how to win the election. The bickered with one another over angels on pinheads, and lost sight of the country's problems. Consider the inordinate amount of legislative time, and political capital, spent on winning votes in Parliament to establish an independent planning commission (IPC), about which the public had no knowledge or interest, and which the Conservative-led administration abolished within weeks of coming into office. To which burning social issue was the IPC the answer? Which socialist values did it embody?

Senior ministers plotted endlessly against Gordon Brown – ineffectually and ineptly, it turns out. They could see the problems up close, but they failed to act. They became too familiar with the trappings of power: the cars, the private offices and the grace-and-favour residencies. The opportunities were there for Labour to champion change, on reform of the welfare system, on reform of the MP's expenses system, on democratic accountability for MPs, on reform of social housing. One by one, the opportunities were lost. The Conservatives became the party of change; Labour the party of stasis. Labour politically calculated itself to death. That's why the Conservatives are in government, and Labour is not.

Rather than presenting a shopping list of policies, this book sets out a broad argument for the kind of party Labour must become, and the approach to politics and campaigning we must adopt. It looks afresh at Labour's sacred trinity of values – equality, liberty and community – and assesses their place in the modern world. Without such a restatement of values, all policy deliberation is sterile. It looks at how an emboldened approach to the decentralisation and devolution of power, not just from one group of politicians to another, but from the politicians to the people, can shape and inform Labour's recovery. In this task, the ideals of libertarian socialism, and the anti-big-state, 'localist' instincts of radicals and reformers are dusted down and brought into play. It will be a disaster for Labour if it is painted as the party of the big state, with higher taxes and more public spending, and the Tories are the party of the small state, with lower taxes and less public spending. That narrative puts Labour on the wrong side of the public's instincts, and will cost the party even more public support at the next election than it squandered at the last. Voters will swallow cuts to local services if the alternative is Labour's higher taxes.

Labour's Revival aims to show how Labour can reconnect with the five million people who have stopped supporting us since 1997, and how a new leader can build support amongst new voters, especially young people. It aims to paint a useful backcloth for Labour's new leader to begin leading the party into a period of renewal. The argument is simple: Labour must own the future, be the party of change and modernisation, and reach out to a new coalition of voters.

Labour's new political approach must be built on three pillars:

- Labour as the party of aspiration and fairness, with a more equal distribution of wealth, assets, and opportunities, so everyone can liberate their talents, and none is held back by where they live or who their parents are.

- Labour as the party of real democracy, passing power to the people, in real, practical ways that people can experience for themselves.
- Labour as the party of a mutual economy, where co-ops, mutuals and social enterprises become the norm not the exception, where the long-term interests of communities, consumers and the environment outweigh short-term profits and avarice.

A political journey

I joined the Labour Party in early 1987, after joining the National Organisation of Labour Students (NOLS) in my first term as an undergraduate at Salford University in 1986. Like Tony Blair (who had been the Labour candidate in a parliamentary by-election in my home constituency when I was fifteen) I was not born into the Labour Party; I chose it.

I grew up in Gerrards Cross, a small commuter town in south Buckinghamshire. Local families (although not mine) had swimming pools, stables and three cars. No wonder Tony Blair lost his deposit.

Like many young people in the 1980s, I was enraged by the treatment of the mining communities (although they were remote and alien) by the Thatcher government during the 1984–5 strike. Their treatment seemed so *unfair*. I missed out being active in the miners' strike (apart from throwing coins into buckets, and arguing for the miners' cause in the school playground).

I admired the miners' struggle from afar, which appeared noble, heroic and romantic in my teenage eyes, although it was obvious even then that Arthur Scargill was a disastrous tactician. About this time I picked up a copy at a church jumble sale of Alan Clark's *The Donkeys*, about the infantry in the First World War and their inept generals. 'Lions led by donkeys' seemed like an apt description of the miners and their union bosses.

I loved Red Wedge, the collective of musicians and bands which formed in the 1980s to support the Labour Party. When I first met my life-long friend Ruth Turner when she was seventeen (she was later Tony Blair's political secretary at 10 Downing Street) I identified her as a kindred spirit because of the Red Wedge badge on her jacket lapel. The lyrics of Billy Bragg, Paul Weller, the Communards and a band called the Housemartins, whose lyrics combined Jesus and Marx (later famous for an *a cappella* Christmas Number One), opened a world of socialist slogans and political anger. The Greater London Council (GLC) under Ken Livingstone opened London's parks to free concerts with political themes. I remember the Jobs for a Change festival in Battersea Park in 1985. At the last night of the GLC in 1986, before it was abolished, I first heard 'The Red Flag' sung by a thousand voices.

The 1980s was a time of great causes. I was treasurer of the university anti-apartheid society, raising money for the Anti-Apartheid Movement and the ANC (then branded as a terrorist organisation by the government). The campaign against the Conservative Party's Clause 28, which sought to demonise gay relationships, witnessed a wonderful outpouring of political activism and campaigning. We marched through the streets of Manchester and London in support of gay rights and equality. We joined the National Union of Students (NUS) demonstrations in support of free education. At a lobby of Parliament in 1988, the police used cavalry to disperse the crowd on the south side of Westminster Bridge. Being on the wrong end of charging police horses, with their riders waving batons like swords, was a truly frightening experience.

We threw eggs at visiting Tory politicians, including Margaret Thatcher. We chanted slogans and sang songs of protest. We sat down outside Downing Street to protest against homelessness, and outside the South African embassy to protest against apartheid. We knew the words to 'The Red Flag', 'Bandiera Rossa', 'The

Internationale' and 'Red Fly the Banners, O', which had scores of verses, each increasingly sectarian and outrageous.

At university I started to read books and pamphlets about politics voraciously. Few were on the official reading list – it was a personal journey of discovery. I was an inattentive student, despite my politics tutor David Marquand's best efforts. I came away with the 'activists' degree', a 2:2 (or 'Desmond'), which reflected the hours I had spent on political campaigning with the students' union, anti-apartheid society and Labour club rather than writing essays and revising.

The year the Berlin Wall came down, a friend gave me a copy of *The Future of Socialism* by Tony Crosland, which I read cover to cover in the Christmas holidays. I read Aneurin Bevan's *In Place of Fear*, which I admired for its lucidity and passion. *The Ragged Trousered Philanthropists* by Robert Tressell was another favourite. Giles Radice's book *Labour's Path to Power* captivated my imagination, with its explanation of revisionism, and how it could help Labour back to power.

There was a pamphlet by Bernard Crick and David Blunkett that set out an unofficial statement of Labour's aims and values, which seemed so much more practical than the doctrines of Marx, Engels and Trotsky to which anyone in student politics is subjected. It revealed a compassionate, non-doctrinaire ethical socialism, rooted in values which reflect, not clash with, decent British values. I have read Crick, and admired Blunkett, ever since.

I read *News from Nowhere* by William Morris, with its description of a society without conflict, hunger, exploitation or pollution. Above all, I read George Orwell. I had studied *Nineteen Eighty-Four* and *Animal Farm* at school in Amersham, taught in a way which managed to avoid any mention of Orwell being a socialist. At university I was introduced to his political works: *The Lion and the Unicorn, The Road to Wigan Pier, Homage to Catalonia*, and the great essays such as 'Politics and the English Language'. Orwell was and remains my literary hero.

Through this heady mix of campaigning, music, books and

magazines such as *Tribune, Marxism Today* and the *New Statesman*, I came to join the Labour Party, and became immersed in its debates and culture, and I've been there ever since, through the good times and the bad. Supporting the Labour Party is like following a football team – the sense of camaraderie, the ups and downs, the triumphs and disasters, the complaints about the manager. Your heart tells you 'this time', even when your head tells you otherwise.

People who are not much interested in politics, or view it with disdain, have trouble understanding what motivates people in political parties. Political activists combine the fanaticism of football fans, the dogged determination of Jehovah's Witnesses, the tribal loyalty of religious cults and the blind optimism of Pollyanna.

The party represents the extended family, with the disputes and fallings-out that mark all families. The annual trip to Brighton or Blackpool for conference is the family gathering. Within politics are the decent people, the caring people, the people who civilise our society and make our democracy work.

You have to get the balance right between a political life and time for family, friends and other pursuits. The socialist writer G. D. H. Cole was right when he wrote, 'I distrust a man for whom the socialist ideal, or any other ideal, looms so large as to cover the whole of life'.[2]

I hope I've succeeded. When I look at my two sons, I know there are more important things than Prime Minister's Questions (PMQs) and Fabian pamphlets.

Denis Healey once complained that Margaret Thatcher had no 'hinterland'. I was fortunate to visit Healey in his London flat in St George's Square a few years ago. It reflected his interests in music, art, photography and poetry. But there was no sign of a political life anywhere. He might have been a retired diplomat, publisher or travel writer. That seemed rather healthier than the politicians whose homes are crammed full with photographs, portraits and caricatures of themselves.

On moving to London to work at Labour Party headquarters,

another part of my political journey was undertaken. It was the recognition that for all the youthful excitement of going on demonstrations, and the intellectual stimulation of political arguments, it all counted for nothing if your party was in opposition. It was Neil Kinnock as leader who sought to focus minds on the task of winning. Kinnock combined the oratory of his hero, Aneurin Bevan, with the practical tasks of creating a party capable of winning elections. It was exciting to be young and in the audience for one of his great speeches. They lifted and soared. They aroused indignation and passion. They gave the party a sense of mission, without false hope. Like many people whose political education took place when Kinnock was leader of the Labour Party, the commonly held view of him as a 'windbag' or an ineffectual leader seems entirely unfair and unfounded.

The policy review process that Kinnock led after 1987, culminating in a new approach to markets, state ownership, disarmament and Europe, and a new statement of aims and values, was Labour's real 'Clause IV moment'. It was painstakingly hard work, and involved many people having to relinquish their cherished beliefs, not least Kinnock himself, who was a life-long CND member and oversaw the change from unilateral to multilateral disarmament. Being slow and deliberative, like slicing salami, it lacked the drama of Tony Blair's theatrical renunciation of Clause IV. But it laid firm foundations for Blair's modernisation of the Labour party in the 1990s.

In 1990 I was elected chair of the NOLS, largely thanks to the support of the previous chair Simon Buckby. In the lead-up to the 1992 election, we were charged with winning over the student vote for Labour, against the backcloth of the poll tax, the first Gulf War and the change from Thatcher to Major. During my year as NOLS chair, the nomination papers for Labour candidates for the NUS executive failed to be submitted on time. This meant that Labour would lose control of the NUS. Kinnock's office, and party managers Joyce Gould and Sally Morgan, took a dim view of this prospect, as did our candidate for president, Stephen Twigg. My solution was to run a lively campaign to 're-open nominations', which succeeded, and Labour stood, and won its places on the NUS executive. Several careers, and my reputation, were saved.

My first job was in Parliament, as researcher to a Labour frontbencher. Working in Parliament was a huge thrill and privilege. Our offices in the Norman Shaw Building were next to Frank Field's. He would dim the lights and play classical music. Around the corner was Peter Hain, always writing a book or pamphlet. In the corridors you could bump into Michael Foot or Tony Benn. At that time Labour's parliamentary researchers included future ministers such as James Purnell, Yvette Cooper, Pat McFadden and, in the Leader's Office, Charles Clarke. Parliament is an awe-inspiring place to work.

I was there during the last months of Margaret Thatcher's period as prime minister, the Conservative Party's leadership election, the build-up to the 1992 election, and Black Wednesday on 16 September 1992, when sterling was ejected from the exchange rate mechanism and the Conservative Party cost the country £3.3 billion trying to prop up the pound. One billion dollars of that went straight to the currency speculator George Soros. The Conservatives' opinion poll ratings nose-dived and didn't really recover until David Cameron (who was the special adviser at the Treasury during this period) became Tory leader.

My policy area was the environment. Following the Green Party's success in the 1989 European elections, the mainstream parties began to take the environment more seriously. In the 1992 election, though, it was the dog that failed to bark. Labour's press conference on the environment, scheduled for many months as part of the campaign 'grid', was cancelled at the last minute because of an almighty row over the party's election broadcast featuring a little girl needing treatment for her ears. The 'war of Jennifer's ear' which followed dominated the campaign for several days, and culminated in Kinnock's press officer blowing a gasket live on TV. It was not Labour's finest hour.

Labour's defeat in the 1992 general election was an important moment for those that went through it. The shadow Cabinet researchers were relocated to Labour HQ at Walworth Road, the legendary building close to Elephant & Castle in south London. It had a party shop selling books and political ephemera, a canteen and a library (run by a young Southwark councillor called John McTernan, later Tony Blair's political secretary), and it ran a fully staffed magazine.

It was entirely unsuited for a general election campaign. The 'economic secretariat' (shadow chancellor John Smith's team) were in the building next door. In the days before mobile phones and email, they may as well have been on the moon.

The shadow Cabinet researchers were in the basement. It was like working on a submarine. When they let us out on the day before polling day to help in a marginal seat, it was like being released from prison. I found myself blinking in the daylight outside Barons Court Tube station in west London with Jenny, the daughter of playwright Michael Frayn, wearing 'Time for Change' T-shirts and leafleting the commuters. That was when it dawned on me that Labour was going to lose. It's when they won't look you in the eye.

The lesson of defeat was that Labour hadn't changed enough, despite all the modernisation since the 1980s. This wasn't a lesson taken to heart by Labour's next leader, John Smith. His untimely death, and his innate decency, have ensured that Smith is fondly remembered in Labour Party circles. As a party press officer I met him several times. Once, before a TV interview, he showed me how to put on make-up. He was a good man. But there was a growing sense of frustration amongst young members, and others, that the project to modernise the Labour Party had stalled. There seemed to be a sense that 'one more heave' would be enough to win next time.

The Labour MP Nick Raynsford wrote an article for *Fabian Review* that summed up how many of us felt. It warned that Labour was 'sleepwalking into oblivion' by simply hoping the Tories would lose.

When John Smith died, there was a huge outpouring of grief. Outside Labour HQ a mountain of flowers grew, much like the ones, although not on the same scale, that sprang up when Princess Diana died three years later. It seemed obvious to modernisers like me that the replacement should be Tony Blair. Whatever the psychodrama that was being played out between Blair, Gordon Brown and Peter Mandelson behind the scenes, it was crushingly obvious to me and my friends that Blair was the modernising candidate, whose hard-headed work as shadow home secretary had brought us new respect and support, who spoke the language of Middle England, and who could win us an election. The Fabian Society's work on Labour's 'southern discomfort' showed that the party needed to win in the south. To elect another Scot as leader, after a Scot and before that a Welshman, seemed like idiocy. Whatever Gordon Brown's attributes in 1994, his ability to reach out to new voters across England was not one of them. It had to be Blair.

It would of course have been much better if Blair and Brown had both contested the Labour leadership in 1994. Blair would have won and Brown would have been defeated. Brown would have gone on to become chancellor in Blair's government, but perhaps without the burning sense of entitlement and destructive jealousy that soured the relationships at the top of government for a decade.

Such was the generosity of donors to Blair's election fund that a sizeable sum was left over after his victory. It allowed a new organisation and magazine to be established: Progress, still going strong fifteen years later. It was established by Derek Draper and run by Kate Dixon. The guest of honour at the launch party was James Callaghan. Progress was a platform for modernisers and a place for discussion. Writers over the years included Blair, Alan Milburn, Stephen Byers, Liam Byrne, Patricia Hewitt, Hazel Blears, Ruth Kelly, David Miliband, James Purnell and many others (including myself).

I was a candidate in the 1997 general election, taking on Teresa Gorman in the Essex seat of Billericay. It was a fantastic experience. The local party members were generous and welcoming. I commuted over from my home in Hammersmith every weekend and several evenings a week. We ran street stalls and organised petitions, knocked on doors, and spoke to people on the streets of Pitsea, Laindon, Wickford and Billericay. You could tell that the Conservatives' grip on the voters of Essex was slipping away.

Importantly, you could tell it was coming Labour's way. When Blair came to neighbouring Basildon to support Labour's Angela Smith, it was like Beatlemania. On the night, we won Basildon with a majority of over 13,000. In Billericay, where Labour had come third in 1992, we came second on a swing of over 17 per cent. Labour's share of the vote in 1992 had been 20 per cent. In 1997 it went up to 37 per cent. Teresa Gorman's majority collapsed, from 21,000 to 1,356. In the 2010 general election, in the new seat of Basildon & Billericay the Conservative majority was over 12,000 and Labour's share of the vote was back down to 23 per cent.

The experience of the campaign in 1997 taught me that Labour is capable of winning support in places like Billericay that can all too easily be dismissed as 'true blue' or 'too affluent'. It would be nice to think that they were voting for me, but of course they weren't. Individual candidates make only a marginal difference in elections, unless they've done something very very bad. The people of Essex were voting for a modernised Labour Party which shared their concerns and spoke their language. New Labour, with no apparent sense of irony, described itself in this period as 'the political wing of the British people'. Today that sounds absurd, but it makes the point that Labour had aligned its policies and campaigns with the best instincts of the voters.

On 1 May 1997, the British Labour Party, historically one of the least successful socialist parties in the world, won 419 seats to the Tories' 165, giving a Labour majority of 179. Aside from the stage-managed crowds waving Union Jacks in Downing Street, mostly comprising party staff and members of Mitcham & Morden Constituency Labour Party, there was a real, tangible enthusiasm for New Labour. People smiled at each other in the street. There was a genuine sense that something important had taken place.

For the first time in the party's history, people who hadn't voted Labour pretended that they had. There was a 'feelgood factor' in those weeks – Tony Blair in Downing Street, Britain winning the Eurovision Song Contest, and the sun shining.

The first Labour Cabinet, the product not of Blair's choosing but of the election of the shadow Cabinet the previous year, included John Prescott, Robin Cook, Jack Straw, Harriet Harman, David Blunkett and Gordon Brown. Although only a handful of the new government had any ministerial experience, they were a generation steeled by opposition and the long march to electoral success.

In so far as any politician has 'name recognition', the leading lights of the Cabinet – Blair, Brown, Prescott, Cook, Blunkett, Straw – were people the public knew and could recognise. It was a Parliamentary Labour Party that did not yet include Douglas Alexander, Ed Balls, Liam Byrne, David Miliband, Ed Miliband, Jon Cruddas or Andy Burnham, and a Parliament without George Osborne, David Cameron or Nick Clegg.

In June 2010 Tony Blair spoke at the Institute for Government and claimed one of his biggest regrets was wasting much of Labour's first term in power dismantling what the previous Tory government had done. I disagree with that analysis. I think the biggest mistake the Labour government made was its pledge to stick to the Conservatives' spending targets for the first three years in office, coupled with a reluctance to truly embrace public service reform. Much of the increase in public spending, and the important reforms such as academies and NHS foundation trusts, came in the second term. After 9/11 the second term was distorted and dominated by foreign affairs, not domestic reform.

The biggest changes came with the constitutional reforms – to the House of Lords and the devolved assemblies in Scotland, Wales and London. The peace process in Northern Ireland was also a vital part of Labour's work. A concerted effort to tackle poverty saw the introduction of tax credits and the national minimum wage, action to tackle rough sleeping, and investment in schools and hospitals.

But Labour's first term was broadly social democratic, without any attempt at transformation. A national minimum wage helps the very poorest workers, but it does not transform society. With a huge parliamentary majority, and a Conservative Party in utter disarray, Labour should have moved further and faster. Hindsight is a wonderful thing.

During Labour's period of office, I remained a loyal supporter, willing to speak up in public or on the airwaves for unpopular policies and help out at unwinnable by-elections. I spoke on public platforms in support of British and American military intervention in Iraq and Afghanistan, not because of some arcane reasoning by the attorney general, but because I wanted to see the Taliban and the Ba'ath Party eradicated, just as a previous generation had defeated the Nazis. Free from any burdens of office, I am able to say that my support was on the basis of regime change, so that Afghani girls could attend schools and Saddam Hussein could face trial for the massacre at Halabja. Socialists like Michael Foot, George Orwell and Tony Benn signed up to defeat the Nazis. Why shouldn't socialists want to see the overthrow of the despotic and murderous regimes of our own times?

I was elected to the Fabian Society executive and enjoyed a year of office as chair. I wrote a pamphlet on reforming the monarchy, *Long to Reign over Us?*, which made the headlines and was ritually denounced by the Labour leadership. I compiled and edited a book of Tony Blair's speeches and articles going back to the early 1980s, which he was later kind to enough to praise.

I was briefly editor of the Labour Party's members' magazine, but working under Labour's legendary general secretary, Margaret McDonagh, was a little like being the editor of a newspaper owned by Rupert Murdoch. In 2001 I was Labour's candidate in the Sussex constituency of Lewes, which includes Newhaven, Seaford and Polegate on the edges of Eastbourne. The local Lib Dem MP was not overly troubled by my efforts. His majority went from 1,300 to nearly 10,000. It was an enjoyable campaign, in the company of kind, decent people, largely conducted in pubs. *The Guardian* asked me to write a weekly campaign diary for their website, alongside candidates from the other parties. The young hopeful they asked to write the Conservative entries was David Cameron.

In the 2005 general election I assisted Labour minister Hazel Blears on her tour of marginal seats, from deepest Essex to the Isle of Anglesey. Hazel is a formidable campaigner, able to strike up a conversation or take on an argument with anyone, anywhere. There is more than a touch of Barbara Castle about her. She has an innate confidence in working people's ability to take control of their own lives, and a deep distrust of political elites and 'Fabian' types who want to 'help people'. In the 1950s, her family got a letter from the council telling them their house was being demolished as part of the 'slum clearances'. I would guess that her reluctance to place too much faith in bureaucracy stems from that time. She belongs to a Labour tradition of self-help and co-operation, and was never willing to compromise her politics to play silly Westminster games. She was subject to a great deal of patronising by parliamentary colleagues, especially the members of Labour's aristocracy.

Following the 2005 general election, sensing Labour's time was running out, I was keen to become a special adviser to the Labour government. Special advisers occupy a unique place within Whitehall. Each secretary of state can appoint two special advisers (or 'SPADs' in the jargon). Some ministers of state also have a SPAD if their workload demands it. SPADs are political advisers, not civil servants, but they work within Whitehall departments or at Number 10. They are appointed directly by the Cabinet minister. There are no job advertisements in the newspapers, interview panels or aptitude tests. When the secretary of state resigns or is sacked, the SPADs lose their jobs instantly and are asked to leave the building. When you arrive at the department with your minister the civil servants applaud you; when you leave they bundle you out of the building.

I was interviewed by Patricia Hewitt, the newly appointed health secretary, and was offered the job at the end of the interview. Patricia is one of the brainiest people I have ever met; I spent most my time working for her feeling inadequate. She had been Neil Kinnock's press secretary in the 1980s. She had championed reforms to give women a greater role in politics and society. She had a strong grasp on the complexities of health service reform, and drove forward necessary but unpopular policies. She was loyal and kind to her staff, and was decent and sincere. When she joined Geoff Hoon in an unsuccessful attempt to stir up opposition to Gordon Brown's leadership she ended her parliamentary career on a discordant note, which was a shame given her years of service.

The SPADs' office is in the Department of Health's HQ at Richmond House, opposite Downing Street. It's cramped and over-crowded, but the door leads directly into the secretary of state's office, which counts for a great deal in Whitehall. I worked with Liz Kendall (now an MP) and the health policy adviser Matthew Swindells, one of the architects of Labour's health policy. The Number 10 health adviser was Paul Corrigan, who I had known many years earlier at Walworth Road.

Tony Blair invested a great deal of political time and effort in the elaborate programme of reform in the health service. The policy, designed to bring down waiting lists by using private healthcare suppliers, and to give more power to patients through greater choice, was driven from Downing Street. Number 10's political office kept the pressure up on ministers for further, faster reform of the NHS and regular 'stocktakes' with the PM, to deliver real changes that would be felt by patients. Under a sustained assault from the Tories, and the health service unions and professional bodies, Patricia led a reform programme which yielded improvements in patient care. One of the key areas was tackling NHS organisations' financial deficits, which became a huge political issue. Some parts of the NHS had spent more than even their massively increased budgets had allowed for, and so were having to retrench. The opponents of Labour's plans, to the left and to the right, presented this to the public as 'cuts'. When Patricia addressed the Royal College of

Nursing (RCN) in April 2006, she was barracked and booed as part of an organised protest. The irony, with hindsight, is that this period will be seen as a golden age of NHS funding and performance as cuts and longer waiting lists become a reality.

The job of special adviser is relentless. There's no time for friends and family. Phone-calls come at all hours, from early dawn to midnight. At 10.00 p.m. on Saturday, SPADs would take part in a Number 10 conference call to discuss the political stories in the first editions of the Sunday papers, and the 'lines to take' for the Sunday political programmes. I have spent many Saturday evenings in a restaurant car park or hallway of someone's house with the phone to my ear during a party or dinner.

The flipside of the job is that you are often in the room when important issues are discussed or decisions taken. At health, the SPADs formed part of a move within government to harden up Labour's anti-smoking policy. It culminated in the ban on smoking in public places, which has already been shown to have improved thousands of people's lives. I like to think that I had some small part in a process, ably led by the public health minister Caroline Flint, which will lead to longer lives for tens of thousands of ex-smokers.

All the SPADs were expected to attend a meeting on Friday lunchtime at which the political secretary (at this time John McTernan) would set out the political strategy for the days ahead. The advisers to Gordon Brown rarely, if ever, attended these Friday sessions. This was at the height of the so-called 'TB–GBs', the protracted war of attrition waged against Tony Blair by supporters of Gordon Brown. Brown's team was semi-detached from the rest of the government, waiting in the wings for the top jobs they felt they deserved. The thrill of walking down Downing Street, knocking on the door and entering the Tardis-like building never leaves you. It is like a football fan walking out onto their team's pitch, or a music fan joining their heroes on stage. Some weeks the Friday meeting would take place in the Cabinet Room, so we would sit around the table where the political dramas of the past 200 years had been played out. Against one wall is a library of books, each presented and signed by an outgoing member of the Cabinet. For a political book junkie, it is the ultimate collection.

In 2006, Tony Blair appointed Hazel Blears to the Cabinet as party chair, and I joined her as special adviser. My new colleague was Andy Bagnall, a legendary Labour organiser, who had recently lost his seat on Croydon Council thanks to Labour's disastrous local government election performance. The role of party chair, being appointed by the party leader rather than being elected, lacked legitimacy with party activists. In the absence of a government department, it was not respected within Cabinet. We toured the country in support of local Labour candidates and activists. Hazel won plaudits for her energy and commitment to Labour's cause, but it was an uphill struggle.

Hazel, along with five others, stood for the deputy leadership of the Labour Party in 2007 when John Prescott and Tony Blair stood down. The front-runner throughout was Alan Johnson. On the day, television news announced that he had won. The results were announced to a special Labour Party conference in Manchester. We had arranged a series of hand-signals with Caroline Flint, Hazel's campaign manager, who would know the result before it was announced. She signalled to Hazel's team sitting in the conference hall that Harriet Harman had won, for which the signal was a hand on the heart. I assumed Caroline had indigestion. We couldn't believe it. When the result was announced, Alan Johnson's SPAD, sitting in the row in front of us, was filmed exclaiming 'Oh f*ck'. Harman had won thanks to 'transfers' from Jon Cruddas's supporters after three other candidates (Hazel, Hilary Benn and Peter Hain) had been eliminated.

Gordon Brown appointed Hazel as secretary of state for communities and local government, her dream job. Andy and I went with her to Eland House in Victoria. It had been the Office of the Deputy Prime Minister under John Prescott, until he was stripped of many of his responsibilities following newspaper revelations about his affair with Tracey Temple, his diary secretary. We arrived to find that much important spade-work had been done by Hazel's predecessor, Ruth Kelly: there was a good set of officials, in the private office, in the press office and at the senior ranks of the department. The department ranged across wide areas – from the redevelopment of the Thames Gateway, to tackling Islamist extremism, to council housing, to major planning decisions. As I describe later, many of the radical suggestions and initiatives that Hazel brought to the government, especially to devolve power to councils and communities, were stymied by Number 10. It was frustrating for her and her advisers.

In one area above all Hazel showed real guts: tackling violent Islamist extremism. Within the Labour government there were differing views about how to deal with groups claiming to represent Britain's Muslim communities. Some wanted an 'open door' policy, with anyone, regardless of how odious their views on women, gays or parliamentary democracy, able to meet with government ministers. Others wanted to challenge these views and give a platform to the very many British Muslims who do not follow Islamist ideology.

Hazel created forums for young Muslims and women to engage with their government. She gave vocal support to moderate and mainstream Muslim voices, especially at the grass roots, and sought to isolate extremists and apologists for terrorism. This was important work which formed a key plank of Labour's counter-terrorism strategy, 'Contest', which the current government seems intent on scrapping. It also led to some titanic, and unresolved, rows between ministers about how to engage with Islamist organisations.

When the first email came to me on a Friday in May 2008 from the *Daily Telegraph* asking about the expenses and tax affairs of my boss, I had little clue that it was part of a scandal that would envelop the whole of the political world, end several careers and lead to Hazel's resignation from the Cabinet. Like many MPs and Cabinet ministers, Hazel was accused of 'flipping' the designation of her primary home to avoid paying capital gains tax (CGT).

Hazel Blears is the least materialistic or avaricious person I have ever met. She is also the most straightforward and plain-spoken (a trait that got her into political hot water from time to time). The idea that she would construct some cunning artifice to deliberately avoid a tax for which she was liable was preposterous. We checked with the tax office and they confirmed that she was not liable to pay any CGT; her tax affairs were in order and up to date. Then Gordon Brown made an intervention that falsely accused her of a misdemeanour, as he had done with Peter Watt, the Labour general secretary who had been forced to resign a few months earlier (and subsequently vindicated). The prime minister told his regular press conference (where the first few questioners had been primed by his spin doctors to ask about Hazel) that her behaviour was 'wholly unacceptable'. By singling her out from the pack, Brown made her position impossible. Why did he do it? It might have been that he overstepped the mark in an effort to look tough on expenses. It might have been an attempt to divert attention away from others in the Cabinet with dodgy expense and tax affairs. It might have been revenge for perceived political disloyalty.

For the next few weeks until her resignation, Hazel's life was hell. She was subject to the full media treatment: cameras in the front garden, neighbours' doors knocked on, her elderly relatives door-stepped. It felt like living in a pressure cooker. She was wrong to resign on the eve of local and European elections, and knew it instantly. Of course it made no difference whatsoever to the results of the election, which was a rout for Labour. I drafted her resignation letter, and saw her off from the back entrance of Eland House, past a scrum of cameras, and into the ministerial car for the last time. She was well on the way from Euston to Manchester when I got a call from the *Evening Standard* after an eagle-eyed and long-lensed photographer had noticed the tiny writing on her silver brooch 'Rocking the Boat' alongside a picture of the owl and the pussycat. It was a present from her husband. I don't think she wanted to rock the boat. I think she just wanted to get home to her beloved Salford.

As a special adviser during the change from Blair to Brown, I saw the triumphs and disasters of Labour's last term from a ringside seat. From the highs – the smoking ban – to the lows – the 10p tax debacle – I was fortunate to witness some of the machinations from inside the tent. I think that political observers think that inside government there exists a carefully worked-out plan that is slowly revealed to the outside world. My experience is of controlled chaos. Sometimes there's a plan, which seldom survives for long. More often there's just a series of spasms of activity, crisis management and rows between politicians. One of the tasks written into the special adviser job description is 'long-term policy-making'. At best long-term meant 'until the next election'. At worst it meant 'surviving to the end of the day'.

Under Blair, there was a frenetic burst of activity right up until the moment of his departure. Under Brown, there was one crisis after another, some external such as the collapse of the housing market, some home made such as the fiasco over 10p tax or the Gurkhas. I found my time working for a Labour government exhilarating, exhausting and at times infuriating. I also met and worked with some brilliant people with a strong sense of public service who wanted to create a better world. And I never forgot that there are scores of talented people who want to work as special advisers, and that I was very privileged to have had the opportunity. It is not a chance that the next generation of Labour activists are likely to have for many years.

We are all shaped by our experiences. In my twenty-five years in politics I have seen Labour rise and fall. I have lived through its greatest defeats and its greatest victories, and seen its most successful leaders and its least successful leaders up close. I maintain the view, shaped all those years ago when I joined the Labour Party, that politics is the answer to whatever problem you pose. There's a book called *In Defence of Politics* by a socialist academic, Bernard Crick, who pops up a lot in this book. *In Defence of Politics* makes the point that for all its flaws and faults, democratic politics is the tool and tactic of social progress.

The day-to-day conduct of politics, and the exercise of power, may be unedifying, disgusting even. But if the art of politics is married to the application of values, the result can be greater human happiness. At Tony Blair's last PMQ in the House of Commons, he said:

> Some may belittle politics but we who are engaged in it know that it is where people stand tall. Although I know that it has many harsh contentions, it is still the arena that sets the heart beating a little faster. If it is, on occasions, the place of low skulduggery, it is more often the place for the pursuit of noble causes.

That sums up my view: politics should be, and at times is, about the pursuit of noble causes. What follows is a personal view, a modernisers' manifesto, on how Labour can rise to prominence once again. You can't live through the fall of the Berlin Wall, the end of apartheid, peace in Northern Ireland and the election of Barack Obama without understanding the power of hope. All socialists should be optimists, because we believe that tomorrow can be better than today. A new generation is taking over in the Labour Party. With them comes new hope that the oldest of values can be enacted in the most modern of settings.

I've spent a quarter of a century attending meetings, knocking on doors, writing pamphlets, articles and speeches, and helping politicians both in power and in opposition. The great heroes of politics are not the famous names, but the activists and volunteers who make it all work. Without them, there is no democracy, no social progress.

Paul Richards

August 2010

Part One

1. All the way for this?
New Labour in office 2007–10

'Had she come all the way for this,
To part at last without a kiss?'

William Morris, 'The Haystack in the Floods' (1858)

Like the maiden in Morris's poem, Labour supporters have a right to feel disappointed by the party's final years in government. It was a period which saw Labour's position decline and authority leach from the government. Major planks of New Labour's reform programme, such as NHS reform, were slowed or halted. Initiatives on welfare reform, housing reform, and direct democracy were shelved. Schemes such as the Eco-town building programme were a victim of the collapse of the construction sector. The government was buffeted by events, most of which were handled deftly. But it was the victim of unforced errors, of both policy and presentation. Internal discipline all but broke down inside Parliament, and dozens of MPs announced that they would not be standing again. The scandal over expenses rocked the whole political establishment, but Labour, having more MPs, suffered disproportionately. The financial meltdown dominated the pre-election period. Labour's courageous, and correct, handling of the banking crisis was not translated into electoral support. The turning point was the disastrous miscalculation over whether to call an election in October 2007. After that, Labour's opinion rating never recovered, despite some claw-back as the election got nearer.

The curry house coup

Tony Blair announced in September 2006 that he would be leaving office the following year, at a school, flanked by Alan Johnson, with noisy demonstrating schoolchildren in the background. His departure date was earlier than he intended because of pressure put upon him by a group of Labour MPs who publicly demanded that he 'step aside' in a letter earlier in the month, and by the resignation from government of seven of the signatories (one minister and six parliamentary private secretaries).

There was immediately intense speculation about the true nature of these demands, the degree to which they were part of a co-ordinated plot to bring down the prime minister, and whether they were being co-ordinated by allies of Gordon Brown. Some of the letter signatories were traced back to a dinner at the Bilash restaurant in Wolverhampton in the West Midlands on 31 August. The *Express and Star* newspaper spoke to witnesses who remembered a group of seven, including Tom Watson and Siôn Simon (both of whom signed the restaurant's visitors book). The media dubbed the letter and resignations 'the curry house coup'. Then it emerged that Watson had visited the Scottish home of Gordon Brown. Watson told the *Express and Star*:

> I could not get into the hotel I wanted to go to, so I called Peter Snape (Mr Watson's predecessor as West Bromwich East MP) to ask if he could recommend any hotels up there from his golfing visits. He suggested the St Andrew's Bay Hotel, and as we had a present for little Fraser (the Browns' new baby), we decided to call in at

their home on the way. At no point did we discuss the 2001 intake's letter with the Chancellor. That would have been quite inappropriate. The conversation was about teaching Malachy to read, and how young Fraser was getting on.

Blair's people at Number 10 were in no doubt that it was a co-ordinated plot, nor were they in any uncertainty as to who was behind it. I spoke to Benjamin Wegg-Prosser, one of Blair's inner team, who was organising a counter-letter of support for the PM, on the day of the resignations. He made it clear to me that 'someone was trying to bring down the government'. Blair's autobiography, *A Journey*, records that 'I never had any doubt that Gordon did not merely know of it all but had organised it'. The *Daily Telegraph* reported that by the 2008 reshuffle Brown had rewarded most of the plotters with ministerial posts and other jobs.

We may have to wait a long time to know what conversations took place about the coup against Blair, and who knew what and when. We will probably never know the unvarnished truth, as nothing was written down, and recollections will dim with time. My personal view is that some very ambitious and highly political people behaved in an entirely political way. Unlike later plots against Brown, which lacked any guile or an agreed alternative candidate, the curry house plotters had a candidate in the wings and the prospect of their own advancement to spur them on.

I think some of the signatories regretted it with hindsight, especially when Brown led Labour into a terrible defeat. The result of the plot was that Blair brought forward the date of his departure from office by a few weeks, to 27 June 2007, but was made to look like he was being bundled from office. It was an unedifying spectacle. From that humiliating departure, Brown never recovered.

Gordon Brown's leadership election

After years of slick presentation under Tony Blair, Gordon Brown promised to be 'Not Flash, Just Gordon'. An early sign of the new approach was on Friday 11 May 2007 at the trendy Imagination Gallery in London, when Brown launched his leadership bid. The teleprompter screens, usually transparent to the audience, appeared opaque. Worse, the camera point was fixed so that the screens came between the camera and Brown. The result was that his face was totally obscured, ruining the live coverage of his speech for the television audience. It was a terrible start to the campaign.

To become a candidate for Labour leader, you must be nominated by fellow MPs. The threshold was forty-five names. Brown got over 300, substantially more than there are current Labour MPs. There was a tiny handful of refuseniks, including Charles Clarke and Siobhain McDonagh. Once Brown got enough MPs to ensure there were not enough left over for another candidate, he was the only nominated candidate, and therefore elected. From the left of the party Michael Meacher and John McDonnell tried to get enough nominations. Even when Meacher stood aside, McDonnell did not have anywhere near forty-five supporters.

There has been a debate ever since as to whether Brown should have faced a contest to be leader. The argument runs that the Labour Party should have been offered a choice, and candidates should have been tested in a six-week campaign with hustings and media scrutiny. You can't blame Brown, or his campaign manager, Jack Straw, for wanting to win outright. Brown enjoyed support from across the Parliamentary Labour Party (PLP), including Tony Blair and a raft of 'Blairite' ministers. It was a moment of rare unity. The alternative was to whip Brown supporters into nominating another candidate to create a false contest. This is what David Miliband did to ensure Diane Abbott appeared on the ballot paper in June 2010 in the leadership contest. It is also what John Smith did in the 1992 leadership election to ensure Bryan

Gould was nominated. Smith went on to win nine to one. Brown was the overwhelming choice of the MPs, and if it had come to an election, Brown would have won in the constituency and union sections too.

The first months

At just before 2 p.m. on 27 June 2007, Gordon Brown visited Buckingham Palace to be invited to form a government by the Queen. By 3 p.m. he was in Downing Street. There was no handover between the political staff who worked for Tony Blair and the ones coming in for Brown. One lot left, and the other lot arrived. Some of the outgoing team joked about removing the Gs and Bs from the Downing Street computer keyboards. One suggested leaving bags of something noxious in the cupboards.

Team Brown arrived with a supreme sense of entitlement and confidence to a largely non-vandalised 10 Downing Street. Outside their boss quoted his old school motto, 'I will do my utmost'.

Brown reshuffled the Labour Cabinet with a deftness that had always eluded Blair (some suggested the smoothness of the reshuffle was because unlike Blair, Brown didn't have Brown to contend with.) He awarded places in government to each of the six contenders in the deputy leadership; only Jon Cruddas, who had had a successful campaign, coming an unexpected third, refused a post as housing minister. The reshuffle was conducted from the prime minister's office behind the Speaker's chair in the House of Commons. The media were denied their usual vantage point at Downing Street to see the ministerial comings and goings, sackings and promotions.

Brown did not purge those ministers closely associated with his predecessor. David Miliband was made foreign secretary, Jacqui Smith went to the Home Office, and James Purnell was given culture, media and sport. Patricia Hewitt and Margaret Beckett left the government with little fuss. In each department, Brown's loyal supporters were given junior roles, to build a new cadre of future Brownite ministers (and, some suggested, to serve as 'commissars' in departments with Blairite secretaries of state).

In an eye-catching move Brown brought in the GOATS ('Government of All the Talents'), including CBI boss Digby Jones, heart surgeon Ara Darzi, Admiral Sir Adam West, and former United Nations deputy secretary general Sir Mark Malloch Brown. Gordon Brown even offered to make Lord Ashdown, the former Liberal Democrat leader, secretary of state for Northern Ireland.

The Governance of Britain

Jack Straw's reward for his successful running of the Brown leadership campaign was the first significant piece of government business, launched as a green paper within days of the new government, called *The Governance of Britain*. The document had four chapters, on:

- limiting the powers of the executive by moving certain royal prerogative powers to Parliament, reviewing the post of attorney general, looking again at the way in which ecclesiastical, judicial and public appointments are made and reassessing ministers' involvement in the honours system;
- making the executive more accountable through enhanced parliamentary scrutiny, boosting the profile of the regions within both government and Parliament, and reforming the operation of the Ministerial Code;
- reinvigorating our democracy through reform of Parliament (including House of Lords reform) and the electoral system, and improving direct democracy at both national and local level:
- focusing on the citizen and the state by carrying out a review of citizenship, developing a 'British statement of values' and

giving further consideration to a 'British Bill of Rights and Duties' and/or a written constitution.

It was a bold statement of reform. Unfortunately, little work had been done to prepare the ground for its publication. There was no coalition of support within the Cabinet for many of the proposals. For example home secretary Jacqui Smith was opposed to a British Bill of Rights and Duties because of the power it would hand to the judiciary.

The Labour Party has been notoriously split down the middle on reforming the electoral system for the House of Commons, despite commissioning the Plant report into reform in 1990, and promising a referendum in the 1997 election manifesto. That area of work went untouched until the election of 2010, when a referendum on the alternative vote system was promised. House of Lords reform remained unfinished, after a promising start. Attempts to bring in systems of direct democracy were stifled. Suggestions for elected local boards for health and policing were strangled at birth (only to reappear in the Coalition Government Agreement in May 2010). The radicalism of *The Governance of Britain* was blunted within months, and none of its major planks were enacted. It looks now like a colossal vanity project: the legislative equivalent of the Dome.

The significance of *The Governance of Britain* was that it implied something important: that the new government had a plan for what it wanted to do. The production, like a rabbit from a hat, of such far-reaching reforms suggested that the Brown Number 10 would be a power-house of new ideas. It hinted that there would be more to come. As a special adviser working for the government in this period, my expectation of a 'first 100 days' burst of government activity was shared by many of my colleagues, ministers and Labour MPs. We waited and waited, and nothing happened. Instead of strategic, planned activity by the new government, the void was filled with reactions to events.

An eventful summer

On 29 June 2007, two car bombs were discovered, by accident, in central London. One was planted outside Tiger Tiger, a nightclub on Haymarket, the other just off Trafalgar Square. Both were made from gas canisters, petrol and nails, and were triggered by a mobile phone. Had they exploded, hundreds of people would have been killed or injured. A another attack took place at Glasgow airport the following day. The attacks on London and Glasgow were the work of Islamist terrorists. Two men were arrested. One died from the fire he caused at Glasgow airport, the other was sentenced to thirty-two years in prison. On 30 June Gordon Brown convened Cobra, the UK's emergencies committee which brings together the emergency services, intelligence agencies, armed services, civil service and ministers. It is named after its original location, Cabinet Office Briefing Room A. It lies in the depths of the Cabinet Office, with a central table and big screens around the walls.

In June and July 2007 parts of the UK were hit by floods, which made many families homeless. English towns and cities including Gloucester, Cheltenham, Tewkesbury, Grantham, Louth, Mansfield, Oxford, Hull, Harrogate and parts of Sheffield were hit by floodwaters. The Atomic Weapons Establishment at Burghfield was put out of action for a year. David Cameron's constituency of Witney was flooded, at the same time as he was on a much-criticised visit to Rwanda. John Healey was appointed minister for floods, and toured the stricken areas. Brown convened Cobra again on 22 July, and announced £200 million more for flood defences by 2011. Some of this additional budget was put together by raiding departmental budgets, for example Communities and Local Government (CLG), by phoning the relevant Cabinet minister personally.

In early August a case of foot-and-mouth disease was discovered in Surrey and traced to the Institute for Animal Health, a government research lab in Pirbright. Again, Brown took charge, convening Cobra once more and breaking off from his family holiday in Dorset.

Brown announced a toughening-up of the laws on cannabis, and as a reflection of his Calvinism, a review of the super-casinos announced under Blair. Civic and community leaders in Manchester, where a super-casino had been promised to regenerate the eastern part of the city, were dismayed. Brown insisted that an alternative package of support be assembled. As the package developed, it seemed to become ever more fanciful, with promises of a David Beckham football academy, a business school run by *Dragons' Den* presenter Peter Jones, and the relocation of the Royal Opera House.

During these months Brown appeared to the nation as a prime minister in charge, taking control of the tiller during national crises and steering the ship to safety. His approval rating hit 48 per cent. On 27 July 2007, Labour's rating was at 41 per cent, against the Tories' 32 per cent, in the *Telegraph*/YouGov poll. This was the 'Brown bounce' that had been promised by a change of leadership. A decent 10-point lead would return Labour to power for a fourth term with a working majority. The Labour Party looked to its leader and saw a steady pair of hands. Increasingly, the Tory Party looked to Cameron and saw a liability.

A lack of respect

The problem for Labour in this period was that its reputation for sound handling of the nation's affairs was based on unpredictable events, not a strategic plan of reform and change. It wasn't a case of Labour's strategy being knocked off course by unforeseen events like bombs, floods and diseases. There was no strategy. The only tactic that seemed to be at play was to distance the new prime minister from the old one, with reversals over drug classification and casinos. The 'respect agenda' which Blair announced in 2005, whereby local communities were given extra powers and support to tackle anti-social behaviour, was dropped in late 2007. Louise Casey, the energetic and effective official in charge of the policy, was sidelined. *The Times* reported on 11 January 2008 that 'The dismantling of the whole Respect agenda took place quietly last year as Gordon Brown sought to distance his government from key policy areas of his predecessor'.[1]

Respect was a popular initiative. It connected politicians directly to the concerns of voters, especially those on tough estates. It empowered people to take on gangs, prostitutes and drug dealers. It made people on low incomes think twice about the old axiom that politics can't make a difference. It rewarded, through the 'Taking a Stand' awards, brave citizens who stood up to anti-social behaviour. It was scrapped because it was considered 'Blairite' but not replaced with anything as effective or resonant. I have no doubt that dismantling the 'respect agenda' cost the Labour Party votes from working-class voters at the 2010 election.

One or two presentational difficulties

The presentational disaster of the campaign launch, with the teleprompter obscuring the prime minister's face, was not the end of the presentational difficulties; it was only the beginning. It started with a face you couldn't see, and ended, in Rochdale, with a voice that shouldn't have been heard.

The media, and the right-wing blogs (especially the Guido Fawkes blog), started to highlight every presentational problem or error. It became the gift to a hostile media that kept on giving.

A YouTube video of Brown picking his nose whilst sitting on the front-bench went viral, and was seen by millions.

In May 2009 Brown was photographed in front of a swastika at Prendergast-Hilly Fields College in Lewisham, south-east London. The display was part of a project on the Second World War. The 'snappers' encouraged Brown to have his photo taken with the offending symbol in the background, and no-one stepped in to stop it.

In November 2009, *The Sun* ran a story about Jacqui Janes, the mother of Grenadier Guardsman Jamie Janes, who was killed in Afghanistan, receiving a handwritten letter from the PM which misspelled their names. Some government insiders considered that *The Sun* had over-stretched itself, and that Brown should be commended for writing personally to every service family to suffer a loss.

New advisers came and went with a brief of sharpening up the communications. Usually they fell foul of the inner circle around Brown. When Nick Stace, the PR supremo at the Consumers' Association, was brought in, he told me that he expected some resentment, even briefing to the press, from the old guard. What he didn't expect was that he would be attacked in phone briefings to journalists whilst he was still in the room. Stace resigned, and went to live in Australia. Stephen Carter was brought into Number 10 from a solid background in public relations. A presentation he gave to political staff not long after arriving showed the 'political positioning' of the party leaders as seen by focus groups. Clegg was a bunny rabbit, Cameron a rattlesnake, and Brown was seen as a grizzly bear.

The 'dividing lines' that Carter showed us in March 2008 were:

Us	*Them*
Leadership	Salesmanship
Opportunity	Privilege
Resilience	Recklessness
Experience	Youthfulness
Internationalism	Parochialism
Fairness	Selfishness

By September, Carter had left Number 10, and joined the government as a minister in the Lords.

Should presentation matter? In an ideal world, prime ministers would be judged on their ability to lead, to govern, to make the right calls, and the values systems that guide them. The trivial details shouldn't count for anything. Yet in an unforgiving 24-hour media environment, with a camera phone and link to YouTube in the hands of every other citizen, the modern politician has to be media savvy and wise to every potential pitfall. It's not an environment that would have suited Churchill or Lloyd George, who each had their quirks and peccadilloes. Gladstone spent his evenings attempting to 'save' prostitutes. Asquith's vice even gave us a new word: 'squiffy'.

Brown was the first prime minister in the age of Twitter, and would be the first to admit he didn't sit easily in it. In February 2010 Brown told *The Guardian*, 'Look, I'm not a PR executive. I'm not someone who automatically thinks that communications are my strongest card. I think I could have been far better at presenting my case.'

The election that wasn't

On Friday 5 October 2007 the usual Friday special advisers' meeting took place. Unusually it was in a formal room in the Cabinet Office, rather than one of the dining rooms at Number 10. There was no doubt in anyone's mind that a general election was about to be called. Gordon Brown's political secretary, Joe Irvin, made it clear that although no decision had been taken, one was about to be made, and that special advisers had to be ready. The talk was of downloading useful documents and data on memory sticks, because once the election was called, special advisers would be banished from government departments and reassigned to the party headquarters in Victoria Street in London.

Hundreds of people in politics have their own story about the 'election that wasn't'. From the Labour Party general secretary Peter Watt, who describes in his book the limousines circling around Parliament Square,[2] to the lorry driver who turned up on

Monday 8 October at party HQ with a load of desks and chairs for the extra election staff, to the sound engineer who was told to cancel his holiday to be ready to support the press conference on Monday, to the candidates who spent the weekend printing election addresses. At the party conference a week earlier, the talk had been of nothing else. Candidates were phoning their agents to arrange election launches. The Labour Party machine was cranked up. Adverts for new campaign staff were placed in newspapers. Special advisers were asked to work up sections for the manifesto. Hazel Blears and I had a meeting to discuss the communities and local government contribution to Labour's manifesto with Ed Miliband. I have the resulting drafts on a computer file somewhere.

On Saturday 6 October I went out campaigning in Putney with Labour's candidate, Stuart King. We were joined by a news crew from Channel Four, who were filming 'marginal' seats of the sort Labour might hope to take back from the Tories in an autumn election. The next day Gordon Brown stunned us all by announcing on *The Andrew Marr Show* that there would be no election, nor one the following year. I couldn't believe that Brown, a student of Labour history, would repeat the mistake made by James Callaghan in 1978, when he avoided an October election, despite making most people think he was going to call one, and instead going to the country in 1979 after the worst winter of industrial disputes anyone could remember.

This was Brown's equivalent to Black Wednesday, when the Tories threw away their reputation for economic management. Brown's strengths were supposedly as an astute political leader. What he lacked in Tony Blair's people skills and emotional intelligence, he made up for in strategic insight and deftness of touch. He was supposed to be good at politics. That reputation was irreparably damaged on Sunday 7 October 2007. The opinion polls nose-dived and never recovered. Within a week, the Conservatives were ahead in the polls by 10 points.

Labour's problem was compounded when Brown told reporters at a press conference that the opinion polls had had no bearing on his decision. This was plainly nonsense, and everyone knew it. A more deft response might have been to say, 'Of course the opinion polls matter. I'm not going to hold an election before I have to, if there's the prospect of a Tory government.' The actual reason given, to allow the British people to see what kind of leader Gordon Brown is, had most of us holding our heads in our hands. Those Brown aides who had been arguing most strongly for an autumn poll were blamed for the debacle and briefed against in the press. David Cameron struck home with his jibe in the Commons: 'He's the first leader to cancel an election because he thought he was going to win.'

The man charged with organising 'the election that wasn't', Peter Watt, put the final bill at £1.2 million pounds. Labour Party members' money down the drain, and an election dodged that Labour would almost certainly have won.

The elections that were

There was plenty of evidence of a significant fracturing in Labour's electoral coalition between 2007 and the general election. When real elections took place, voters across the country had their opportunity to pass verdict on the Labour government.

Early successes in Southall and Sedgefield
The Ealing Southall and Sedgefield parliamentary by-elections were held on the same day, 19 July 2007. In Sedgefield, Tony Blair's seat since 1983, Phil Wilson won with a majority reduced from 18,000 to just short of 7,000. The Conservatives were pushed from second to third place.

In Southall, Labour's candidate Virendra Sharma won, albeit with a majority half of the 2005 result. The Conservatives' campaign was a shambles. Their centrally imposed candidate, Tony Lit, split the local party when a photograph of him with Tony Blair at a Labour

Party fundraiser the previous month found its way into the press. The week after the by-election the polls showed Labour on 40 per cent, with the Tories on 33 per cent. The *Daily Telegraph* reported that 'Ed Miliband, the Cabinet Office minister, has started work on Labour's manifesto for the next general election. Mr Miliband began the task "actively" on Saturday, Downing Street sources told the BBC. The news is likely to increase speculation that the prime minister is thinking of calling an early election.'

Boris beats Ken in London

If you were to ask the question a few years ago which politician would have the largest personal mandate in the country, it is unlikely that the answer would have been Boris Johnson. Ken Livingstone gained more votes in 2008 than in 2004. But Boris won, with 1,168,738 first- and second-preference votes to Ken's 1,028,966. Johnson's team ran a sophisticated election machine, targeted at 329 of the capital's 625 wards. Work was put into the outer London boroughs, where the Tories have done better since the days of the GLC. Lynton Crosby, the right-wing Australian election strategist, was brought in to give the campaign focus. Johnson played on his celebrity and anti-politics persona.

Labour's campaign was conducted against the noise of the 10p tax row in the background. Livingstone was subject to a concerted campaign of vilification by the *Evening Standard* newspaper. His willingness to share platforms with hard-line Islamist preachers undermined key parts of his coalition. On the day, it all came down to turnout. Labour's vote held up. The Tories persuaded more people to vote for them.

On the same day, Labour suffered its worst local election results for forty years, coming third behind the Liberal Democrats, with a national share of the vote of 24 per cent. Labour lost 331 council seats from an already low base.

The loss of London was a body-blow to the Labour government. The mood amongst Labour politicians and advisers was angry in the aftermath, and the question of leadership was aggravated once again. The feeling was that if Labour could lose in London, a Labour city for over 100 years, with its historic associations with Herbert Morrison, Ernest Bevin and Clement Attlee, it could lose anywhere. In the elections that followed, that proved prophetic.

The 'toff strategy' fails in Crewe & Nantwich

The Crewe & Nantwich by-election was held on 22 May 2008, following the death of the veteran Labour MP Gwyneth Dunwoody. The Labour Party made a string of errors in the campaign. The first was to select Gwyneth Dunwoody's grieving daughter Tamsin as its candidate. Tamsin Dunwoody was a member of the Welsh Assembly until she lost her seat to the Conservatives. She was born in Devon, educated in London and Kent, and lived in Wales. She had no tangible connection to the constituency.

The second error was to attempt to portray the Conservative candidate, Edward Timpson, as a 'toff'. Timpson, a lawyer, belongs to the Timpson family which owns the successful chain of key cutters and shoe menders. To even the most blood-thirsty of class warriors, mending shoes and cutting keys is hardly exploiting the proletariat. Even John Prescott must get his heels fixed. Young people, including a member of Number 10 staff (subsequently photographed), wore top hats as a 'stunt' to highlight Timpson's supposed blue blood. The political backlash was deafening. It looked chippy and it drew attention to a lack of underlying political message.

When Dunwoody was revealed to have her own entry in *Burke's Peerage and Gentry* under her full name, Tamsin Dunwoody-Kneafsey, the 'toff' strategy fell to bits. There was a 17 per cent swing from Labour to Tory, and the Conservatives notched up their first by-election gain since 1982. Timpson retained the seat at the 2010 general election with a majority of over 6,000.

Henley: 1066 and all that

At the Henley by-election on 26 June 2008, caused by Boris

Johnson's resignation to take up the role of London mayor, Labour's vote collapsed. The party's candidate, Richard McKenzie, came fifth, behind the Greens and the British National Party, on an 11 per cent swing away from Labour. Only 1,066 people voted Labour, less than 5 per cent of the electorate. This was a truly terrible result for Labour. Although few doubted that the Tories would retain this safe seat, I was concerned at the time about the underlying current. In a private political note to Hazel Blears I suggested:

> In real elections, people who voted Labour are either switching or staying at home. In affluent, southern Henley, 6,800 people voted for the Labour Party in 2005. In the by-election this year it was 1,066. That means that nearly six out of seven people changed their minds about Labour in this southern seat between 2005 and 2008. This is how the south is thinking right now. They like Cameron because he is one of them. They don't like Gordon because he is foreign to them.

Haltemprice & Howden

Labour Party strategists rather spoiled the fun in the Haltemprice & Howden by-election on 10 July 2008 by not standing a candidate. The by-election was triggered by MP David Davis, trying to make a point about civil liberties. Twenty-five fringe candidates stood, including the National Front, David Icke and the Church of the Militant Elvis Party. On a 35 per cent turnout (the voters obviously thought it a waste of time) Davis won with 64 per cent of the vote.

The revolt in the heartlands: Glasgow East

Later the same month, there was a by-election which Labour took much more seriously. The majority for the victorious Scottish Nationalists on 24 July 2008 may have only been 365, but for Labour to lose in Glasgow East felt like a political earthquake.

The seat comprises tough estates, including Easterhouse, where 30 per cent of the working-age population is on unemployment or incapacity benefit, and nearly 40 per cent of children grow up in homes where there is no adult in work. Nearly 40 per cent of adults smoke, and on average there are twenty-five drug-related deaths a year. In parts of the constituency, male life expectancy is just fifty-four, lower than Gaza. Glasgow East was the third safest seat for Labour in Scotland.

Labour's leader in Scotland, Wendy Alexander, resigned days before the contest over false allegations and media reporting about financial donations. It appeared that Labour had some trouble finding a candidate for the seat. One potential candidate, George Ryan, failed to turn up to the selection meeting and then withdrew. *The Scotsman* then reported that at least two others had been offered the role as candidate. Labour lost on a massive swing to the SNP.

The weekend following the defeat the Labour Party went straight into its national policy forum at Warwick University, to formulate the manifesto. The main work of the forum was to thrash out policy positions with the trade unions, but the buzz around the event was whether Gordon Brown could survive as leader. The presence of David Miliband added to the intrigue.

Labour did not make the same mistake in the Glenrothes by-election in November 2008. The headteacher of Gordon Brown's old school was selected as the candidate, and Labour won the seat with a slightly increased majority.

The unnecessary by-election in Norwich

The Norwich North by-election was a by-product of the expenses scandal. Ian Gibson, the left-wing Labour MP for the seat, had sold his flat below market value to his daughter. He was referred to the 'star chamber', comprising members of the National Executive Committee, to judge if he had brought the party into disrepute, and should be endorsed as a Labour candidate. He had the backing of his local party. The 'star chamber' barred him from standing as a Labour candidate, and he resigned immediately, triggering a by-election.

The perception in Norwich was that Ian Gibson's 'crime' was that he sold a flat at below market value to help his daughter. So if he had sold it at a profit and pocketed the cash, like so many other Labour MPs, would he still be the MP for Norwich North? His treatment made the Labour Party look authoritarian and, worst of all, unfair.

Labour's high command seemed to write off Norwich North from the start. The party's 'get out the vote' teams on polling day were probably not encouraged by the story in *The Times* that morning that 'Gordon Brown has indicated that he does not believe that Labour will win today's by-election in Norwich North'. On the morning of the by-election, the Cabinet was meeting in Cardiff, a mere 272 miles away. Labour lost the seat to the Tories on a 16.5 per cent swing.

Number 10 attempted to dismiss the defeat as the electorate taking their revenge for the expenses scandal. But that didn't stack up, because the Labour candidate wasn't involved in the expenses scandal. Independent candidates such as Craig Murray failed to break through. Norwich North was not a 'weathervane' seat, which switches between Labour and Tories depending on who has formed a government at Westminster. It is a seat which has remained stubbornly Labour, apart from the years of the party's electoral collapse in the 1980s. In 1970, when Labour lost nationally, Norwich North returned a Labour MP with a majority of 6,696. In 1979, with Callaghan losing to Thatcher, Norwich North re-elected the ex-Labour Cabinet minister David Ennals with 50 per cent of the vote and a majority of 5,592. The Conservatives' Chloe Smith won the seat again in May 2010 with a majority of just under 4,000, and a 40 per cent share of the vote.

Labour wins in Glasgow

The last by-election of the parliament was held on 12 November 2009 in Glasgow North East, following the resignation of Speaker Michael Martin. Labour's Willie Bain won with a thumping 8,000 majority over the SNP. The Tories got just 1,075 votes, and the Liberal Democrats came sixth, with less than 500 votes.

The row over 10p tax

On the wall of the Labour Party chair's office in the House of Commons was a series of framed posters from the 2001 general election, with slogans demonstrating Labour achievements. One of them was 'Introduced 10p Tax Rate'. Sitting in that office as chancellor, Gordon Brown announced on 21 March 2007 that Labour was scrapping the 10p tax rate, I wondered if I should turn the poster to the wall. In his final Budget Brown announced he was axing this starting rate of taxation and slashing the basic rate of income tax from 22 per cent to 20 per cent. It was immediately calculated that more than five million low-income earners, including those with an income of less than £18,000, would be worse off. For Labour people, this was seen as a disaster. It had us scratching our heads – why was Gordon doing it?

On 1 April 2008, with Brown at Number 10 and Alistair Darling at Number 11, the new tax measures came into force. Backbench Labour MPs, in response to their constituents' concerns, furiously lobbied the government. At the beginning, they were told they were wrong, and that no-one would be worse off. At a meeting of the PLP on 21 April 2008, Brown rejected suggestions that the move would hurt poor people, and demanded that MPs showed him their constituents' pay slips to prove otherwise. Angela Smith (the Sheffield MP, not the Basildon MP of the same name) threatened to resign as a ministerial aide and had to be persuaded to stay by the PM. phoning from a visit to see George W. Bush in Washington. Frank Field MP tabled an amendment to the Finance Bill, which was swiftly signed by more than forty Labour MPs. Eventually, under pressure, the government conceded that those who lost out would be compensated. On 1 May, with the 10p tax row ringing in their ears, the voters delivered a crushing defeat to Labour at the local elections and in London.

The 10p tax debacle drew attention to a deep-seated problem within the Brown Downing Street. Firstly, when Field warned of problems down the track at the time of the Budget in 2007, he was dismissed as a troublemaker. The people around Brown seemed to view MPs through the prism of 'with us or against us'. It was like a tribe, surrounded by enemies. Field, a long-term critic of Brown, was plainly in the 'against us' camp, and so anything he said must be an attempt to undermine Brown. Then when MPs started to complain, the response was not to listen, but to tell them they were wrong. Even with mounting evidence to the contrary, Downing Street held the line that no-one would be worse off. It became a test of loyalty. Polly Toynbee, who had agitated for Blair to be replaced with Brown, wrote that the 10p tax fiasco caused 'inestimable harm'.[3] The point was that the row, the ill-feeling it generated within the Labour Party, and the impact on the poorest pockets and purses, was entirely self-inflicted. It was self-harm on a grand scale.

The narrowest of margins: forty-two days' detention

I have never witnessed a political operation like the one mounted to win the Commons vote on forty-two days' detention of terror suspects in June 2008. In the end, it was the votes of the Democratic Unionist Party (DUP) which gave the Labour government its majority of nine. Thirty-six Labour MPs rebelled against the three-line whip. Accusation flew around Westminster about deals, bribes and inducements of all kinds. The rumours were that the DUP had been offered extra financial grants for its constituencies. A handwritten letter from the chief whip, Geoff Hoon, to Keith Vaz MP found its way into the media. It suggested that Vaz would receive a 'suitable reward' for his 'help' with the vote. There was certainly a lot of arm-twisting and cajolery going on around Westminster.

Brown was right to press ahead with forty-two days' detention. Counter-terrorism was an issue that was at the front of his mind every day of his period of office. The security services kept him up to date with the number and manner of terror plots against the UK. In

December 2008 on a visit to Pakistan, Brown revealed that twenty plots against the UK had been planned in that country. He received immediate updates of British casualties in Iraq and Afghanistan, and dispatched handwritten letters to the families of dead soldiers. In an article in *The Times* Brown argued:

> Some have argued that I should drop or significantly water down the 42-day limit. But having considered carefully all the evidence and arguments, I believe that, with all these protections against arbitrary treatment in place, allowing up to 42 days' pre-charge detention in these exceptional terrorist cases is the right way to protect national security.[4]

It may have cost a great deal in political capital, and in the case of Northern Ireland actual capital, but the cost of backing down would have been much worse.

Ayo Gurkhali!

A full year before David Cameron and Nick Clegg formed a coalition government, they had worked together to humiliate and defeat the government in the House of Commons on the issue of the rights of Gurkhas to settle in the UK. In April 2009 Gordon Brown became the first prime minister since James Callaghan to lose the vote in an opposition day debate, further damaging the status of the government.

It could have been so different. Most British people have an enormous affection and respect for the Gurkha regiments. I can remember seeing Gurkha soldiers on the train between London and the army base in Beaconsfield in their spotless uniforms and shining brasses. Their role in the First and Second World Wars was the stuff of legend, but their decisive contribution in the Falklands War was recent, and very real. When their champion, Joanna

Lumley, daughter of a Gurkha officer and national treasure, wrote to Downing Street to point out the unfairness of Home Office rules which forbade veterans from living in the UK after their service to this country, a fleet-of-foot leader might have spotted a golden political opportunity. The rules could have been swiftly altered and Gurkhas invited to Downing Street. Imagine the photo-opportunities on the steps of Number 10.

Instead Lumley's letters were ignored and went unanswered. Her campaign was relentless, and ministers found themselves defending the indefensible, on orders from Downing Street. I was told at the time that the home secretary, Jacqui Smith, wanted to allow the Gurkhas a right to settle here but was overruled in a Cabinet committee. Because Cabinet committees are secret, I have no proof. In a straight PR scrap between winners of the Victoria Cross led by Joanna Lumley, and politicians from a record-breakingly unpopular government, who would your money be on?

I was furious with my party at the time, and respected the twenty-seven Labour MPs who voted with the Lib Dems and Tories to win the right of all Gurkhas to settle in the UK. It associated Labour with unfairness in the public's mind, and yet again it was self-inflicted damage.

'YouTube if you want to'

One of the jobs of the special adviser is to 'ghost-write' articles for their political boss, which then appear in the name of the politician. It's a common practice across the political parties. Toby Helm from *The Observer* approached me at the end of April 2009 to see if Hazel Blears would write a political comment piece. She agreed, and on Friday 1 May, following a painful trip to the dentist, I tapped out a piece and emailed it to her for her sign-off. Like all ghost-written pieces it reflected her views based on discussions in the office, and after some amendments, she signed it off. It is reproduced below in full.

'When Gordon Brown leads Labour into the next general election, our campaign must rest on three pillars: we need to fight on a platform of practical policy, not personalities; once we have a solid offer, we need to sell it in plain words, directly to the voters; and our campaigns, communications and policies need to show we are still in tune and in touch with people.

First, we must fight the election on policy. No government after 12 years in office can compete on slick presentation and clever soundbites; we can leave that to the Tories, who have an impressive spin operation and many admirers in the press.

This Labour government has the right policies, and the recession has brought this into sharp relief. While our efforts have been focused on saving the economy, jobs, businesses and homes, the Tories have had little to say. And when they do speak, they get it wrong. The idea that the answer to global recession is spending cuts and tax breaks for the most affluent is not shared anywhere else in the world. The recession has tilted public opinion throughout the developed economies towards the idea of active, interventionist governments.

But this meta-narrative needs to be supported by practical policies. The recession is not the excuse to row back on public-service reforms; it should be the catalyst for more decentralisation of power to citizens and communities, and more choice within public services for the people who use them. Getting NHS waiting lists down, improving school standards, tackling street gangs, reforming the welfare system to get people off benefits and into work – those issues haven't gone away because of the recession, and they need to be at the top of the government's agenda now.

The second pillar is effective campaigning and communications. Labour ministers have a collective responsibility for the government's lamentable failure to get our message across. All too often we announce new strategies or five-year plans, or launch new documents – often with colossal price tags attached – that are received by the public with incredulity at best and, at worst, with hostility. Whatever the problems of the recession, the answer is not more government documents or big speeches.

People want to look their politicians in the eyes and get their anger off their chests. We need a ministerial 'masochism strategy', where ministers engage directly and hear the anger first-hand. I'm not against new media. YouTube if you want to. But it's no substitute for knocking on doors or setting up a stall in the town centre.

Third, we need to have a relationship with the voters based on shared instincts and emotions. We need to start showing we understand the instincts, fears, hopes and emotions of the broad mass of British people. We approached the Gurkha issue purely rationally and were mown down by a wave of emotion in support of these brave, loyal fighters. We put ourselves on the wrong side of the British sense of fair play, and no political party can stay there for long without dire consequences. So we need to plug ourselves back into people's emotions and instincts and sound a little less ministerial and a little more human.

Labour's standing has taken a titanic battering in recent weeks. But there's still time for Labour to recover, because for all the swagger and arrogance David Cameron has still not sealed the deal with the public.'

Hazel was very keen to avoid it being seen as an attack on the prime minister, hence the opening line. She also was keen to share the responsibility for the 'battering' that Labour had had. It is hard to disagree with a word of the article in hindsight – the analysis is spot on, and had the advice been followed, Labour might still be in office.

At the time, though, it was taken as just such an attack, not least because journalists from *The Observer* released it to broadcast media at around 7 p.m. on the Saturday before publication. Some of the people around Brown judged others by their own standards, and saw plots in every corner.

The expenses scandal

From the inside, enduring the expenses scandal of 2009 felt like being under siege. Day after day, new revelations from the *Daily Telegraph* brought parliamentary reputations crashing down. MPs wandered around Westminster like the prisoners on death row. There was no joy in others' misfortune. The entire political class was under assault. One Conservative MP, Nadine Dorries, suggested that she 'feared a suicide' from amongst her parliamentary colleagues. The details of individual MPs' cases, from outright fraud to cunning accountancy, accumulated to a wave of anger amongst the public. It didn't matter that MPs had not broken any laws, rules or regulations, or that they had followed to the letter the advice from the House of Commons authorities, or their accountants, or Her Majesty's Revenue and Customs. 'I was within the rules' became as hollow a defence as 'I was only obeying orders'. Margaret Beckett was booed and barracked on the BBC's *Question Time* in Grimsby when she tried it in May 2009.

It is a rare moment when a Westminster issue becomes the subject of angry comment at the nation's water coolers and school gates. The lasting impression, only partially assuaged by the election of so many new, untainted MPs in 2010, is that Parliament is full of politicians who are in it for what they get for themselves, fiddling the hard-working taxpayer and living a life of luxury and perks. The detachment of the political class from the rest of society is at its most acute since the extension of the franchise in the late nineteenth century.

Gordon Brown's response was to devise a system of attendance allowances to replace expenses, and announce it on YouTube, without consultation. The other party leaders rejected the idea, and Brown's solution was stillborn. Both the idea of an attendance allowance, which reflects some of the worst practice in the House of Lords and the European Parliament, and the method of communicating it, via a medium which made the prime minister look ridiculous, were flawed. It also allowed David Cameron to appear in control of events, and in charge of his own party.

The degree of public alienation and anger could have been avoided. It could have been avoided, firstly, with an expenses system familiar to anyone working for a company, charity or public body: clear rules on what can and can't be claimed for, all claims backed up by genuine receipts, and a fundamental rule that expenses are there to replace out-of-pocket expenditure, not to provide an additional source of income. And anyone found breaking the rules would be subject to immediate sacking. Parliament has yet to introduce a proper system of expenses. The new Independent Parliamentary Standards Authority had a difficult start to its life with complaints from MPs that the system doesn't work, and the resignation of its chief executive in June 2010.

Secondly, the collapse in public trust in Parliament could have been avoided if members of the public had a mechanism for holding their MPs to account, through a system of 'recall'. All of the anger could have been channelled into democratic activity – petitioning, public meetings and by-elections – leaving our democracy stronger, and the public more, not less, engaged. A system of recall was proposed by Hazel Blears, and blocked by Gordon Brown.

Plots, coups and resignations

As soon as Labour's poll ratings went thought the floor in autumn 2007, murmurings began about the possibility of removing Gordon

Brown from the leadership. Recent events had shown that it was possible for a party to remove a leader considered to be an electoral liability and replace them with someone with more vote appeal. The Liberal Democrats got rid of Charles Kennedy, then Menzies Campbell, and ended up with Nick Clegg. The Conservatives replaced Iain Duncan Smith with David Cameron. The blueprint for Labour had been designed by Brown himself. The Labour Party, lacking in any practical constitutional means for removing a leader, was shown how co-ordinated resignations from government could force a sitting prime minister from office.

None of the grouplets of MPs who wanted to replace Brown ever stood any chance of success. Firstly, they lacked any strength in numbers. There were small groups of MPs willing to act in concert, for example the one including Joan Ryan, Siobhain McDonagh, Janet Anderson, David Cairns and others, who wrote letters demanding that ballot papers should be issued for a leadership contest in September 2008. The Downing Street tactic was to 'out' potential plotters by naming them to journalists, then demanding public demonstrations of loyalty. Those whose loyalty could not be offered were sacked. It was more *Goodfellas* than government.

Secondly, there was no obvious candidate. Unlike the plotters against Tony Blair, who had an obvious replacement in mind, the plotters against Brown were divided on who the replacement should be. Some longed for Alan Johnson to replace Brown; others wanted David Miliband. On 29 July 2008, the week after Labour's defeat in Glasgow East, Miliband wrote an article in *The Guardian* which ended with the words 'New Labour won three elections by offering real change, not just in policy but in the way we do politics. We must do so again. So let's stop feeling sorry for ourselves, enjoy a break, and then find the confidence to make our case afresh.' It felt at the time like a standard was being planted in the ground. But apart from an appearance on the Jeremy Vine show, nothing happened. MPs went on their holidays, and Downing Street planned its revenge.

It came at the Labour Party conference, when in his speech Brown said, 'It's no time for a novice.' On the surface it was an attack on the then untested David Cameron. But Damien McBride, the prime minister's communications adviser, told the broadcasters covering the speech to cut away to David Miliband, sitting on the front row in the audience, when the 'novice' line came up. This, coupled with the infamous photograph of Miliband with a banana, ensured that Brown's supremacy was assured, until the next time.

In June 2009, several ministers resigned from the government. Only James Purnell did so explicitly in protest against Brown's continuing leadership. He did it out of frustration, not because he thought anyone would follow him. Like Tony Benn, he left Parliament in order to spend more time in politics.

Of the others – Jacqui Smith, Hazel Blears, John Hutton and Caroline Flint – none was co-ordinated with one another, or with a single outcome in mind. Hutton seemed to want a quiet life. Flint was frustrated at being treated like 'window dressing'. One by one remaining ministers pledged their loyalty, and the threat, such as it was, passed. There was talk of email plots, and letters, and lists of names. Perennial critics such as Charles Clarke continued to voice their concerns. In January 2010 Patricia Hewitt and Geoff Hoon attempted to trigger a last-minute leadership ballot, but it fizzled and failed.

Brown, surrounded by loyal supporters, was always much safer than the media believed. The plotters were always more disorganised and disparate than the media (and Number 10) believed. Reporters from the *Mail on Sunday* believed it had unearthed a plot when they saw several women ministers entering Jacqui Smith's London home, which they had under surveillance. They dubbed the group the WAGs – Women Against Gordon. In reality it was just a regular 'girls' night in' which this group regularly took part in at each other's flats.

The PLP lacked the vicious instinct for self-preservation that the Tories have displayed many times. It was only natural that future leadership contenders like Ed Balls and David Miliband should have been 'on manoeuvres' during this period – sounding people out and weighing up the options. But there was never a serious threat. Perhaps the Labour Party is just too sentimental? Although the pollsters Philip Gould and Deborah Mattinson independently claim that Labour would have won the election with a different leader, it is doubtful that a party that had just gone through the mightiest assassination since Julius Caesar could present a united front to the voters a few weeks later. It didn't happen, so we'll never know.

The financial collapse

The defining issue of Brown's premiership was the financial crisis. It allowed him to draw on his long experience as chancellor, and to impose his authority on the government. A tangential affect of the global meltdown was that it kept Gordon Brown in office. Few Labour MPs would move against the prime minister as people were losing their businesses, homes and jobs. People who went to see him in Number 10 reported that Brown was in his element, taking control of the situation and making swift decisions. It was a time of incredible economic change: the run on Northern Rock, the collapse of the banks, the credit crunch and the trebling of oil prices.

The government's response in October 2008 was to establish the national economic council, a kind of economic war cabinet, to manage the crisis. It replaced the old Cabinet sub-committee which looked after economic affairs. Brown pressed ahead with a bold response to global meltdown. He nationalised Northern Rock, recapitalised the banks to the tune of £500 million, cut VAT to 15 per cent to boost consumer spending, then took controlling shares in the Royal Bank of Scotland and HBOS-Lloyds TSB to prevent their collapse. Not a single bank collapsed, and not a single penny was lost from anyone's savings or bank account.

The hottest ticket in town in April 2008 was for the G20 summit in London, with Barack Obama as the headlining act. It was Brown's finest hour as prime minister. I saw him at St Paul's Cathedral, with Australian PM Kevin Rudd, on the eve of the summit. He made a brilliant speech, which argued that 'the globalisation that has done so much to improve choice, driven down the cost of everything from computers to clothes and lifted millions out of poverty has also unleashed forces that have totally overwhelmed the old national rules and the systems of financial oversight'.

A huge amount of government time and effort was put into the event, and into persuading other countries to follow Britain's lead. It paid off. The world's richest nations pledged trillions in fiscal stimuli, and Britain looked to the world like the pace setter. The team at Number 10 imbued the G20 with a huge amount of hope. There was a conviction that it would allow the prime minister to show a positive side to the public, and show him to be a leader on the world stage. Unfortunately the public don't pay much attention to international summits, and by the time of the election it had been forgotten.

Summary

Gordon Brown's period as Labour prime minister was both a personal and a public tragedy. It was a personal tragedy because after wanting to be prime minister for so long, and pursuing the office so determinedly, it was clear within a few days that he seemed to be hating every minute of it. He was subjected to fierce and cruel attacks in the media and blogosphere. Rumours about ill-health and eccentric behaviour swirled around Westminster. The incident described in Andrew Rawnsley's book when the prime minister physically assaulted a member of his team was common knowledge amongst special advisers long before it appeared in print. In reality, we heard much worse.

Andrew Marr on his BBC show, on Sunday 3 October 2009, asked the PM if he was reliant on prescription drugs, reflecting a rumour doing the rounds on the internet that he was on medication.

The Tories, in full Flashman mode, attacked Brown for throwing mobile phones and mistreating his staff. After a year of Brown's tenure at Number 10, the Tories issued a dossier listing 'a year of gaffes, tragedy and farce' including photo-opportunities gone wrong, and quotes from unnamed Cabinet colleagues calling him 'mental'. It is impossible to imagine any other world leader getting the kind of humiliating treatment that was meted out to Gordon Brown. It was relentless, cruel and destabilising.

The commentariat and MPs might forgive bizarre behaviour and some presentational difficulties if there was a strong sense of forward momentum. There wasn't. It was quickly obvious that the years brooding in internal exile in the Treasury were not spent constructing a programme for government, just plotting to destabilise potential rivals and hasten the departure of the incumbent. On arrival at 10 Downing Street, it felt as though Brown didn't know what to do next.

The Brown administration was characterised by contradictions. The lofty aims of alleviating global poverty were undermined by hired political thugs proposing to smear political opponents. One of the best-read, most academically gifted prime ministers we've ever had was also capable of great rages and violence. He was the biographer of James Maxton, the Red Clydesider, who was willing to pander to the *Daily Mail*. He expected total loyalty, yet was prepared to throw people such as Peter Watt to the wolves.

In an era of psychobabble and celebrity disclosure, Brown refused to let his emotional side show in public. In July 2009, I wrote a piece for the Fabian Society referring to Brown's

> pure rationalism, his command of numbers and statistics, and his belief in the power of argument. It is lazy to attribute Brown's moral compass to being a son of the manse. Intellectually, he is a modern-day David Hume or

Adam Smith. He is an Enlightenment thinker in the age of emotion.[5]

In the Enlightenment, it was Reason that counted. In our touchy-feely world, people expect their leaders to emote.

How will history judge Gordon Brown? Strong government intervention to shore up the banking system will be seen as decisive and bold. If David Cameron governs for two terms, Brown will have the misfortune to be a prime minister with a short period in office wedged between two prime ministers each with a decade in the job. In the sweep of history, such a short period in office will be easily overlooked, and, like James Callaghan, history will note that Gordon Brown is a prime minister who never won an election.

2. The election campaign

'That was a disaster. Should never have put me with that
woman. Whose idea was that?'

Gordon Brown (2010)

If you seek a metaphor for Labour's 2010 general election campaign,
it is the moment on Friday 30 April that Omed Rashid lost control
of his green Volkswagen Golf after clipping a refuse truck at
Hockley Circus outside the New Bingley Hall conference centre in
Birmingham. Mr Rashid ploughed into a bus stop, causing his car a
great deal of damage, but escaping unhurt. The crash happened as
Peter Mandelson was speaking a few yards away at the press launch
of the last posters of Labour's campaign.

The posters were a series of slogans in child-like handwriting
urging people to vote Labour. They suggested that children would
want their parents to vote to secure their children's future. 'Vote
Labour for Us' and 'Don't Forget to Vote Labour, Mum' were two of
the slogans. To the untrained eye they merely looked amateurish.
Some people wondered, given the prime minister's notoriously
poor handwriting (caused by his partial blindness), whether he'd
written them himself.

Mandelson, flanked by Gordon Brown, Alistair Darling, Harriet
Harman, Andy Burnham and Yvette Cooper, paused momentarily
as the sound of screeching brakes and a loud crash could be heard.
Brown took a step back, but remained unflappable. The journalists

and camera-crews ran to the scene, and recorded with glee that Labour's poster launch had been a 'car crash' event. They couldn't believe their luck.

Ms Denny and the NHS

The metaphor is not simply that Labour's campaign was a car crash. After the speeches, health secretary Andy Burnham introduced Gordon Brown to a local woman, Jacqueline Denny, who had, the previous day, being given the all-clear for breast cancer by her local NHS. She had phoned Labour's West Midlands headquarters because she wanted to thank them for investing in cancer treatment. Ms Denny's story, her positive encounter with the prime minister and the wider message about Labour's policy to fast-track cancer patients was lost in the media coverage of Mr Rashid's written-off Golf.

The media had collectively decided that Labour was going to lose the election. The journalists following the Labour campaign were on the lookout for gaffes, banana skins, and examples of incompetence. Never mind the substance, the investment, the reform, the voters' lives improved. The car crash was just too good to ignore.

People not posters

By the time Labour entered the 2010 general election, no-one was listening to it any more. The party struggled to get its message to cut through to the public. It was hamstrung by a lack of funds and a lack of experienced personnel. Some campaign staff were still being recruited after the election had been called. For many, it was their first election campaign. They were like the eager young subalterns recruited by Kitchener, about to go over the top. Labour's battle-hardened veterans of 1997 were long gone.

The date of the election – 6 May – had been anticipated for two years. On 12 March 2008 Martin Kettle accurately predicted the date on the Guardian website.[1] He claims to have been the first to do so. For most of the following period, people in the political world had 6 May 2010 pencilled in. Gordon Brown announced the date of the election at 10.47 a.m. on 6 April, following the traditional audience with the Queen, and after an egg on toast for breakfast, calling it 'the least well-kept secret of recent years'. He travelled to Rochester in Kent, appearing in Morrisons, the first of several visits to supermarkets in the campaign. Labour's candidate Paul Clark lost the seat.

Labour's manifesto, *A Future Fair for All* (a title first used by the party at its 2003 conference), had a cover variously described as 'art nouveau', ripped off Tory posters from the 1920s, or Maoist.

It was authored by Ed Miliband (and a cast of thousands) and focused on the economy, especially green and digital industries, reform of public services, and revitalising the democratic system. It included pledges for a national care service for elderly people, more time off work for new fathers, a mechanism for recall of MPs, and a referendum on the alternative vote system for the House of Commons.

The launch on 12 April, at the new acute wing of the Queen Elizabeth hospital in Edgbaston, Birmingham, was accompanied by a cartoon which showed a family being offered a 'new industrial revolution' and 'an active democracy'. Peter Mandelson described it as 'Blair-plus', which caused some consternation amongst his colleagues and confused its author, who told the BBC, 'I don't know what that means.' The launch event was marred by the revelation that the young activist Ellie Gellard, chosen to introduce the prime minister, had called for him to resign after Labour's defeat in Glasgow East in 2008. She had written on her blog, The Stilettoed Socialist, 'Get your coat. Time's up.'

Brown's visits were built around appearances at places such as Glyndŵr University in Wrexham, Asda in Weymouth, Asda in

Telford, Asda in Colindale, Leamington Spa (with Ross Kemp), a steelworks in Sheffield, Yeadon Health Centre in Leeds, a mixed housing development in Burnt Oak, the Concourse shopping centre in Skelmersdale, the National Glass Centre in Sunderland, and of course Rochdale. It was a hyper-energetic leader's tour, criss-crossing the nation. Labour strategy was for Brown to focus on Sure Start centres, health centres, and other examples of Labour investment, and at the same time meet voters in shopping centres and supermarkets, at railway stations and in the street. There were no large-scale events for the faithful in the style of Neil Kinnock's Sheffield Rally in 1992. This was the 'canteen campaign', designed to introduce the prime minister to small groups of voters in their own communities.

Two of Brown's set-piece speeches stood out during the campaign. The first was at the Royal College of Nursing conference in Bournemouth on 26 April. Drawing on his own experience, he told the delegates, 'We feel like parents who have been in the presence of angels dressed in nurses' uniforms performing the most amazing works of mercy and care.' Brown was rewarded with a sustained and genuine standing ovation.

Brown's speech to Citizens UK, a community organising movement, at Methodist Central Hall in Westminster was hailed as the best of the general election. Punctuated by enthusiastic applause and cheering, Brown allied himself with the great progressive causes, from the abolition of slavery to the election of Barack Obama, and in a personal testimony told the crowd:

> He taught me, my father, that life was about more than self-interest, that work is about more than self-advancement, that service is about more than self-service, that happiness is about more than what you earn and own. My parents taught me the fundamental values of taking responsibility, doing your duty, being honest, looking out for others.

It was an oratorical *tour de force*, and for once Brown seemed utterly in his element, free from any artificial straitjacket, and speaking from his heart. Many Labour candidates, staring defeat in the face, wished that Brown had found his voice in time to save their seats. It was just three days before polling day.

Douglas Alexander MP, one of the three campaign supremos, declared that the campaign would be about 'word of mouth', which has the advantages of being trusted and cheap. Interviewed by *The Guardian* he said he had been in discussions with Barack Obama's team for over a year, and that 'their key campaigning insight in an age of cynicism about politicians is word of mouth. The Conservatives are fighting a broadcast election in a networked age. What we are going to offer is not a one-way communication, but one-to-one communication.'[2]

In a message emailed to party members he said, 'Members of social networks, whether that is the book club, the coffee morning, the sports and social clubs, or whether it's being online, each one of us has a role to play in communicating Labour's message.'

This was certainly the first election whereby those people on Facebook, Twitter, YouTube and other forms of social media could follow the election, spoof it and comment on it, purely online. But the election campaign itself, and its outcome, were not shaped by social media.

The trade union Unite funded a virtual 'phone-bank' which allowed supporters to go online and dial up potential Labour voters in eighty-four target seats. Unite's post-election analysis suggests that over 51,800 phone calls were made through the Unite phone-bank operation. In the top ten key seats over 219,000 direct mails were sent out and over 307,000 emails. In the most marginal seat of Hampstead & Kilburn, held by Labour with a majority of forty-two, over 18,000 direct mails were sent out and 19,000 emails, and with the phone-bank the party managed to reach almost 50 per cent of the constituency's Unite members, who numbered nearly 1,300. This type of campaigning, modelled on the United Steelworkers of

America's campaign in the USA, is effective because it empowers individual members to talk to others.

Posters not people

Labour's poster campaign was best forgotten. One poster featured David Cameron as Gene Hunt, from the hit BBC series *Ashes to Ashes*, with the slogan 'Don't let him take Britain back to the 1980s.'

The programme is a *Sweeney*-style cop show set in 1982, but with a time-travelling policewoman from the 2000s to highlight the differences in attitudes and culture. Gene Hunt is the anti-hero: tough, northern, not adverse to planting evidence or beating up suspects, the epitome of life before 'political correctness'. The point of Labour's poster was that David Cameron would be a throwback to the 1980s.

It failed on several levels. The obvious one was that to compare the somewhat effete Cameron with a rough-and-ready cop did him a favour. But beneath the surface was a failure to understand that for many millions of people the 1980s were not the time of bleak de-industrialisation and demonstrations that Labour activists remember. They were a time of economic boom, personal prosperity and a prime minister that they admired. For voters in their forties and fifties, the 1980s was the decade of their youth. They would love to be taken back to the 1980s.

It turned out that the poster was the work of a 24-year-old amateur called Jacob Quagliozzi, a Labour supporter from St Albans, who entered a competition organised by the party's advertising agency, Saatchi & Saatchi. It was launched by two brothers, both in the Cabinet, Ed and David Miliband, in Basildon.

The Tories were swift to launch their own take it online. 'Fire up the Quattro. It's time for change' adapted one of Gene Hunt's catchphrases. Underneath, in smaller writing, the poster read 'Idea donated by the Labour Party'. Cameron told the media: 'I think there will be thousands of people, millions of people, in the country who wish it was the 1980s and that police were out there feeling collars and nicking people instead of filling in forms.'

The Tories had learned fast the benefits of subverting and sabotaging their opponents' posters. In the first week of January 2010, the Tories launched a 1,000-poster raid on the UK, costing over half a million pounds. The original poster was a large headshot of David Cameron, with the slogan 'We can't go on like this. I'll cut the deficit, not the NHS'. In previous elections, if you wanted to deface a political poster you needed a ladder and a spray can, and you faced the possibility of arrest. By 2010, all you needed was a computer. Hundreds of spoof posters appeared on www.mydavidcameron.com, with slogans from 'Vote Conservative or I'll kill this kitten' to Cameron as Elvis with 'we can't go like this. With suspicious minds.' It was the best example of how new media, along with some creative citizens, can subvert the parties' official campaigns and invent new, funnier, more telling versions of posters and campaign slogans. The 2010 election saw the end of billboard advertising in British politics as a significant part of campaigns, although it is doubtful that they ever had much impact. From now on, campaign strategists will find more effective ways to spend their war-chests.

The television debates

The major innovation in the 2010 was not Twitter or YouTube but television. A mere half-century after the first presidential television debates in the USA, Britain got its first party leaders' debates, live, over three successive Thursday nights hosted by Sky, ITN and the BBC. The British political class has been debating whether to hold debates for decades. Part of the pre-election ritual is for the leader of the opposition to challenge the prime minister to a televised debate, and declare them a coward when they refuse. The received wisdom has been that challengers have nothing to lose from debates, whilst incumbents have everything to lose, and so refuse them. Labour leader Harold Wilson challenged Tory prime minister Alec Douglas Home to a debate in the 1964 general election, just four years after the famous Kennedy–Nixon debates in the USA. Douglas Home rejected the idea, saying 'You'll get a sort of *Top of the Pops* contest' and worrying that the best actor, with the best scriptwriter, would become prime minister. James Callaghan offered to debate Margaret Thatcher in 1979, but she shrewdly turned him down. He was the last PM, until Brown, to agree to take on his opponent live on TV.

It must have seemed like a good idea, with his party 15 points ahead of Labour, for Cameron to call for a debate. Perhaps he assumed Brown would simply say no. As the election got nearer, and the polls narrowed, it seemed more foolhardy. The biggest error made by the Conservative camp was to concede a space on the platform to Nick Clegg, leader of the Liberal Democrats. Cameron's appeal from 2007 to 2010 was built on not being Gordon Brown. It was quickly apparent in the first TV debate that Nick Clegg wasn't Gordon Brown either. Cameron had a serious competitor for the anti-government vote. Clegg's easy debating style, his addressing of audience members by name, and his technique of looking down the barrel of the camera to speak directly to the audience at home are all easily taught presentational devices. Cameron and Brown both attempted to make alliances with Clegg on points of argument. 'I agree with Nick' became the catchphrase, not just of the night, but of the rest of the campaign, with Lib Dem HQ commissioning posters and T-shirts with the slogan.

Because he was a relatively unknown figure, his appearance alongside Cameron and Brown brought him to attention of millions of people for the first time. The first debate, on ITV, was watched by 9.9 million viewers. The second, on Sky News, Sky 3 and also on the BBC News Channel, attracted four million viewers. The final debate, hosted by the BBC at the University of Birmingham was watched by 8.6 million people.

There was a yellow surge. The instant opinion polls conducted straight after the first debate was aired declared Nick Clegg the stand-out winner. Research by YouGov for *The Sun* rated Clegg 'most impressive' by 51 per cent, a lead over Cameron on 29 per cent and Brown on 19 per cent. A ComRes poll for ITV News also found that Clegg was rated as the winner by 43 per cent of the 4,032 viewers polled, nearly double Cameron's score of 26 per cent and Brown's 20 per cent.

It was, as the pundits said, a game-changing moment in the campaign.

Each event was accompanied by a 'spin room', a crowded space filled with journalists and camera crews mixing with spin doctors and politicians, each trying the shape the coverage of the debate and claim their guy had won. It was like 3 a.m. in the bar at the Grand Hotel Brighton, or the Metropole Blackpool during a party conference: packed, hot and filled with political hyperbole. Marina Hyde, for *The Guardian*, compared it to Mos Eisley spaceport in Star Wars: 'You will never find a more wretched hive of scum and villainy.'[3]

It is hard to imagine that British general elections will not have televised debates from now on, although in the US, after Kennedy–Nixon in 1960, it was fourteen years before the next one. No prime minister will be able to resist the pressure. At the next election, if Cameron and Clegg are still prime minister and deputy prime minister, the dynamic will be wholly different from 2010. A Labour opposition leader will be taking on two members of the government. The phrase 'I agree with Nick' is unlikely to pass their lips.

The person who gained the most of the television debates was Nick Clegg. The person who lost most was David Cameron. Only Gordon Brown, by starting out behind and staying there, did not confound anyone's expectations.

The Importance of Mrs Duffy

When Gillian Duffy was a child in the 1950s, her 'Red Flag'-singing father taught her three things that mattered: education, the NHS and caring for vulnerable people. In a life supporting the Labour Party, working for the Co-operative Society in Rochdale, and working with disabled children, she put that teaching into effect. As a retired widow, who intended to vote for Labour's Simon Danczuk in the Rochdale constituency, Mrs Duffy was the perfect person to meet the prime minister.

The television footage shows Mrs Duffy being led by the arm by Sue Nye, now Baroness Nye, the prime minister's long-standing aide, although it is unclear who first brought Mrs Duffy to meet the PM and the candidate. The exchange between the Labour voter and the PM was typical – the kind of encounter experienced by every Labour candidate several times a day. Mrs Duffy asked about her personal taxes, the national debt, immigration from eastern Europe, and closed the conversation by congratulating the local education service, which was serving her grandchildren well. It was all caught on camera, with the sound provided from Sky News via a clip-on microphone, and 'pooled' to other broadcasters. Aides considered it a job well done.

What happened next is the stuff of election legends and Gordon Brown's nightmares. The clip-mic attached to Brown's lapel continued to record the sound of Brown complaining about the meeting with Mrs Duffy:

> BROWN: That was a disaster. Should never have put me with that woman. Whose idea was that?
> AIDE: I don't know, I didn't see.
> BROWN: Sue's, I think. Just ridiculous.
> AIDE: Not sure if they'll go with that one.
> BROWN: Oh they will.
> AIDE: What did she say?

BROWN: Everything. She's just this sort of bigoted woman
who said she used to be a Labour voter. Ridiculous.

Within minutes, the audio clip of this exchange in the car was being
broadcast, and not long after that it was being played to Mrs Duffy.
In 1997, one of the iconic moments of the election was the look
on Stephen Twigg's face when the returning officer announced
that he had beaten Michael Portillo in Enfield Southgate. In 2010,
the lasting image is Mrs Duffy's look of surprise and shock when
she heard for the first time a Labour prime minister calling her a
'bigoted woman'. It was heart-breaking to watch.

Brown instinctively understood the scale of the disaster. He
cancelled his engagements and returned to Rochdale to apologise
to Mrs Duffy in person. Mrs Duffy refused to join the prime minister
on the front step of her home for a reconciliatory photo-opportunity.

The incident was damaging to Labour for many reasons. Firstly,
it was another unforced error on the campaign trail, distracting
attention away from whatever message Labour hoped to sell
that morning. It added to the sense of a campaign out of control.
Secondly, it reflected badly on Gordon Brown himself. When he
heard the recording in the studio for Jeremy Vine's programme
on Radio 2, he visibly crumpled. Whether it is fair or not, it made
Brown sound like a man who said one thing in public and another
in the privacy of his car. His aide appeared afraid to contradict
his boss and tell the politician that the conversation was neither
'ridiculous' nor a 'disaster'. Often it is the job of aides to placate
and reassure politicians, especially in the fraught atmosphere of an
election, when nerves are frayed and sleep a luxury. The aide in the
car did not seek to reassure Brown, but simply said 'I don't know. I
didn't see'. It appeared as though Brown sought to 'blame Sue' for
the 'disaster'. After months of damaging speculation about Brown's
personal management style, this brief private conversation seemed
to reinforce all of the negativity.

The real damage was not caused by what Brown said to Mrs Duffy, but what Mrs Duffy was saying to Brown, and especially the points on eastern European immigration. Immigration from eastern Europe has transformed many parts of Britain. It is a legitimate concern for millions of people. Mrs Duffy did not use any xenophobic or racist slang. By asking the question, she was speaking for millions of her fellow citizens. To dismiss her as 'bigoted' was not just an irascible politician being rude about a Labour-voting grandmother, and getting caught; it spoke to a much wider belief that politicians are out of touch on the issue of immigration, and that voters are 'forbidden' from talking about it.

Later, in the middle of the Labour leadership campaign, Brown's closest ally, Ed Balls, said that the Mrs Duffy incident showed that Brown had failed to understand the potency of the immigration issue:

> On immigration, I said to him that you should be talking about immigration the last year and a half and that we were making a mistake by brushing it under the carpet. And to be honest, I think Gordon's answer to Mrs Duffy showed he'd not been having the conversation, because what she said was the kind of things being said by Labour supporters, and in some cases former Labour supporters over the last year and a half, which was: 'Look, we're not racist, and we support our EU membership and we know that immigration's important for the NHS, but look what it's doing to my community, to my child's job prospects, our housing queues.'[4]

The lasting legacy of the Mrs Duffy incident is that immigration is central to the debates about Labour's future. The leadership contenders each addressed it head on in the debates and hustings over the summer of 2010. In any future election, no Labour leader will make the mistake of sweeping such a salient concern under the carpet. Future Labour politicians will seek to ensure that the party and electorate never again become so dislocated on an issue.

Mrs Duffy has a place in the footnotes of political history. She only popped out for a loaf of bread.

A tale of two campaigns

Political strategists talk of the 'air war' (broadcasts, advertising, online) and the 'ground war' (canvassing, direct mail, street stalls etc.). In the 2010 election it was as though Labour was fighting two distinctly different elections. In the absence of financial support from the centre, Labour candidates raised their own funds and ran their own campaigns. On a good day, the national Labour campaign did very little damage to their prospects of election; on a bad day, it undermined local campaigning efforts.

The clear lesson from the campaign is that where local candidates were supported by active community-based campaigns, built on years of incumbency, with local issues at the fore, they stood a much better chance of winning.

In every election, mythologies are created. For Labour, success in Edgbaston is fast becoming the stuff of legend.

Caroline Badley, the local campaign organiser, makes no apology for modelling the campaign on Obama's bid for the White House, especially the use of community activists and volunteers, rather than relying on a dwindling band of Labour Party members. She wrote: 'This activist recruitment project started as the Obama campaign for the White House came to a successful close. Neither of us went over to the States but many people we knew had gone over; as they came back the excitement about the movement that Obama had built was palpable.'[5]

The campaign in Edgbaston drew up a 'local manifesto' based on extensive 'manifesto meetings' with local groups to determine the most important issues to key sections of the electorate. They used volunteers, especially young people, to recruit more volunteers, who were then trained, and empowered to go off and campaign.

This was consciously modelled on Obama's 'ground game' in the 2008 election, which, instead of treating volunteers as unpaid labour, gave them training and responsibility. In the Labour Party, activists are usually treated as drudges, given mountains of leaflets or addresses to canvass, in exchange for a biscuit and a cup of tea.

The combination of a local manifesto, a respected Labour candidate, Gisela Stuart, who made much of her capacity to 'think for myself', and a total separation of the dismal national campaign from the energetic local campaign (Stuart told *The Guardian* afterwards: 'I had no idea about what was going on. I didn't hear about "bigotgate" for about twelve hours, and then it was only because a voter told me'),[6] meant that Labour held a seat that few believed would not go Tory. The Edgbaston campaign was cited by Ed Miliband as he launched his leadership campaign as an example of the way ahead. His brother David pledged to fund training for 1,000 community volunteers during his leadership campaign.

In many constituencies, the Labour candidate was newly selected. In some seats, candidates were selected at the last minute, and had few local connections or roots, despite their own personal qualities and attributes. Several candidate selections were rocked by controversy and created bitter internal divisions.

In Liverpool Wavertree the former director of Labour Friends of Israel, Luciana Berger, was selected to replace Jane Kennedy. As a young Jewish woman from London, she immediately faced some local hostility, inside and outside the Labour Party. This despite being the great niece of Manny Shinwell, one of the Red Clydesiders of the 1920s, Labour MP and minister, and former chair of the Labour Party, which makes her minor Labour royalty. Peter Kilfoyle, the retiring MP for Liverpool Walton, called her a 'student politician' and highlighted what he called the 'growing influence' of Labour Friends of Israel. Berger did herself no favours in an interview when she admitted to not knowing who Bill Shankly is. Ricky Tomlinson, star of *The Royle Family* and a supporter of Militant in the 1980s, threatened to stand against her under the banner of the Socialist

Labour Party (SLP), the splinter organisation formed by Arthur Scargill. Tomlinson failed to be selected by the local branch of the SLP and did not stand. Luciana Berger was elected with an increased Labour majority of 7,167.

In Stoke-on-Trent Central the television historian and biographer of Friedrich Engels Tristram Hunt was selected in March 2010 from a shortlist which did not contain any candidates who lived in Stoke. His friendship with several people in Labour's high command, including Peter Mandelson (who attended the launch of Hunt's *The Frock-Coated Communist*), led to accusations that he had been 'parachuted' into the seat. The secretary of the local constituency Labour Party, Gary Elsby, a regular contributor to the comments section of political blogs, resigned in protest and stood in the election as an independent. Hunt was elected with 12,605 votes, a majority of 5,566. Gary Elsby came seventh, with 399 votes, behind UKIP and the BNP, lost his deposit, and was expelled from the Labour Party for standing against an official candidate.

Gloria de Piero was famous for being GMTV's political reporter, and was reputed to have been Tony Blair's 'favourite political reporter'. She resigned from GMTV to seek a Labour seat, and in March 2010 she was shortlisted in Ashfield, Derbyshire, where the sitting MP, Geoff Hoon, was standing down. She faced harsh criticism from within the local Labour Party for being based in London (although de Piero is from Bradford, the daughter of Italian immigrants). Many people in the Labour Party knew her as a Labour activist and campaigner before her television career. In a seat which had seen little community campaigning by the former MP, who did not live in the constituency, de Piero faced a tough fight. She won with a slender majority of 192, after a swing to the Lib Dems of 17.2 per cent.

Chris Leslie was the last Labour candidate to be selected. Leslie beat Tory grandee Marcus Fox in 1997, but lost the Shipley seat in 2005. He ran Gordon Brown's leadership campaign in 2007 (albeit against no opposition), and there might be a link between that, and his shortlisting in Nottingham East, a seat with which Leslie had no obvious prior affinity. Leslie won the selection on 14 April 2010 from a shortlist of nine, including three councillors, and Byron Taylor, from TULO, the trade union–Labour Party link organisation. Controversially, he was chosen by a 'special selections panel' of the Labour National Executive, rather than local party members. He was strongly supported behind the scenes by Ed Balls, whom Leslie nominated for the party leadership once he had won the seat. Hard-working and likeable, Leslie will without doubt win over the sceptics.

Summary

Neil Kinnock said that elections are won in years, not weeks. By the time the election was called, even the most brilliant, well-funded and imaginative Labour campaign could not have saved the Labour Party from defeat. A manifesto offering to scrap income tax, introduce ten new bank holidays and give free chocolate to every voter would still have failed to win them over. People were uncertain about the economy, not longer terrified by the Tories, and overwhelmingly bored with Labour. Labour struggled to get its message through a media which was mostly hostile, with the exception of the *Mirror*. The expenses scandal had exacerbated anger towards the political class as a whole, but did not cause Labour to be disproportionately punished, nor did independents standing on 'anti-sleaze' platforms perform well. In Salford, the candidate put up by local left-wing groups to unseat Hazel Blears came fifth and lost his deposit.

But the record of the government in the years preceding the election, and above all Labour's failure to be the party of exciting progressive change, contributed to one of its worst defeats. Gordon Brown's unpopularity, especially in the south of England, contributed to the defeat, but was not decisive. John Major in 1992, and Tony Blair in 2005, were not 'popular'; they were respected, and represented parties who the voters preferred to the alternative. In 1979, James Callaghan was more popular than Margaret Thatcher, but she still won the election, and the two after that.

Labour lost not because of a gaffe-prone campaign, nor because the Tories were warmly embraced. Labour lost because it had forgotten the lessons it learned in the 1990s, conceded too much of the centre ground to the Tories, lost authority on the economy, and lost touch on issues such as immigration and anti-social behaviour. It had ceased to be New Labour, and paid the price.

3. The election result:
surviving the car crash

> BLACK KNIGHT: 'Tis but a scratch.
> ARTHUR: A scratch? Your arm's off!
> BLACK KNIGHT: No, it isn't.
> ARTHUR: Well, what's that then?
> BLACK KNIGHT: I've had worse.
>
> *Monty Python and the Holy Grail* (1975)

On 6 May Labour suffered a terrible defeat, but many in the party felt that somehow it could have been worse. Douglas Alexander, Labour's election co-ordinator, wrote on Labour List a week after the election:

> And amidst the disappointment of this week we can all take heart from a central insight of this campaign – that committed and engaged volunteers, campaigners and candidates still do matter, and indeed were the decisive factor in so many of the seats that denied David Cameron the majority to which he has long felt he was entitled.

The polls pointed to a Conservative victory for much of the period leading up to polling day. David Cameron's election as leader of the Conservative Party on 6 December 2005 caused the first, small, Conservative opinion poll leads over Labour for a decade.

Throughout 2006, Labour and the Conservatives took it in turns to lead in the polls. Labour enjoyed a boost after Gordon Brown became leader in June 2007. But after November 2007, when Brown cancelled plans for a much-heralded general election, the Conservatives were consistently ahead in the opinion polls, with leads over Labour that would have given them overall majorities in the House of Commons.

On 7–8 May 2008, YouGov for *The Sun* gave the Tories a 26 per cent lead. Throughout 2008 and into early 2009, the Tories had double-digit leads over Labour. On 28–31 May 2009, IPSOS Mori showed a 22 per cent lead. For most of the Brown premiership, the Labour Party considered itself to be a dead man walking. Labour's defeat felt inevitable, and the attitude of ministers was to try to secure as much of their shopping list of policies as possible in the time left. It was like an episode of *Supermarket Sweep*. No-one in government seriously contemplated a fourth term in office. Only at the start of election year, and during the campaign itself, did the Tory lead get smaller, and the prospect of Cameron not winning outright become a serious prospect.

On 6 May, by denying the Conservatives an outright victory, many Labour campaigners felt a overwhelming sense, not of defeat, but of relief.

Added to this was the sense of satisfaction that the Liberal Democrats, despite their leader dominating the television election debates, had a terrible night. Of the twenty seats that were most susceptible to a Lib Dem victory, only three (Eastbourne, Wells and Solihull) were taken. Far from achieving a breakthrough, the Lib Dems actually lost five seats overall (they gained eight, but lost thirteen), and won just fifty-seven seats. The Liberal Democrats under Nick Clegg secured just 1 per cent more of the vote than they managed in 2005 under Charles Kennedy.

Labour's overarching narrative of the election – it stopped the Tories gaining a parliamentary majority – was repeated by the party's spokespeople on election night and in the weeks that followed. Through repetition, it became established as the story of what happened on the night. That message gave some comfort to Labour's campaigners and supporters, although not so much to the ninety-seven Labour candidates who stood in what had been Labour seats and saw them go Tory, Lib Dem or Green.

On election night, despite the mounting losses and high-profile casualties such as former home secretaries Jacqui Smith and Charles Clarke, there were some surprising successes for the Labour Party. In Birmingham Edgbaston, one of the Conservatives' top target seats, Gisela Stuart, the sitting Labour MP, would have lost her notional majority of 1,555 on a minuscule swing of 1.5 per cent. Yet on the night, thanks to a campaign fast becoming legendary (described in more detail on pages 48–9), Labour won with a majority of 1,274.

In Westminster North, Labour's Karen Buck, first elected in 1997, beat her Conservative challenger, Joanne Cash, with a majority of 2,216. Labour's notional majority in this seat was 2,120. Cash, a lawyer and Cameron A-lister, had resigned as the Conservative candidate three months before polling day after many months of internal scrapping between her and some members of the local Conservative Association. Much of the internecine feuding could be followed on Twitter. Following an intervention from David Cameron (who was at Eton with her husband, Octavius Black) and other party officials, Cash was reinstated as candidate. Her campaign was fatally destabilised, and she failed to win.

Another Conservative A-list candidate to fail to win was Shaun Bailey in Hammersmith, a seat with a notional Labour majority of 3,673. This seat, with new boundaries in 2010, contains huge contrasts in income and occupation, from the White City estates to leafy Ravenscourt Park and Brook Green. This part of west London is classic swing territory, and again Labour could take great satisfaction in seeing Andrew Slaughter returned as MP.

In Islington South & Finsbury, Labour's Emily Thornbury saw off a challenge from the Liberal Democrats. A notional Labour majority of 484 was turned into a real one of 3,569.

At the first meeting of the Fabian Society executive following the election, its chair, Sadiq Khan, was warmly applauded for retaining Tooting for Labour. Even a notional Labour majority here of 5,169 was not considered safe. A majority for Labour of 2,524 was judged a success.

In London and elsewhere on 6 May there were council elections as well as the general election. Labour did better than expected. In London, Labour controlled seventeen boroughs to the Tories' eleven. Labour won each of the directly elected mayoral elections in Hackney, Lewisham and Newham. In England and Wales 386 new Labour councillors were elected. Labour gained outright control of Liverpool, Coventry and Oxford city councils, Doncaster and St Helens metropolitan borough councils, Hartlepool and Hastings borough councils, and ten London boroughs: Brent, Camden, Ealing, Enfield, Harrow, Hounslow, Islington, Lewisham, Southwark and Waltham Forest.

In Barking & Dagenham Labour won every single seat on the council, defeating twelve BNP councillors and one Tory. The BNP suffered a severe thrashing in the parliamentary seats of Barking, where its leader, Nick Griffin, came third, and Stoke-on-Trent Central, where it had campaigned hard. Across the country, of the twenty-eight BNP councillors previously elected, twenty-six lost their seats. The anti-BNP campaign Hope Not Hate, bringing together the *Mirror* newspaper, trade unions, *Searchlight* magazine, Billy Bragg and anti-fascist campaigners, deserves credit for the BNP's defeat, alongside local Labour candidates and their supporters.

In the East End, Labour's Rushanara Ali defeated the Respect Party's candidate in Bethnal Green & Bow, won in 2005 by Respect's George Galloway. Next door in Poplar & Limehouse, Labour's Jim Fitzpatrick saw off Galloway, to keep an area, previously represented by Clement Attlee and George Lansbury, firmly Labour. In Rochdale, home to Mrs Duffy and location of the encounter that will haunt Gordon Brown forever, Simon Danczuk managed to beat the Lib Dem candidate and win the seat back for Labour.

There was even comfort to be taken from the result in Luton

South, where the television celebrity Esther Rantzen, running on an anti-sleaze ticket, was beaten by Labour's Gavin Shuker, a 28-year-old local church pastor. Rantzen came fourth and lost her deposit, despite an energetic campaign. It was a result of very little overall psephological significance, but sometimes the little things can give disproportionate pleasure.

Real pleasure should be taken in the result that eighty-one women Labour MPs were elected, more than in all the other parties put together.

Unlike in previous elections when a Labour government was removed from office, there were not any high-profile Cabinet casualties. Ed Balls scraped home with a slim majority of 1,101, defying a strong Tory attempt at 'decapitation', backed by Obama-style online fundraising. Other Cabinet ministers such as Jack Straw, Alistair Darling, John Denham and Ben Bradshaw, who might have been under threat in a Labour meltdown, kept their seats.

By the morning of 7 May Labour could survey the battlefield and conclude that although it had lost, no-one else had won. The negotiations to form a coalition government allowed Gordon Brown to remain in Downing Street, and Labour ministers remained ministers following the election, at least for a few extra hours.

The traditional brutal shock of a party being defeated, and being ejected from the citadels of power within a few hours, simply didn't take place. Death, when it came to the Labour government, was slow and suffocating, whereas normally it comes as a bullet to the back of the head. Add to this the unexpected pleasures of the thorough rout of the fascist BNP, the loss of seats for the Liberal Democrats, the failure of the anti-politics, celebrity and independent candidates to break through (Wyre Forest's independent MP, Richard Taylor, lost his seat to the Tories), local government and mayoral election successes, and the triumph, against the run of play, of some Labour candidates such as Gisela Stuart, Karen Buck, Ian Austin, Ed Balls and Simon Danczuk, and it painted a picture for Labour activists that in some way Labour had done well.

In the weeks following the election, thousands of people joined the Labour Party, many of them former Lib Dem supporters disgusted with their party forming a coalition with the Tories. Every constituency party in the country saw new members coming through on local membership lists, after years of decline. It added to the strange sense of optimism.

In May 2010, Labour was like a driver emerging unscathed from the wreckage of a terrible car crash: jubilant to have survived, glad to be still alive, and unlikely to be overly concerned with the cause of the accident.

The scale of Labour's defeat

The results of the 2010 election put Labour into a kind of torpor. In May and June 2010, as newly elected or newly returned Labour MPs congregated in Westminster, and as Labour activists and councillors met at conferences organised by Compass, Progress and the Fabian Society, the mood was defiant and optimistic. In Portcullis House as the new parliament met, new Labour MPs hugged, kissed, swapped campaign stories, debated the party leadership question, schemed over the election of select committee chairs, wrote their maiden speeches, and interviewed for new members of staff. There was a 'first day of school' atmosphere, with new members clutching induction packs and maps of the Houses of Parliament. When a defeated former MP appeared, with a box of belongings taken from a freshly vacated office, it was like the appearance of a ghost at the feast. Parliament belongs to the victors; if you're defeated you're not invited in.

In summer 2010, the Labour Party was a party in denial. This was partly explained by the Labour campaign co-ordinator, Douglas Alexander, at a Progress conference in May 2010 as being because, although Labour had slumped to a 1983-style share of the vote, the party had managed a 1992-style share of the seats. Because of this anomaly, it felt better than it was.

In 1983, Labour's heavy defeat was clear for all to see. Well, not quite all: Tony Benn called it a triumph because there had been 'eight million votes for socialism'. Labour won just 27.6 per cent of the vote, and 209 seats in the House of Commons, a net loss of 51.

In 1992, Labour gained forty-three seats, and lost one. The Tories gained three, but lost forty-four. There was a 2.2 per cent swing from the Conservatives to Labour. Labour won 271 seats. The Tory government, under John Major, had a majority of twenty-one. Labour won 34.4 per cent of the vote. This election, far from being seen as a defeat, was viewed as the platform for victory next time (and so it proved).

In 2010, the Labour Party won 258 parliamentary seats: far more than in 1983. But it had made a net loss of ninety-seven seats. Labour's share of the vote in 2010 was just 29 per cent, marginally ahead of the result achieved under Michael Foot (27.6 per cent). Foot led a party which won 8,456,934 votes in 1983. Under Gordon Brown, Labour won 8,609,527 votes (from a bigger electorate).

It is suggested that Brown spent some of this time considering how he would be judged against his predecessor Tony Blair, as is only natural. After May 2010, the leader Gordon Brown is most likely to be compared with, in terms of electoral performance, is not Blair but Foot.

Labour's defeat in 2010 can be compared with previous elections in terms of share of the vote, total number of votes, and number of seats in Parliament (see Table 1 overleaf.) We can see that although Labour lost over 940,000 voters between 2005 and 2010, it had already lost over a million between 2001 and 2005, and nearly five million since the landslide of 1997. Labour's decline began almost as soon as it had peaked in 1997. The period 2005–10 served to speed up the process.

On share of the vote, Labour's result in 2010 is truly abysmal. It compares badly with the *annus mirabilis* 1997, of course, but also with years of Labour's defeats such as 1979 and 1992. It is the party's second lowest share of the vote since 1918.

Table 1

General election	Labour share of vote	Total number of Labour votes	Labour seats	Winner
1979	36.9%	11,532,218	269	Conservatives
1983	27.6%	8,456,934	209	Conservatives
1987	30.8%	10,029,270	229	Conservatives
1992	34.4%	11,560,484	271	Conservatives
1997	43.2%	13,518,167	418	Labour
2001	40.7%	10,724,953	413	Labour
2005	35.2%	9,552,436	355	Labour
2010	29.0%	8,609,527	258	Con/Lib Dem

In 2010 young adults deserted the Labour Party. In 2005, Labour was 18 per cent ahead of the Tories amongst 25–34-year-olds. At this election, Labour was 5 per cent behind.

Although no Cabinet minister lost their seat, an army of junior ministers was rejected at the ballot box: armed forces minister Bill Rammell, health minister Mike O'Brien, care services minister Phil Hope, third sector minister Angela Smith, solicitor general Vera Baird, transport ministers Chris Mole and Paul Clark, justice minister Claire Ward, and minister for disabled people Jonathan Shaw.

The numbers demonstrate what every Labour campaigner and candidate knows from their conversations with the voters: huge numbers of people, most of whom voted Labour in the past, deserted the Labour Party in 2010. The Labour Party's electoral coalition, rebuilt in the 1990s after a decade in opposition, has now fractured, and is disintegrating fast.

Labour's retreat into the heartlands

To understand the nature of Labour's defeat, you have to understand what kinds of people turned away from Labour, and where they live. Labour did better in some regions than others, and with some social groups than others. There was no uniformity to the swing away from Labour.

For example, in six UK regions and nations, Labour had a lead over the Conservatives in 2010: Scotland, Wales, London, North East, North West and Yorkshire & the Humber. In Scotland, Labour's lead was 25.3 percentage points, with the Tories on just 16.7 per cent. In summer 2010, Labour enjoyed double-digit leads over the SNP ahead of the Scottish parliamentary elections in 2011. In the Northern region, Labour's share of the vote was 42.5 per cent, a 16.6 point lead over the Tories. In the North West Labour's lead was 10 points. Even in London, where the Tories won the mayoralty in 2008, Labour had a narrow 2.2 point lead in 2010. The Tories' attempts to win support in the North of England, and especially the great northern cities, did not bear fruit. In Scotland and Wales they seem to have given up altogether.

Labour held its own in Scotland, Wales, in the traditionally Labour towns and cities of the north of England, and in inner London. These are the Labour heartlands which return Labour MPs through thick and thin, in all but the most unusual of electoral circumstances: cities such as Liverpool, Manchester, Leeds, Hull, Sheffield, Salford, Bradford, Newcastle, Glasgow, Stoke-on-Trent, Nottingham, Birmingham and the East End of London; and towns such as Wigan, Barnsley, Blackburn, Halifax, Hartlepool, Easington and Bolsover. Urban areas which once knew mining, weaving, spinning, shipbuilding, steelworking and iron forging. The places that returned James Keir Hardie, Aneurin Bevan, Clement Attlee, Barbara Castle and Ernest Bevin to Parliament. The homes of the Independent Labour Party, the Co-operative Guilds, the National Union of Mineworkers and the Transport and General Workers' Union. These are the constituencies which voted Labour in 2010: heartland seats, rich in Labour history and tradition, rejuvenated and renewed thanks to Labour's investment, but which combined can never add up to a Labour majority in the House of Commons.

In other regions, Labour was all but annihilated.

If you leave London by way of the Labour constituency of Edmonton, in the north of the city, and travel due north, the next Labour seat you come to is Great Grimsby, on the banks of the Humber.

Labour's killing fields were below the line which stretches from the Wash to the Severn. Once Labour was the party of the commuter-belt and suburb, of the rural market town, and of the English seaside resort; no longer. Labour in Essex, Kent and Sussex was wiped off the map. The icons of New Labour's advance – Basildon, Brighton, Hastings, Hove, Crawley, Dover, Thanet, Gravesham and Dartford – have all been relinquished to Labour's opponents. Reading, Watford, Milton Keynes, Hemel Hempstead, St Albans and Welwyn Hatfield are all true blue. Apart from London, the South West, South East and East regions of England saw the biggest swings away from Labour, and the loss of the most seats.

Seventy per cent of the 938,000 votes Labour lost were in the east, south-east and south-west. Labour's share of the vote in the south east (outside London) fell by a third to just 16 per cent (roughly the same as the Conservatives' dismal share in Scotland). In the south west it was 15 per cent and in the east of England it was 20 per cent. Thirty Labour MPs lost their seats across these regions.

There are now just ten Labour MPs across the East, South East and South West regions of England. They have a combined majority of around 35,000 votes (see Table 2).

Labour's level of representation across these huge swathes of England is more like a small minority party, not one which forms governments. But even Labour's southern representation is skewed towards southern towns and cities, with six out of the ten seats in Southampton, Luton and Bristol. From Chichester across to Dover, and from the English Channel up to the banks of the river Thames, there are no Labour MPs at all.

This matters more than simply the absence of Labour MPs to make up a parliamentary majority. It matters more than just that

Table 2. Fire next time? Labour's MPs in the south, south-west and south-east

Constituency	MP	Majority
Southampton Itchen	John Denham	192
Plymouth Moor View	Alison Seabeck	1,588
Luton South	Gavin Shuker	2,329
Southampton Test	Alan Whitehead	2,413
Exeter	Ben Bradshaw	2,721
Bristol East	Kerry McCarthy	3,722
Oxford East	Andrew Smith	4,581
Bristol South	Dawn Primarolo	4,734
Slough	Fiona Mactaggart	5,523
Luton North	Kelvin Hopkins	7,520

millions of people in the south who need Labour representation are unlikely to have it.

The retreat into the Labour heartlands, and the forced evacuation from the southern parts of England, affects what kind of party Labour becomes. It affects the development of Labour's policies, and the presentation of them to the public.

It is of course a foolish caricature to suggest that voters in the north all work in factories, belong to trade unions and read the *Mirror*, whilst voters in the south work for small IT firms, belong to golf clubs and share David Cameron's politics. There are aspirant middle classes in every town and city; there are struggling families across the country. There is fantastic opulence in Cheshire, and terrible poverty on the English south coast.

The fact remains that the way issues are perceived, and people's sense of priority, are not the same throughout the UK. Wage levels, house prices, patterns of immigration, availability of school places, access to GPs, length of journeys to work, proximity of close family members: these things are different in Crawley than in Chorley.

The peril in Labour's retreat into its geographical heartlands is that it is replicated in a political retreat into its policy heartlands too. If Labour further surrenders issues such as tackling anti-social behaviour, controlling immigration and reforming the benefits system to reward hard work, then it will never regain the seats, and the support, it lost on 6 May. Unless Labour can connect with many millions of people living in towns and villages across the southern parts of England we will never again form a government.

This was a problem familiar to those of us active in the Labour Party in the early 1990s. Between 1992 and 1994 the Fabian Society produced a trio of pamphlets addressing Labour's challenge in winning support in the south: *Southern Discomfort, More Southern Discomfort* and *Any Southern Comfort?*. The author was Giles Radice MP, the Labour revisionist writer and thinker, and the research was supplied by Stephen Pollard, then researcher at the Fabian Society, and now editor of the *Jewish Chronicle*. Much of the fieldwork was conducted by Deborah Mattinson, a long-serving Labour pollster, in Gravesham, Harlow, Luton South, Slough and Stevenage, seats which Labour failed to win in 1992 (but went on to win five years later; today only two of the five still have Labour MPs).

The conclusion of *Southern Discomfort* was that 'Labour suffers from a crippling political weakness in southern England'. After the 1992 election Labour held only ten seats out of the 177 outside London and south of a line from the Wash to the Bristol Channel. After 1987, that number was just three. The authors went on, 'Labour cannot win without doing better in the south. In several ways the key to a Labour victory lies in the south.' Crucially, the pamphlet makes the point that Labour's 'southern problem' was more than just a question of geography. Seats outside of the south that failed to win had 'southern characteristics': a suburban location, high home ownership, above average numbers of white-collar and skilled manual workers. Labour had failed to adapt to changing social attitudes and patterns of work, wealth and home ownership.

The work of the Fabian Society was studied by Tony Blair, Gordon Brown and Peter Mandelson, and helped to inform Labour's approach after Blair became leader in 1994. In his 1996 speech to the Labour Party conference, Blair told the story of the voter he met in the 1992 campaign. The story is probably an amalgam of encounters with the electors, and focuses on one man in the Midlands, rather than the south, but it encapsulates New Labour's approach to the changes in British society:

> I was canvassing in the Midlands on an ordinary, suburban estate. I met a man polishing his Ford Sierra. He was a self-employed electrician. His Dad always voted Labour, he said. He used to vote Labour too. But he'd bought his own house now. He'd set up his own business. He was doing quite nicely. 'So I've become a Tory,' he said.
>
> He wasn't rich. But he was doing better than he did, and as far as he was concerned, being better off meant being Tory too.
>
> In that moment, he crystallised for me the basis of our failure, the reason why a whole generation has grown up under the Tories.
>
> People judge us on their instincts about what they believe our instincts to be.
>
> And that man polishing his car was clear. His instincts were to get on in life. And he thought our instincts were to stop him.

What New Labour achieved – an electoral coalition across all nations, regions and social classes of the UK – replicated what Clement Attlee's Labour Party achieved in 1945. George Orwell described the new elements of the coalition joining its traditional working class base as: 'skilled workers, technical experts, airmen, scientists, architects and journalists.'[1]

In March 2008, Deborah Mattinson presented private findings to Labour staff which showed that Labour was losing voters in the south, and particularly that the Conservatives had won over large numbers of skilled and semi-skilled workers in occupational classes

C1 and C2 in southern marginals. In *Progress* magazine in early 2008, Giles Radice wrote that the issue of 'southern discomfort' was raising its head again. He warned that Labour's policies, and especially the budget that year, did not connect with southern C1/C2 concerns like crime, immigration and interest rates.

At the same time former home secretary Charles Clarke circulated privately a 'doomsday list' of Labour seats that would fall if just 7,500 voters switched from Labour in twenty-four seats in the south. Like Cassandra, Clarke's predictions were proved to be accurate, but ignored at the time by Downing Street. Most of the MPs who were wheeled out by Number 10 to denounce Clarke lost their seats, as did Charles Clarke in Norwich South.

The flight of the C2s

On the definition of the Market Research Society (MRS), C2s are:

- all skilled manual workers, and those manual workers with responsibility for other people;
- retired people, previously grade C2, with pensions from their job;
- widows, if receiving pensions from their late husband's job.

This group comprises roughly one-fifth of the UK population.

Behind the marketing jargon are millions of people who comprise 'hard-working families' with few assets, job insecurity, fluctuations in income and high levels of debt, and who have one or two pay cheques between them and financial ruin. Immigration, taxation, welfare reform, crime and anti-social behaviour, and job opportunities are the issues that candidates reported coming up again and again, alongside the 'Gordon' issue.

It was the C2 group that swung behind Margaret Thatcher in 1979 and 1983, animated by issues such as the 'right to buy', curbs on trade unions, and tough law and order policies.

There were falls in support for Labour in occupational class DE (low-skilled and unskilled workers, people living on benefits, unemployed people, casual workers). Labour broadly held its support amongst C1s (junior managers, non-manual workers) and ABs (managers, professionals, businesspeople).

On 6 May 2010, the C2 vote collapsed for Labour. In 2005, 43 per cent of C2 voters voted Labour. In 2010 just 23 per cent did. This represents an earthquake in voting behaviour.

The shape of Mosaic

Mosaic is a method of segmenting the UK population for marketing purposes. It has also been enthusiastically embraced by Labour Party strategists as a tool for targeting different forms of political messages, based on voters' social status, incomes and media consumption. Mosaic divides the adult population into eleven main groups, and over sixty smaller groups, and gives each group a name to describe their attributes. For example 'Symbols of Success', 'Happy Families', 'Suburban Comfort', 'Ties of Community', 'Urban Intelligence', 'Welfare Borderline' and 'Blue Collar Enterprise'.

Immediately following the election, the core team of Labour election strategists analysed the results of the election based on Mosaic, and some of the findings were published by former chief secretary to the treasury Liam Byrne MP in a pamphlet for *Progress* within a few days of the defeat.[2]

The analysis showed that Watford, Bedford and Ipswich had much higher than average numbers of residents from the Mosaic group known as 'Suburban Mindsets' – maturing families on mid-range incomes living a moderate lifestyle in suburban semis.

Thurrock, Stevenage, Harlow, Thurrock and Waveney each had a large proportion of residents characterised as 'Ex-Council Community' – often lower-skilled workers, but on reasonable incomes, living in right-to-buy homes – and 'Industrial Heritage' –

those families and couples owning affordable older-style housing in communities historically dependent on manufacturing.

Portsmouth North, Gillingham, Chatham & Aylesford, Dartford and Reading West all had significantly higher than average numbers of voters in Mosaic's 'Suburban Mindset' group, plus (apart from Reading) large numbers from the 'Industrial Heritage' group. Crawley had a very large number of local residents in the 'Ex-Council Community' group.

Kingswood, North Swindon, South Swindon and Gloucester all had much higher than average numbers of 'Suburban Mindset' residents. In Hove and Brighton Pavilion, there are quite different trends to other seats in the region. Here, Mosaic group 'Liberal Opinion' make up 48 per cent and 59 per cent of local residents respectively. Stroud too is a slightly different seat, with a very high proportion of families (nearly 20 per cent) from the 'Professional Rewards' group – experienced professionals in successful careers, enjoying a reasonable degree of financial success.

In the West Midlands fourteen out of the sixteen seats Labour lost have a higher than average number of residents in the 'Industrial Heritage' group; around ten of the lost seats have almost double the average number from this group.

In the North West five seats have twice the average number of residents from 'Industrial Heritage'. A further four seats had higher than average numbers of residents in the 'Suburban Mindset' group.

In Yorkshire and Humberside all the seats lost have a higher than average number of residents in the 'Industrial Heritage' group; two – Pudsey and Elmet & Rothwell – have much higher than average numbers of residents in Mosaic's 'Suburban Mindsets' group.

In the north Labour lost both Stockton South and Redcar, both seats where the fall-out from the closure of the Corus steelworks had a negative impact. In Redcar, Mo Mowlam's old seat, there was a 22 per cent swing from Labour to the Lib Dems. Carlisle, on the other hand, is a seat with a high number of local residents from either the 'Suburban Mindsets' or 'Industrial Heritage' groups.

Byrne's pamphlet made the important point that of the ninety-seven seats Labour lost, forty-four had new candidates following the retirement of the sitting Labour MP. These retirements were announced during the twenty-four months leading up to the election, creating the impression of a Parliamentary Labour Party having a collective mental breakdown.

Byrne also points that New Labour's covenant with the people – if you work hard, we will help you get on in life – was stretched to breaking point through the recession. Immigration and the conviction that some people got a better deal from the government by relying on benefits were the issues coming up time and time again during the campaign.

Summary

Labour lost the election on 6 May, but is taking its time to realise the true scale of the disaster. Because of the nature of the defeat, the fall from office was cushioned. For Labour to even begin its process of revival, it needs to understand why so many voters, especially in the southern parts of England, and in other marginal seats, switched their votes from Labour to other parties, mostly the Tories. Although Labour's support has been in gradual decline since the high-water mark of 1997, between 2005 and 2010 it went over the cliff. This was especially true of C2 skilled workers – the hard-working fifth of the population who are concerned with immigration, housing, welfare reform and job security.

To win again Labour must rebuild its electoral coalition, but this task is made harder by the absence of Labour MPs in most of the southern and eastern parts of England to articulate the aspirations of people in commuter towns, market and county towns, and coastal resorts. There is a danger that Labour may retrench into its heartlands – urban areas with Labour traditions – and fail to speak in a language that non-urban voters can understand.

New Labour's triumph was to be able to reach out, reassure and retain the votes of people who had never voted Labour before, in places such as Basildon, Watford, Milton Keynes, Crawley and Hastings. These are the people who work hard to pay their mortgages, take foreign holidays, own a car, and are prepared to go to extraordinary lengths to give their children a leg-up in life. New Labour chimed with this kind of aspiration. It understood why families would want a conservatory, give their children music lessons or buy a better car. Labour's failure in recent years has been to alienate and repel those same voters. The grave threat is that Labour looks like being solely the party of welfare dependants, minorities and trade union men and women. The challenge now is to build a platform that appeals not just to the people living in places represented by Labour MPs, but also people represented by Tories and Liberal Democrats.

Part Two

4. Voices and inspirations

> 'For me, New Labour . . . wasn't at all about changing the basic values or purpose of progressive politics; on the contrary, it was about retrieving them from the deadweight of political and cultural dogma that didn't merely obscure those values and that purpose, but also defeated them.'
>
> Tony Blair, *A Journey* (2010)

Labour's revival need not start at some kind of political Year Zero. There are thinkers, writers, movements and campaigns which can offer Labour some illumination as it grapples its way forward. A new leadership of the party should look to the past as well as to the future. Without an understanding of the past, its tragedies will be repeated and its triumphs will fail to inspire.

Since rejecting, as a student, Marxism-Leninism twenty-five years ago, I have never trusted anyone who adopts wholesale the theories of a great thinker or system of thought. It hampers independent inquiry, stifles curiosity and leads inevitably to disillusionment. The strength of British socialism is its variegation and granularity. It is built on the militancy of the shop stewards' movement; the donnishness of the Webbs; the vision of the Rochdale Pioneers; the romance of Bevan; the calculation of Wilson. Socialism has room for the miner and the millionaire. British socialism is like a rainforest – a single entity, yet rich in diversity, curiosity and life. And endangered.

They say you should never meet your heroes. Anyone working

in or around politics knows that politicians have feet of clay. The romantic hero of the party conference or the passionate advocate on BBC *Question Time* can be a cruel employer, a merciless bully, or tortured by self-doubt. It is a strange that a party founded on principles of co-operation and brotherly love has within it so many schemers, fixers, plotters and egotists. Politics, unlike any other pursuit, attracts both the worst of people and the best; the most noble and the most venal.

Sometimes in the newspapers you read people's 'perfect dinner party guest-list', which includes some combination of Buddha, Einstein, Gandhi, Mozart and Elvis Presley. I imagine a dinner party comprising the greats from Labour's pantheon would be a living hell. Imagine the arrogance of Crosland, the waspishness of Castle, the terseness of Attlee, the flamboyance of Bevan and the puritanism of the Webbs around a single table. Add William Morris passing judgement on your soft furnishings, Orwell obsessing with the cleanliness of your house, and H. G. Wells trying to seduce the female members of your household. You would be longing for them all to leave.

Yet within this infinite variety are some writers, thinkers and political leaders who can give inspiration, encapsulate an idea or instinct, or provoke a fruitful train of thought. As Labour starts its journey to revival, it should mount the steps to the attic and dust down some volumes which were hidden away during its New Labour obsession with modernity.

None should be swallowed whole; each is of its own time and place. On the following pages are a few of the people who can give inspiration, and serve as a reminder that everyone in the Labour Party is standing on the shoulders of giants. They are the thinkers, writers and activists who have developed and deepened our understanding, through word and deed, of Labour's values. Each has something to say to our own times, our own preoccupations and concerns.

1. The Levellers: soldiers for democracy

If you walk down Putney High Street towards the river, past the cinema, you come to St Mary's Church. On this spot in 1647 a group of soldiers and officers, fresh from the front line of a bloody civil war, came together to debate issues which resonate in our own times, and in every society around the world. The Putney Debates, conducted within the Parliamentary forces of Oliver Cromwell, pre-date the great social and political struggles of the next 350 years. Within Cromwell's forces were the Levellers: democrats, egalitarians and civil libertarians who wanted England to be a democracy within a framework of civil rights and fair laws. Opposing any suggestion of a deal with King Charles, Thomas Rainsborough MP, speaking for the Levellers, made the famous demand for democracy:

> For really I think that the poorest he that is in England hath a life to live, as the greatest he; and therefore truly, sir, I think it's clear, that every man that is to live under a government ought first by his own consent to put himself under that government; and I do think that the poorest man in England is not at all bound in a strict sense to that government that he hath not had a voice to put himself under.[1]

The Levellers were a faction within the Parliamentary forces in the English Civil Wars. They were drawn from the lower middle classes – artisans, shopkeepers and tradesmen – and organised around local chapters, arranged on democratic lines. They used the newly affordable medium of mass-produced print to produce political pamphlets and a newspaper, *The Moderate*. There were Levellers inside Oliver Cromwell's New Model Army, fighting the Royalists, and in the civilian population, especially in London. They supported Cromwell, but as the leadership of the Parliamentary forces became more dictatorial, they opposed his growing power.

They were Christians, believing from their study of the Bible that human rights were innate and granted by God. Therefore no man, be it a king, priest or landowner, should have the power to exercise dominion over anyone else. The Leveller demands were distilled into a declaration called the Agreement of the People. Its third edition, drafted by the Leveller leadership in prison, is a remarkable document. It was written in 1649, yet it prefigures the American and French Revolutions in the eighteenth century, the Reform Acts and the Chartists in the nineteenth century, and many of the debates still going on today.

The Agreement of the People includes demands for:

- an extension of the franchise to all men, except servants and those living on charity, over the age of twenty-one;
- the power to recall members of Parliament at any time;
- a parliament of 400 MPs, with constituencies of equal size;
- annual elections for MPs, with MPs receiving salaries;
- religious toleration, abolition of tithes and elections for priests;
- free courts, and restriction of the death penalty to cases of murder and treason;
- trial by jury;
- army officers to be appointed by the parliament, bringing the army under democratic control;
- reform of the tax system to introduce progressive income taxes;
- freedom of the press.

The basis of a civil rights agenda is here, with a separate judiciary, a right to be tried by your peers, and freedom of religion. The democratic reforms – extension of the vote, payment for MPs, an end to rotten boroughs and annual elections – were taken up by the Chartists 200 years later. The power to recall MPs was discussed by the Labour government in 2008 and ruled out. It then appeared in the manifestos of both Labour and Tory parties, and is now the Tory-led government's policy. A group of men, during a time of huge upheaval and a war in which more people as a percentage of the population died than even the First World War, constructed a political platform way ahead of its time.

A breakaway faction of the Levellers was called the True Levellers, or Diggers (immortalised in a song by Dick Gaughan and later Billy Bragg). The Diggers believed in an end to private property, and equal shares of the produce of the earth. In 1649, they occupied land at St George's Hill in Surrey for five months and ran a commune. Today St George's Hill is covered with a private housing estate, a golf club and a tennis club, and is home to footballers, television stars and stockbrokers. In 2007, the average house price was £3 million.

Cromwell found the Levellers and the Diggers to be too much trouble. He sent the army into the Diggers' encampment, who, being non-violent, offered no opposition. The Levellers were rounded up and imprisoned or executed. At Burford in Oxfordshire in May 1649, a mutiny by Levellers in the army was crushed. Three Levellers were shot dead.

As a footnote to the story, in 1975 the local branch of the Workers' Education Association (WEA) organised a Levellers' Day in Burford, and asked the Labour secretary of state for energy to speak. Tony Benn has been attending Levellers' Days ever since. The graffiti 'Bollocks to Benn' was hastily removed from a local wall before his arrival. The local MP, Douglas Hurd, complained that a church had been used to celebrate the lives of three 'mutineers', and one year the local Conservative Association booked the church hall for a fictitious jumble sale to sabotage the event.

In March 2010 Douglas Carswell, the Tory MP for Harwich, made the claim that the Levellers would have voted Conservative. Others – Benn, Fenner Brockway and Michael Foot – have claimed the Levellers for the Labour movement. The reality is that you can't ascribe contemporary attitudes and voting behaviour onto people who lived 350 years ago, before the Industrial Revolution and the development of capitalism, any more than you can say that Queen Victoria would have been a Rolling Stones fan, or Boudicca would have shopped at Sainsbury's. It's pure ahistoricism.

The Levellers have something to tell us today about our politics: about the struggles to win a democracy which, though half-finished, we take for granted; about the courage of men willing to debate, dissent, and in the end die for the ideas they believed in; and about the role of visionaries – people whose ideas seem outlandish and dangerous in their own time, yet prove to be true in future decades. Ideas, with courageous people to stand up for them, are the engines of human progress.

2. The pioneers from Rochdale

Co-operation has been a human trait for as long as there have been humans. The first tribes of human beings were communal and collaborative. The survival of each depended on the actions of all. The first application of this natural instinct within the individualistic, exploitative and Darwinian atmosphere of the Industrial Revolution was in the 1760s by weavers in Ayrshire and at corn mills in Kent and Woolwich.[2]

Welshman Robert Owen (1771–1858) devoted his life to developing co-operation, as a practical system in his various attempts at creating a co-operative community, notably at New Lanark in Scotland; and as a theory, in his *A New View of Society*, which argued that humans are shaped by their environments, and therefore decent homes, workplaces and public spaces would make decent human beings. His *Report to the County of Lanark* set out his view that social relations were poisoned by competition and greed resulting from capitalism. He called for 'villages of co-operation' which would cover the country as an alternative to the horrors of laissez-faire industrialisation. In Brighton, Dr William King (1786–1865) founded a co-operative store on Owenite lines and a newspaper, *The Co-operator*. Its slogan was 'Knowledge and union are power. Power, directed by knowledge is happiness. Happiness is the end of creation.' King believed that the answer to capitalism was for workers to accumulate capital themselves, and thus remove the need for capitalists. He also advocated workers' education, improved health and diets.

Owenites were the backbone of the trade union movement in the 1820s and 1830s, both local trade unions and the Grand National Consolidated Trades Union, and the attempt to unite the industrial workers around pay and conditions. In 1832 six agricultural labourers were arrested swearing an oath to form a 'friendly society' (a kind of self-help union) in Tolpuddle in Dorset, and were deported to penal colonies in Australia. The Co-operative Congress met in Manchester, Liverpool and London in the 1830s, with delegates from local co-ops.

In Toad Lane, Rochdale, in 1844, a group of 'pioneers' banded together to start the first successful co-operative business. They started with twenty-eight.* Today, there are 700 million members of co-operatives around the world. The Rochdale Pioneers were motivated by values, and by hunger. Their values reflected the co-operative ideals of Robert Owen, who had developed a theory of co-operation as the route to the liberation of humankind, and the creation of human fulfilment.

This was the Hungry Forties, with unemployment and starvation across the industrial areas. In Ireland a million people starved to death when the potato crop failed. The shop opened just in time for Christmas 1849, selling just butter, sugar, flour, oatmeal and a few candles. They committed themselves to selling unadulterated food, at the correct weights. At a time when most food was filled with ingredients, from sawdust to chalk, to make it go further, and retailers routinely cheated their customers with false weights and measures, these were radical principles.

The Rochdale Pioneers were unemployed men, listed as weavers, tailors, cloggers, wool sorters, joiners and warehousemen, meeting

---

* Or so legend has it, although G. D. H. Cole in his *A Century of Co-operation* (1944) disputes this.

in the local 'Socialist Institute', against a backdrop of Chartist campaigning and Owenism. They set out the laws and objects of the Rochdale Society of Equitable Pioneers:

> The objects and plans of this Society are to form arrangements for the pecuniary benefit and the improvement of the social and domestic conditions of its members, by raising a sufficient amount of capital in shares of one pound each, to bring into operation the following plans and arrangements.
>
> The establishment of a store for the sale of provisions and clothing etc.
>
> The building, purchasing, or erecting of a number of houses, in which those members desiring to assist each other in improving their domestic and social condition may reside.
>
> To commence, the manufacture of such articles as the society may determine upon, for the employment of such members as may be without employment, or who may be badly remunerated.
>
> That as soon as practicable, this society shall proceed to arrange the powers of production, distribution, education, and government, or in other words to establish a self-supporting home-colony of united interests, or assist other societies in establishing such colonies.
>
> That for the promotion of sobriety a Temperance Hotel be opened in one of the society's houses, as soon as convenient.

They asked for no state aid or charity. They did it for themselves. As the penultimate 'object' suggests, the pioneers' ambition was for more than a shop selling foodstuffs, but for a 'self-supporting home-colony of united interests'. In other words – a new view of society.

The principles the pioneers adopted for their co-operative shop in Toad Lane were no less revolutionary:

1. Open membership.
2. Democratic control (one person, one vote).
3. Distribution of surplus in proportion to trade (the 'divi')
4. Payment of limited interest on capital.
5. Political and religious neutrality.
6. Cash trading (no credit extended).
7. Promotion of education.

In these simple ideas rest revolutionary sentiments: democratic control, equality for all members, self-help, freedom of expression and worship, education, and most famously the 'divi', whereby members of the co-op share the profits equally in the form of a dividend. The spread of the co-operative model around the world, and its application to everything from milk production to football clubs, proves that it taps into the best of human nature. The men from Rochdale pointed to a democratic, caring society, and their ideas should take us forward into our own century.

3. William Morris: the dreamer of dreams

William Morris (1834–96) hated the age he lived in. He hated its architecture, its commerce, its poverty, its politics, its industry, but most of all he hated its individualistic, selfish system of values. At the end of his life he explained: 'The study of history and the love and practice of art forced me into a hatred of the civilization which, if things were to stop as they are, would turn history into inconsequent nonsense, and make art a collection of the curiosities of the past.'[3]

He was famously a designer, artist, poet and writer, linked to the Pre-Raphaelite Brotherhood, and later the Arts and Crafts Movement. He longed for pre-industrial forms of production and craftsmanship, and tried to use traditional methods and ingredients in his workshops (including liberal amounts of arsenic). He wrote long Icelandic sagas, romantic verse and regular columns for left-wing publications. Aneurin Bevan learned to conquer his stammer by learning and reciting long passages of Morris's poetry.

Morris was a political activist, beguiled (if not completely seduced) by Karl Marx, and involved in the various socialist sects of his time. He left the Social Democratic Foundation (SDF), a quasi-Marxist group, to form the Socialist League in 1885. It ran local branches and a weekly newspaper subsidised by Morris's profits from selling wallpaper. It was in turn taken over by anarchists, and Morris left.

Towards the end of his life, Morris recanted on his opposition to parliamentary routes to socialism, and conceded the need for a single socialist party. His very last lecture in January 1896, in Hammersmith, took as its theme the need for 'One Socialist Party'. It is doubtful he would have welcomed the foundation of the Labour Representation Committee (LRC), had he lived to see it. He was suspicious of the socialist purity of the Independent Labour Party (ILP) in 1893, which espoused a much more robust, evangelical form of ethical socialism. Despite being influenced by the Christian socialist Charles Kingsley, and going up to Oxford to train for the priesthood, Morris's religiosity was reserved for socialism. The Labour Party's blend of liberalism, trade unionism, Fabianism and parliamentarianism (in his *News from Nowhere* Parliament has become a storage facility for horse manure) would have no doubt had him reaching for his pen.

In 1894, he wrote an account of his political journey in *Justice* magazine, the publication of the SDF, which he had left some years earlier. *How I Became a Socialist* explains his starting point: 'Apart from the desire to produce beautiful things, the leading passion of my life has been and is hatred of modern civilization.'

The alternative to the 'filth' of modernity is socialism, which in Morris's mind is an agrarian, communistic form of life, with small-scale production, a premium on craftsmanship and artistry, and no state. He defines it:

> What I mean by Socialism is a condition of society in which
> there should be neither rich nor poor, neither master nor
> master's man, neither idle nor overworked, neither brain-
> sick brain workers, nor heart-sick hand workers, in a world,
> in which all men would be living in equality of condition,
> and would manage their affairs unwastefully, and with the
> full consciousness that harm to one would mean harm
> to all – the realization at last of the meaning of the word
> COMMONWEALTH.[4]

His greatest legacy to the Labour movement is *News from Nowhere* (1890), an account of an activist returning home from a branch meeting of the Socialist League in Hammersmith to fall into a deep sleep. When he awakes, he is in the socialist future: 'The soap-works with their smoke-vomiting chimneys were gone; the engineer's works gone; the lead-works gone; and no sound of riveting and hammering came down from the west wind from Thorneycrofts.'

Hammersmith Bridge is an ornate paragon of craftsmanship; there are salmon in the clear waters of the Thames. The activist is taken on a journey around London, with healthy citizens living in pure equality, no money, no government, no marriage and no politics. The people live in harmony with nature, work because they enjoy it, take pleasure in crafts, and have few conflicts with one another. Morris's vision echoes Marx's idea that under communism people would be able 'to hunt in the morning, fish in the afternoon, rear cattle in the evening, criticize after dinner.'[5] Unfortunately for women in *Nowhere*, they still have to do all the housework, bring up the children and serve the men with food, but in Morris's vision they seem to enjoy it.

Morris looked like an Old Testament prophet and fulfils that role in the Labour tradition. His vision is inspiring. His politics are uncompromising. He could be dismissed as utopian or 'impossibilist', if it were not for the amount of time, effort and money he expended on what he called 'practical socialism': printing newspapers, leaflets and pamphlets, organising meetings, giving lectures and building socialism as a political force, not just a late-Victorian daydream. He called himself a 'dreamer of dreams, born out of my due time.'[6] Yet he was also every bit as much a political organiser as Keir Hardie, MacDonald or Bevin.

His desire to see an end to mass production and voracious industry, and a return to small-scale local production, seems like a very modern view. His socialism was imbued with environmentalism and an understanding of the brutalising nature of the modern city. He railed against pollution, the destruction of ancient buildings, shoddy goods and poor design. He was a 'green' long before the term was invented. One of his very last lectures was for the Society for Checking the Abuses of Public Advertising, a thoroughly 21st-century matter of concern.

His work directly recruited G. D. H. Cole to the cause of socialism, and he has influenced many thousands of socialists since, not to mention designers, writers and poets. Despite years in the most sectarian of political environments, he retained his faith in humankind and an innate sense of decency. W. B. Yeats wrote of him: 'No man I have ever known was so well loved. He was looked up to as to some worshipped medieval king. People loved him as children are loved. I soon discovered his spontaneity and joy and made him my chief of men.'

Kelmscott Manor, the Gloucestershire palace to arts and crafts that he shared with Dante Gabriel Rossetti, is open to the public. In Bexleyheath you can visit The Red House, which Morris designed and lived in. On Upper Mall in Hammersmith is Kelmscott House, where he died in 1896. Above the coach-house, the William Morris Society have created the sign that the traveller sees in *News from Nowhere*: 'Guests and Neighbours, on the site of this Guest-Hall once stood the lecture room of the Hammersmith Socialists. Drink a glass to the memory! May 1962.'

4. Keir Hardie: the child in the dark

Until the day he died of a broken heart in 1915, Keir Hardie (who like Gordon Brown had the real first name James) carried a silver pocket watch. On it were the teeth-marks of a favourite pit pony who had tried, unsuccessfully, to eat it. The experience of the pits left their mark on Hardie too. He was sent down the mines at the age of ten, and worked as a miner until his early twenties, when the mine owners blacklisted him for agitation. It is hard to know what working for twelve hours a day in the black of a mine tunnel does to a little boy of ten or eleven. Hardie resolved to learn to read and write, to improve his lot, and to improve the lot of every worker like himself. Philip Snowden, a future Labour chancellor of the exchequer, wrote that Hardie was spurred on to learn to read and write when he signed up to the Good Templars, an organisation of the temperance movement, but was ashamed that he couldn't write his own name.

His first chosen tool was the trade union. He organised the Lanarkshire miners and led them into a strike. He rose to become president of the Scottish miners' union. He founded two newspapers, *The Miner* and the *Labour Leader*, and wrote articles throughout his life. Hardie converted to evangelical Christianity. In 1910 he said: 'The impetus which drove me first into the Labour movement, and the inspiration which has carried me on in it, has been derived more from the teachings of Jesus of Nazareth than from all other sources combined.'

He stood for Parliament and came last. In 1892 he stood as an Independent Labour candidate in West Ham South, in the East End of London, and was elected, beating the Tory thanks to a non-aggression pact with the Liberals. He lost in 1895. He turned up to Parliament in a cap, tweed suit and red tie, and caused outrage by refusal to conform to the dress code.

Hardie displayed huge bravery in his political career. He backed suffrage for women, and became a great friend and ally of the Pankhursts. He was arrested at a Suffragette rally in Manchester.

His biographer Kenneth O. Morgan called him 'the greatest-ever male feminist'. He opposed the Boer War. He spoke out against the monarchy and was banned from garden parties. He supported a national minimum wage and a tax-funded health service. He spoke out against racial segregation in the British Empire, especially South Africa, and for self-rule for India.

In 1900 Hardie helped to found the Labour Representation Committee (LRC) and was elected MP for Merthyr Tydfil, one of two Labour MPs. Hardie never found his voice in Parliament; nor did he make a very effective party leader. The compromises and concessions of politics did not suit his evangelical passions and conviction politics. His pacifism led him to oppose Britain's entry into the First World War; he was desperate to persuade the Second International to organise a general strike across Europe to prevent war. He died in 1915, as the few remaining members of the professional British army of the original expeditionary force were dying in increasingly futile trench battles. He was heartbroken at his failure to prevent the carnage.

Hardie never held ministerial office. He never saw the Labour Party form a government. His name is not associated with any great acts of Parliament or reforms. Yet if Morris was a prophet, Hardie was a saint. In the corner of a room in his home in Cumnock in Ayrshire was a walking stick presented to him by his friend and admirer Mahatma Gandhi. Hardie belongs in that pantheon of visionaries and leaders, which includes Gandhi and Martin Luther King, whose power came from their moral force, not any office of state. He built the Labour Party, based on the trade unions and socialist groups, as a great power in the land. His socialism was non-Marxist, based on ethical principles and indignation at injustice. It was a non-theoretical kind of socialism. He was no fool. His education was wide and deep. Yet he rejected theories and text-book definitions, preferring practical answers.

His was not the socialism of the central state. It was based on mutual aid and small local organisations, such as the branches of the miners' federation. He would have been unimpressed with the bureaucracy and alienation that characterised the nationalised industries and welfare state half a century after his death. He was no Fabian paternalist, unlike the Webbs (Beatrice didn't like him). He had a colossal faith in working people's capacity to take control of their own lives.

The causes he chose to champion – feminism, anti-racism, child labourers, anti-imperialism, pacifism – put him on a collision course with the received wisdom of the day, even within the Labour movement. Leaders of the trade unions were touring the industrial areas recruiting workers to the army when Hardie was trying to prevent the war. Yet on each issue, he was right.

In 1897, he issued his Christmas message:

> I am afraid that my heart is bitter tonight, and so the thoughts and feelings that pertain to Christmas are far from me. But when I think of the thousands of white-livered poltroons who will take Christ's name in vain, and yet not see His image being crucified in every hungry child, I cannot think of peace. I have known as a child what hunger means, and the scars of those days are with me still and rankle in my heart, and unfit me in many ways for the work to be done.

The little boy underground in the dark, surrounded by the rough voices of the miners and the stamp and snort of the pit ponies, went on to become an MP and establish and lead a great political movement, but the smell of coal-dust never left his nostrils.

5. R. H. Tawney: 'The democratic socialist *par excellence*'

When Richard Tawney was a young man, he was given a rifle and sent out to France to kill Germans. Our view of the First World

War focuses on the senseless loss of life, rows of gravestones and horror beyond our nightmares. We easily forget that those young men sent from the cities, towns and villages were warriors; they killed the enemy with bullet and bayonet, and sometimes with pick-axe handles, bludgeons and bare fists. Tawney wrote about his experiences in the trenches in an essay, 'The Attack', where he describes shooting enemy soldiers.

Tawney served in the Manchester Regiment. As an act of egalitarianism he refused a commission, choosing to join as a private soldier, and progressed no further than sergeant. For many years he would wear his sergeant's jacket around his Bloomsbury flat. Tawney fought in the Battle of the Somme, and was shot through the chest in the early stages of the battle. You can only speculate at how many other Richard Tawneys – great writers, architects, doctors, world statesmen and inventors – were lost to humanity in the smoke and mud.

He was born in India in 1880. At Rugby School he became friends with 'Billy' Temple, who went on to become Archbishop of York, and at Balliol forged a friendship with William Beveridge, a Liberal, who wrote the most famous social report of the twentieth century. He refused to pay for the conversion of his second-class Oxford BA to an MA (a practice which still continues), on the grounds that such things should be earned, not bought and sold.

He spent his youth working at Toynbee Hall in the East End of London, and as a tutor for the Workers' Education Association (WEA), travelling to Rochdale every week to give lectures to working men.

Tawney was a Christian who became a socialist. He hated the term 'Christian Socialist'. His socialism developed from his experience as a social campaigner in the East End and tutor at the WEA, meeting working-class people for the first time. He consciously rejected charitable works in favour of social reform, and empowering working people through education. He joined the Independent Labour Party (ILP) and the Fabian Society. He stood as a Labour candidate in several elections, but was unsuccessful. In 1935, he was offered a safe seat but declined. Later, he turned down a peerage from Ramsay MacDonald, who he distrusted (rightly as it turned out).

Tawney's great contribution to socialism in Britain was to develop an ethical, compassionate, democratic version, not as some weaker, more conformist, variant of Marxism, but as an indignant, robust, egalitarian and above all distinctive socialism rooted in values. It was a distinctively British socialism, forged in the slums, pubs and factories of the East End and Lancashire, tested through the practical enquiry of working men and close inspection by the Webbs, and anchored in Christian morality and radical Liberalism.

It is a credit to the universal appeal and moral clarity of his writing that Tawney can be claimed by socialists from the left to the right of the Labour Party, and all points in between. Tony Benn argued in 1988: 'For some years Tawney has been quoted extensively by the right wing of the Labour Party who have tried to make him appear as the father of their own school of revisionist thought.' And he proceeds to quote approvingly Tawney's views on class struggle, social ownership and what Benn calls 'socialism in place of the weak and woolly liberalism which has so deeply penetrated Labour politics during the last thirty years'.[7]

When some Labour MPs deserted the party onto whose shoulders they had been lifted to create the Social Democratic Party (SDP) in 1980, they took the name of Tawney with them, as the name of the new think-tank to rival the Fabian Society. The Tawney Society, like the SDP, is now long dead; the Fabians are in rude health.

He wrote academic books on subjects from the link between religion and capitalism to economics in China, but his reputation as a writer rests on two main works, *The Acquisitive Society* (1920) and *Equality* (1931). The first set out his rejection of the need inherent in capitalism to accumulate wealth, and the values of competition and avarice that the economic system bred. He developed the idea of 'function', establishing that no-one should be rewarded without making any tangible contribution. In 1919 Tawney had served on the Sankey commission on the future of the mining industry and argued against the idea that mine owners should be paid for owning land under which was coal. He extended this principle to the rest of the idle classes.

Equality (1931) is the classic socialist exposition of the need for a fairer, more egalitarian society. Tawney's foundation was the Christian ideal of equal worth of each human being. Reflecting his own experience of attempting to liberate the working class, rather than simply ameliorate the worst of poverty, *Equality* argues for a more equal society based on an equitable distribution of assets, wealth and power (the latter firmly linked to the former), so that each person can be self-fulfilled and develop their own attributes and talents. As evidenced by his life-long commitment to the WEA, Tawney saw education as the great liberator. Greater equality would lead to what Tawney calls a 'common culture' and a state of fellowship between human beings. He dedicated the book to the Webbs, but differed from their faith in mechanisms, structures and cold hard facts to deliver socialism. Nor did he wholeheartedly sign up to the guild socialist agenda (see pages 91–2), although he believed in the diffusion of power through society. He wanted cities like Leeds, Manchester and Birmingham to become 'little republics'.

Tawney saw greater equality, not as a leveller, but as the route to new heights of human achievement and attainment: 'The socialist society . . . is a community of responsible men and women working without fear in comradeship for common ends, all of whom can grow to their full stature, develop to their outmost limit the varying capacities with which nature has endowed them.'[8]

He taught at the London School of Economics (LSE), which had been founded by the Fabians, and at Oxford. His pupils included Hugh Gaitskell and Evan Durbin, who he outlived by fourteen years. Born in India, with an Empress on the throne, he died in Bloomsbury, a few weeks before the Beatles had their first hit single. Gaitskell, only months before his own death, spoke at the funeral. He said, 'I think he was the best man I have ever known.'[9]

6. G. D. H. Cole: 'the Bolshevik soul in a Fabian muzzle'

If you want to imagine what George Douglas Howard Cole was like, you could do worse than watch an episode of *Bagpuss*. Oliver Postgate, the creator of the children's animated story, modelled Professor Yaffle, the 'carved wooden bookend' in the shape of a woodpecker, on Cole, his uncle. He is a brilliant, sceptical, and slightly eccentric old academic.

Cole was converted to the idea of socialism by reading William Morris's *News from Nowhere*. As a pupil at St Paul's School, then situated in Hammersmith, Cole was a stone's throw from Morris's former home in Upper Mall, where today the William Morris Society has its offices. The bridge that Morris describes in an early section of the book as 'ugly' would have been seen every day by the young Cole.

At Balliol, Cole joined the Fabian Society, and came under the spell of Beatrice and Sidney Webb. Cole's relationship with the Fabian Society was like that of quarrelsome lovers. In 1915, Cole stormed out of the executive.

His point of departure with the Webbs was the role of the state, and centralised planning and administration. The orthodox Fabian view was that the state could be 'captured' and turned into a benign organ, delivering benefits to the working classes. With the right politicians at the top, and an enlightened class of administrators, the economy and society could be gradually reformed. The Fabianism of the Webbs was essentially elitist. This is what Cole disagreed with. His ideas for socialism were based on self-government for working people, through local units of control and accountability, with different centres of power. This was not 'state' socialism, but something far more radical: the idea that workers could do it for themselves.

Cole did not invent guild socialism, but became the thinker most associated with it. The Guildsmen were socialists who rejected the idea of the central state. They wanted human society organised into 'guilds', both in industry and in the community. In *Guild Socialism* (1918), *Guild Socialism Re-stated* (1920) and *Self-Government in Industry* (1917) Cole elaborated a view of society which was democratic, fraternal and egalitarian. Power was diffused, both in the economy and in society, and democracy placed a duty on citizens to take part. Although a member of the Fabian Society, he was described as a 'Bolshevik soul in a Fabian muzzle'.

Cole described the guild socialist idea as 'a form of socialism designed to oppose the bureaucratic control of state-owned industries and to assure self-government to the producers while safeguarding the interests of the consuming public.'[10]

'Prolific' is an often over-used word to describe writers. In Cole's case it scarcely does him justice. His wife Margaret described him as 'a natural writer almost to the point of disease. Sit him down anywhere, in practically any surroundings, lovely or squalid, still or moving – even put him to bed with a cold – and he will immediately start writing as though a plug had been pulled out.'[11]

He wrote more than twenty-five heavyweight books about political theory, history and political figures from William Cobbett to Robert Owen, including six for Victor Gollancz's Left Book Club. He averaged one every other year all his life. And he also had the energy to write, with Margaret, over thirty detective novels, with titles such as *The Murder at Crome House* (1927), *Death in the Quarry* (1934) and *The Knife in the Dark* (1941).

In 1935 one of Cole's students at Oxford was Harold Wilson, who was recruited to the socialist cause by the professor. Wilson's *Memoirs* fifty years later say:

> I had long held G. D. H. Cole in high regard and found this closer contact with him most congenial. He was a good-looking man, of medium height with a good head of hair, and most attractive in speech and address, except for the manner of his lectures. I had attended a number of them, which he delivered at great speed, eyes down, without

a single note . . . I took to spending most Tuesday and Wednesday evenings with him, helping with copy for and proofs of his articles for the *New Statesman and Nation*. When the work was finished, he used to pour out for each of us a glass of Irish whiskey, which he preferred to Scotch. On one of these occasions he was celebrating his fiftieth birthday. He announced that he had made a resolution, to forswear all reading of books and concentrate on writing them. He was already publishing at least one a year in addition to his other writings . . . It was G. D. H. Cole as much as any man who finally pointed me in the direction of the Labour Party.

He served as president of the Fabian Society 1952–7 and died in 1959.

Cole was inspired by the romance of William Morris, but his contribution is almost entirely cerebral. If Morris was a dreamer, Cole was the builder. What is really exciting about Cole's contribution is that it conceptualised a socialism without a strong central state. Whilst fellow Fabians and Labour Party members were beguiled by the Soviet Union, and a later generation fetishised central planning and nationalisation, equating it with true socialism, Cole mapped an alternative course. He deserves to be read and reread by today's socialists, not for the prescriptions and policies he advocated in his own times, but for the general approach he adopted. Socialism as local ownership and democratic control; citizenship as an active, not a passive, state; democracy as a way of living, not an abstract theory; a small, strategic state atop a panoply of regional, local and neighbourhood bodies and agencies run, owned and accountable to the people: these are ideas whose time has come.

Cole was writing during a grave global crisis and rapid changes in the old political and social order. Our own world is in no less a state of flux and uncertainty. No single theory or doctrine can give all the answers, but Cole comes close.

7. George Orwell: 'the Tory anarchist'

George Orwell (1903–50), whose real name, as everyone knows, was Eric Blair, led an extraordinary life, from imperial policeman in Burma to infantryman in the Spanish Civil War, from MI5 informer to assassin, trained to kill collaborators in the event of a Nazi invasion. He left behind some of the greatest writing of the twentieth century, and succeeded in his life's mission to elevate political writing into an art form. His socialism was shaped by life-changing events, rather than academic study. Like the prime minister, he was an old Etonian, but he never went to university. His education was in the parade grounds of Mandalay, the hotel kitchens of Paris, the back streets of Wigan, the blood-filled gutters of Barcelona, and the air-raid shelters of London in the Blitz.

Orwell developed a faith and confidence in the working-class people he met, the decency of their values and their capacity to make a better world. His great socialist manifesto *The Lion and the Unicorn* stands as a clarion call for democracy, freedom and a less selfish, more egalitarian society. England was 'a family with the wrong members in control'; the war against Nazism had made socialism a necessity:

> We cannot win the war without introducing Socialism, nor establish Socialism without winning the war. At such a time it is possible, as it was not in the peaceful years, to be both revolutionary and realistic. A Socialist movement which can swing the mass of the people behind it, drive the pro-Fascists out of positions of control, wipe out the grosser injustices and let the working class see that they have something to fight for, win over the middle classes instead of antagonizing them, produce a workable imperial policy instead of a mixture of humbug and Utopianism, bring patriotism and intelligence into partnership – for the first time, a movement of such a kind becomes possible.

Orwell was instinctively distrusting of authority, elites and governments. A private education will do that to a chap. At St Cyprian's prep school in Eastbourne he suffered terrible privations and violence, described in *Such, Such Were the Joys*. Across the road from the school was Summerdown Camp, a vast army camp on the side of a hill for wounded soldiers from the trenches of the First World War. What the daily sight of these men in their distinctive blue uniforms, with limbs missing and other horrific wounds, did to the young Eric Blair we can only imagine.

His socialism was heretical. It did not conform into the Marxism of the communists, or the reformism of the Labour Party, although he canvassed for Labour in the 1945 general election. He defied labels, and was too independent-minded to fit into any party, sect or faction (although he joined the Independent Labour Party). He called himself 'a Tory anarchist' until the mid-1930s. After that, experience made him a democratic socialist.

He wrote to his old St Cyprian's schoolfriend Cyril Connolly from revolutionary Barcelona on 8 June 1937: 'I have seen wonderful things and at last really believe in Socialism, which I never did before.'[12] He believed that 'during times of universal deceit, telling the truth becomes a revolutionary act'. He only just got out of Spain alive, before the communists could arrest, and probably shoot, him for being a 'Trotskyist'.

Poverty, squalor and dirt both repelled and fascinated him. His first experience of it was as a *plongeur* in the Paris hotel kitchens and a homeless tramp in the East End of London. Orwell idealised the working class. In *The Road to Wigan Pier* he wrote:

> It is only because miners sweat their guts out that superior persons can remain superior. You and I and the editor of the *Times Lit. Supp.*, and the poets and the Archbishop of Canterbury and Comrade X, author of *Marxism for Infants* – all of us really owe the comparative decency of our lives to poor drudges underground, blackened to the eyes, with

their throats full of coal dust, driving their shovels forward
with arms and belly muscles of steel.

He was an early Tribunite, like Nye Bevan, but wrote his As I Please
column on everything from how to make the perfect cup of tea to
what constituted the ideal pub. He wrote, and advised others how
to write. ('Never use a long word if a short word will do; never use
the passive when you can use the active; have I said anything that is
avoidably ugly?')

Orwell was a man of the left, yet could see right through Stalin,
unlike so many of his contemporaries. His distrust of Stalinism
turned to outright hostility when he saw the communists turn on
the socialists and anarchists in the Spanish Civil War, preferring
to shoot deviants from Soviet communism than the fascists. He
was shot through the throat by a fascist sniper and invalided home.
When the Second World War broke out Orwell signed up to the
Home Guard. Far from being one of 'Dad's Army' he was preparing
(along with Michael Foot) to form an underground guerrilla army
which would attack the Germans behind their lines, and shoot
collaborators. He had seen armed revolution first-hand, and was
ready to take up arms in the British revolution if necessary.

His two last, and greatest, works are *Animal Farm* and *Nineteen
Eighty-four*. *Animal Farm* is an allegory of revolution betrayed, of
the tendency of self-appointed political leaders to aggregate their
power and end up the same as, or worse than, the oppressors they've
overthrown. ('The creatures outside looked from pig to man, and
from man to pig, and from pig to man again; but already it was
impossible to say which was which.') The farm was based on one
in Willingdon, then a village near Eastbourne, which Orwell had
known as a schoolboy at St Cyprian's.

If *Animal Farm* was a 'fairy story', as its subtitle suggests, then
Nineteen Eighty-four is a nightmare: 'If you want a vision of the
future, imagine a boot stamping on a human face – forever.' It was
seized upon by Cold Warriors as anti-Soviet propaganda. But it is a

savage satire on all authoritarianism, of left or right. It was as much about the cold harsh austerity of post-war London in 1948 (Orwell simply transposed the last two digits of the date) as some dystopian future.

Orwell's socialism was humane and practical, in an era of dogma and ideology. He was anti-doctrine; he described the socialist idea in childlike terms:

> The world is a raft sailing through space with, potentially, plenty of provisions for everybody; the idea that we must all co-operate and see to it that everyone does his fair share of the work and gets his fair share of the provisions seems so blatantly obvious that one would say that no one could possibly fail to accept it unless he had some corrupt motive for clinging to the present system.[13]

He was an English patriot, prepared to die for his country, and prepared to die to change his country too. His favourite word was 'decent'.

8. Michael Young (1915–2002)

Michael Young's contribution to the Labour Party and social reform is so great that we can forgive his brief membership of the SDP in the early 1980s. He married a Fabian enthusiasm for facts and research with a practical desire for new forms of social organisation and enterprise, which he set up or encouraged himself. Unlike those social researchers who merely counted and categorised the poor, Young counted, categorised, and then attempted to transform the lives of the poor.

He attended Dartington School in Devon, an experimental, progressive boarding school, which a decade later gave the world Oliver Postgate, creator of *Bagpuss*, and grandson of George

Lansbury. Young graduated from the Fabian finishing school the LSE, and went to work at the Labour Party as head of research. At the age of thirty, Young wrote *Let Us Face the Future*, the party's 1945 manifesto, with its radical simplicity and soaring phraseology (how different from the Labour manifestos of our own times).

Young's political thinking was important because he was prepared to challenge socialist orthodoxies. His classic study *Family and Kinship in East London* (1957), describing the upheaval of Bethnal Green's residents, and their displacement to council estates in Essex, showed that the altruistic instincts of central planners and administrators were destroying community and family life. His novel *The Rise of the Meritocracy* (1959) was a clever satire of a future society run by an elite based on a standardised assessment of intelligence (modelled on the 11-plus) and educational attainment, the opposite of the education he experienced at Dartington Hall. The meritocracy – a word he coined – is a negative form of government, stifling all nonconformity and rewarding uniformity. He regretted the adoption of the term by New Labour politicians, who stripped it of the original meaning and gave it a positive spin.

Young is buried in Highgate Cemetery, but if you seek a monument, look around. Modern Britain is shaped by the movements and institutions he inspired. He spotted the growing importance of consumerism, and founded *Which?* magazine and the Consumers' Association to empower the citizen within the new market places (he even floated the idea of a new consumers' political party). He set up the Institute for Community Studies in Bethnal Green in the East End of London, now the Young Foundation. The Open University, the School for Social Entrepreneurs and the University of the Third Age owe everything to Young's vision. Whilst organising his wife's funeral he saw a need for better training for funeral directors and established the National Funeral College.

He was passionately mistrustful of the central state. His prolific invention of organisations was a reflection of a political conviction that citizens need protection from the state through a strong civil society. He added to the sum of civil society by launching new entrants to it. By empowering individuals through new forms of organization, he hoped to build new forms of egalitarian community. In 2000 he said:

> Were we to evaluate people, not only according to their intelligence and their education, their occupations and their power, but according to their kindliness and their courage, their imagination and sensitivity, their sympathy and generosity, there would be no overall inequalities of the sort we have got used to. Who would be able to say that the scientist was superior to the porter with admirable qualities as a father, the civil servant to the lorry-driver with unusual skills at growing roses? A pluralistic society would also be a tolerant society, in which individual differences were actively encouraged as well as passively tolerated, in which full meaning was at last given to the dignity of man. Every human being would then have equal opportunity to develop his or her own special capacities for leading a full life which is also a noble life led for the benefit of others as well as the self.[14]

On these criteria, Young's own life should be judged a noble one led for the benefit of others as well as the self. Labour should learn the lessons: that with the proper support and leadership, people are capable of extraordinary feats of imagination, innovation and transformation. Young's ideas were often the spark, but his gift was to be able to cut loose his creations as fast as possible, and allow new people to take over. He launched ships; he didn't captain them. The next Labour government must adopt the same approach: to be prepared to let a thousand flowers bloom, to give power and assets to people in the knowledge that they might fail, and to boost a thriving civil society, not simply add new arms to the state.

Summary

The Labour Party can draw on a deep well of experience, tradition and thought. To pretend that New Labour was a 'new party' was always a nonsense. The Labour Party in the 1990s was part of a thread of revisionism which stretches far back into the twentieth century. To suppose that the next phase of Labour, whatever it may be, is purely a product of the early twenty-first century would be equally mistaken. Every generation owes something to those that have gone before. To fail to analyse and understand Labour's past is to risk repeating its errors, or fail to copy its triumphs.

Within the socialist tradition are a great many writers, thinkers, philosophers and political leaders who can provide the modern-day Labour supporter with inspiration and insight. From the Levellers and Diggers, we can take the fight for democracy, civil rights, religious freedoms, and stewardship of the earth's treasures. From the Co-operators we can discover new ways to produce, buy and sell goods and services, to reveal human beings' instincts for collaboration and reciprocity, and to see glimpses of a better way to run our society and economy. From William Morris we get a vision of socialism, with men and women living in tune with the environment, in a world free from war and hunger. Keir Hardie shows us the power of ideas and organisation combined. When we read G. D. H. Cole we discover a socialism, not of the state, but of local guilds and councils, with democracy and self-government a way of life for all. R. H. Tawney teaches us the importance of values in the struggle for equality and an end to selfishness and acquisitiveness. George Orwell offers a dire warning of the dangers of a totalitarian state, of arbitrary power, of repression of the human desire for liberty, and of the crimes committed in the name of socialism. Michael Young teaches us the value of DIY social change – get on and do it yourself!

These socialists represent a tiny fragment of the socialist canon, and a highly subjective selection at that. You could add all manner of people to the list. What this selection aims to show is the strands of thought that run through our history, and what they mean today. Above all, they develop and articulate socialist values in their own times, places and circumstances, in ways which can aid us in the twenty-first century.

5. Labour's values

> 'On a group of theories one can found a school; but on a
> group of values one can found a culture, a civilisation, a new
> way of living together among men.'
>
> Ignazio Silone

Labour is underpinned by a system of values. Labour's values – the values of socialism – are what motivate, animate and guide the party, in its theoretical debates and its practical policies. Without a reassessment of these values, and what they mean in a modern context, Labour's revival will be hamstrung by arguments about policies and personalities, not fundamentals. It is obvious that during the last few years of Labour's rule, the party's values were lost in the foliage of government, and with them a sense of purpose.

The trinity of values that comprises British socialism is liberty, equality and community. This is not simply a straight plagiarism of the French Revolution, despite its obvious similarities with the famous slogan. The values of socialism derive from the various influences that flow into the socialist movement, like the tributaries of a great river. The campaigns for power and democracy fought by the Chartists and the Suffragettes; the romantic utopias of William Morris; Robert Owen's co-operative ideal; the gradualism of the Fabian Society; the practical experience of work supplied by the trade unions; the moral indignation of the nonconformists; the radicalism of the 'New Liberals' who crossed over to Labour; the organising zeal of campaigners against global poverty, apartheid, racism or nuclear weapons; the experience of the women's movement. These forces both reflect and embolden Labour's values.

The point of these values, each of which could legitimately be claimed by other parties and political philosophies, is that they are self-reinforcing and co-dependent. They only work in concert with one another. You can have equality without liberty (in the Soviet Union, most people were equally miserable); you can have liberty without equality (in the USA people are free, yet beset with social problems which restrict their liberty); you can have community without either liberty or equality (the Nazis created a great deal of camaraderie amongst the German people). Only through their interdependence do these values work to create a socialist society.

Labour's values are its anchor; they are what stops it becoming a party of pure pragmatism or ideological extremes. The values stand as judge. They test each act and utterance of Labour's politicians. They serve as a guiding light. They can form, as the Italian socialist Ignazio Silone suggests, the basis for a society, a culture and a civilisation.

Labour should apply its trinity of values to the policy challenges that will emerge in the years ahead. As David Blunkett and Bernard Crick wrote in their *Unofficial Statement of Labour's Aims and Values*:

> Policies must be informed by values and a sense of direction not merely by short-term practicality and expediency. Otherwise policy dwindles into mere pragmatism, always reacting to events, never trying to shape them. Policy must never mean staying in office for the sake of staying in office or trying to win elections simply by reading the momentary popularity of issues on opinion polls.

They should also serve as a way of living, a personal credo and a living example to others. Crick wrote: 'If we can only achieve our aims gradually, we can live by our values now and every day.'[1] It is perhaps the reason that when socialist politicians fall by the wayside, as happened during the expenses scandal in 2009, the fall is that much greater.

It is likely that Labour figures, from Keir Hardie, to Barbara Castle, to John Smith, to Gordon Brown, to David Miliband, would have little difficulty in immediately identifying in one another shared values and recognising common concerns. Yet the policy answers to those concerns, and the methods and tools to apply those shared values, would be almost entirely alien between the generations.

The purpose of having these values is to apply them to the social problems of the day. Labour's values are timeless, because they chime with the better angels of human nature. But obviously the types of issues they must address, and the matter in which they are applied, change from year to year, decade to decade.

Ethical socialism

In the 1990s, as Labour underwent its latest great phase of revisionism, people started to talk of 'ethical socialism' to distinguish it from a socialism dependent on state ownership and control. A socialism without ethics can't exist, but there was a need to make the distinction. The original ethical socialists had been in the Independent Labour Party (ILP), formed in 1893. They were nonconformist Christians, concerned with ending poverty. They were attracted to the utopian visions of Ruskin and William Morris, and the ideals of the co-operators.

Robert Blatchford (1851–1943) wrote *Merrie England* in 1894, an appeal to the working man, 'John Smith', to join the socialist movement. It sold over two million copies within a few years. He also founded *The Clarion* newspaper, and the Clarion Cycling Clubs combined socialist zeal with physical exercise and comradeship.

Later, he supported the Boer War, opposed votes for women and backed the Tories at the 1924 election.

Edward Carpenter (1844–1929) was a leading ethical socialist and advocate for gay rights. Gay himself, he lived openly with his partner in Milthorpe, in Derbyshire, and received guests from the worlds of literature and politics, including E. M. Forster who wrote *Maurice* after a visit. He was concerned with air pollution, vivisection, vegetarianism and women's liberation. He was a founder member of the Fabian Society (and would fit in rather well today).

The ethical socialist pioneers gave the Labour Party a socialism which was non-Marxist, often Christian, rooted in values, passionate about tackling poverty and disadvantage, and concerned with the brotherhood and sisterhood of all humanity rather than prescriptive economic doctrine.

It was this idea of socialism that inspired Tony Blair, a Christian, to join the Labour Party in the 1970s, and gave him the moral basis for his politics. Blair gave a lecture to the Fabian Society in 1994 which identified

> two strands of socialist thought that have dominated the left this century. One is based on the belief that socialism is a set of values or beliefs – sometimes called ethical socialism and closely allied to European social democracy. It does not deny the existence of class divisions but its definition of them is not time bound. The other is a quasi-scientific view of socialism that is based on a notion of economic determinism and a particular view of class.[2]

Clause IV, Part 4

To understand how and why the Labour Party in the twentieth century diverted from the ethical approach of the Christian socialists, the radical liberals, the co-operators and utopians like Morris, you have to go back to Clause IV, Part 4 of the party's constitution: the famous section which committed Labour to 'common ownership of the means of production, distribution and exchange'. It hung like a millstone around the party's neck for eighty years – proof to critics that Labour wanted to seize private property, and evidence to the far left and the party's own left wing that Labour governments always 'sell out'. Labour's ethical socialism was buried under economic doctrine, resulting in a philosophical obfuscation and political muddle which endured for most of the century.

The original words of this part of the Labour Party's constitution read:

1. To organise and maintain in Parliament and in the country a political Labour Party.

2. To cooperate with the General Council of the Trades Union Congress, or other kindred organisations, in joint political or other action in harmony with the party constitution and standing orders.

3. To give effect as far as possible to the principles from time to time approved by the party conference.

4. To secure for the workers by hand or by brain the full fruits of their industry and the most equitable distribution thereof that may be possible upon the basis of the common ownership of the means of production, distribution and exchange, and the best obtainable system of popular administration and control of each industry or service.

5. Generally to promote the political, social and economic emancipation of the people, and more particularly of those who depend directly upon their own exertions by hand or by brain for the means of life.

Inter-Commonwealth
6. To cooperate with the labour and socialist organisations in the commonwealth overseas with a view to promoting the purposes of the party, and to take common action for the

promotion of a higher standard of social and economic life for the working population of the respective countries.

International

7. To cooperate with the labour and socialist organisations in other countries and to support the United Nations and its various agencies and other international organisations for the promotion of peace, the adjustment and settlement of international disputes by conciliation or judicial arbitration, the establishment and defence of human rights, and the improvement of the social and economic standards and conditions of work of the people of the world.

The International section, with its reference to the UN, was added after the Second World War. Part 4 used to appear on the party's membership cards, and was considered to be the sacred socialist text which defined the Labour Party's mission, despite being routinely ignored by Labour politicians, especially when in government.

Clause IV, Part 4 was never intended to become holy writ. Arthur Henderson, Labour's first Cabinet minister, three-times Labour leader, and winner of the Nobel Peace Prize, was the proponent of a constitution for the Labour Party, to put clear red water between the new party and the Liberals. In fine Labour Party tradition, the business of drafting a new constitution was delegated to an eight-member sub-committee of the National Executive Committee (NEC), including Ramsay MacDonald, Sidney Webb and Henderson himself. The remaining places were taken with trade unionists. The sub-committee did not spend long on Clause IV, Part 4, preferring to debate the system for electing internal positions in the party. Two versions were put forward. Henderson proposed: 'To secure for the producers by hand or brain the full fruits of their industry by the Common Ownership of all monopolies and essential raw materials.'

Webb proposed the rather more famous version, which was adopted by the NEC, and by the party conference in 1918. He was clear that the new constitution was essentially pragmatic, not dogmatic. Crucially, it did not commit Labour to nationalisation of the kind that the party pursued in the 1940s and argued about ever after. Writing in 1917 in *The Observer*, Webb made the point that Clause IV

> is a socialism which is no more specific than a definite repudiation of the individualism that characterised all the political parties of the past generations and that still dominates the House of Commons. This declaration . . . leaves it open to choose from time to time whatever forms of common ownership, from the co-operative store to the nationalised railway, and whatever form of popular administration, from national guilds to ministries of employment, and municipal management may, in particular cases, commend themselves.[3]

Its author drafted a text whose meaning was so broad it could appeal to people across the Labour movement, from the co-op, to the unions, to the Fabians, to the Guildsmen, to the municipal socialists. Even the author of Clause IV, Part 4 was pragmatic enough to avoid imbuing it with too much prescription. It was only later, in the 1930s and 1940s, that socialism and nationalisation became synonymous, that state control came to mean the same thing as common ownership, and that socialists forgot the difference between ends and means.

What mattered to Webb was what worked.

Clause IV, Part 4 failed to express Labour's values; it merely expressed an economic policy which fell in and out of practicability and favour as the decades passed since its drafting. Yet it is values which give Labour its life and vitality. How should we describe liberty, equality and community in an age of insecurity and globalisation? That is now Labour's task.

6. Liberty

'The true perfection of man lies, not in what man has, but
in what man is.'

Oscar Wilde, 'The Soul of Man under Socialism' (1891)

The pursuit of individual liberty is what animates socialists. It
connects the modern-day Labour Party with great struggles for
emancipation throughout human history. It allows Labour, in
lofty, idealistic moments, to place itself in an unbroken thread of
historic campaigns and movements, from the Peasants' Revolt to
the Anti-Apartheid Movement, from the Abolitionists to Martin
Luther King. People's desire to be rid of tyranny, slavery, despotism,
dictatorship and servitude echoes down the ages. It was the cause
of the French and American Revolutions, and of political reformers
in Britain, and the language of liberty characterised the early trade
union and Labour movement.

The theme of liberty recurs in Labour articles, speeches and
manifestos. Once, it appeared at the heart of the Labour Party logo,
set against a quill pen and a spade (representing the workers 'by
hand' and 'by brain'), and a flaming torch.

Clement Attlee could argue in 1937, just eight years before Winston
Churchill would accuse Labour of needing a 'Gestapo' to implement
its programme, that Labour's aim was 'greater freedom for the
individual.' He went on: 'British socialists have never made an idol
of the state, demanding that individuals should be sacrificed to it

. . . they appreciate that the wealth of a society is its variety not its uniformity. Progress is not towards, but away from, the herd.'[1]

Yet liberty remains the least understood and most hotly contested of Labour's values. Liberty would be enthusiastically and indignantly claimed by conservatives and liberals as their organising principle and political goal. Conservatives of the Thatcher and Reagan variety saw liberty as a product of free markets, a smaller state and the struggle against communism. Individual liberty is bound up with lower levels of public expenditure, and a reduced apparatus of the state, they say. Reagan said: 'Man is not free unless government is limited. There's a clear cause and effect here that is as neat and predictable as a law of physics: as government expands, liberty contracts.'[2] Yet this idea of liberty simply elevates a small-minded political philosophy into a great goal.

One of the key thinkers behind the Thatcher and Reagan governments was economist and philosopher Friedrich Hayek. Hayek's early works included *The Road to Serfdom* (1944), which made the case for laissez-faire and a smaller state, arguing that 'socialism' (by which he meant a large state) led inevitably to human servitude. One chapter places Nazism (at his time of writing still an extant force) as a product of socialism. George Orwell at his radical best, in reviewing *The Road to Serfdom*, wrote: 'But he does not see, or will not admit, that a return to "free" competition means for the great mass of people a tyranny probably worse, because more irresponsible, than that of the State. The trouble with competitions is that somebody wins them.'[3] Margaret Thatcher read *The Road to Serfdom* in the late 1940s and 'returned to it often'.[4]

A later work by Hayek, *The Constitution of Liberty* (1960), argued that individual liberty (expressed as freedom from the state) was a necessary condition of economic growth and wealth. In 1975, Thatcher met Hayek, and later at a seminar at which a Tory 'wet' was making a presentation, took a copy of *The Constitution of Liberty* from her handbag, slammed it down on the table and said, 'This is what we believe.'[5] It is impossible to imagine any other prime minister being able to say the same about any other book, at any time in our history.

The free-market experiments of the 1980s in Britain and America did not yield greater freedom for the individual. The privatisation of certain state-owned bodies created better, more efficient companies. Labour needs to recognise that the Thatcher government made reforms which were necessary and welcome. It is undoubtedly better to have telecoms in the private sector rather than the state sector. The freedom to choose what colour telephone you want, and when it will be delivered, is without question an improvement on the service people used to get. But better customer service, and greater consumer choice, do not radically enhance the sum of human freedom. For the many millions of people for whom the 1980s represented a major change in their standard of living and way of life, particularly people in the coal-mining and manufacturing sectors, Thatcherism meant less freedom, not more.

Freedom, in this context, was rationed by the individuals' financial circumstances. The rich had more freedom – to access good healthcare and education, to enjoy museums and concerts, to eat fine food and wear designer clothes, and to travel abroad – than the poor. Freedom was no longer conceived to be allocated as a human right, but as a luxury product consumed within a free market, like sushi or cigars.

Neil Kinnock expressed the contradictions in a speech to the Labour Party in 1987:

> I think of the youngsters I meet – three, four, five years out of school, never had a job, and they say to me, 'Do you think we'll ever get a job?' These are young men and women living in a free country but they don't feel free. I think of the 55-year-old woman I meet waiting months to go into hospital for an operation, her whole existence clouded by pain; she is a citizen of a free country but she doesn't feel free.[6]

In the same year his deputy, Roy Hattersley, wrote in *Choose Freedom: The Future for Democratic Socialism* that

> the writings of F. A. Hayek on liberty – and the actions of politicians guided by him – demonstrate that noble aspirations to freedom have, in modern times, been interpreted in the language of class interests. Those who want to maintain and advance their wealth and power have advocated a form of freedom that enables them to do so.

For the Labour Party to convincingly talk about liberty, it needs to know what it means by the term. If we are aggrieved that it has been appropriated by our enemies, then we probably have ourselves to blame.

It is obvious that socialists (and just about everyone else) reject the idea of absolute liberty – the freedom to do whatever you choose. An individual, once beyond infancy, must control his or her instincts within a framework of propriety, morals and the rule of law.

This framework is constantly shifting. A Victorian could walk into a chemist and buy cocaine, opium and heroin over the counter. The age of consent was twelve. No licence was needed to own a gun. Children worked in mines, factories and kitchens, in the armed forces, as prostitutes, and up chimneys. Yet the role of government was tiny, and the size of the state minute compared to the twentieth century. In the 1980s, you could smoke cigarettes in pubs, restaurants, cinemas, at work, and on the London Underground, which usefully provided smoking carriages on the Tube. Today those 'freedoms' seem absurd.

Yet within all forms of society, absolute freedom is restricted. There is no freedom to murder, to assault, to rape, to steal or damage other people's belongings. Only in our darkest nightmares can we imagine a world where individuals can behave with absolute freedom. As John Rawls wrote in *A Theory of Justice*: 'When liberties are left unrestricted, they collide with one another.' Or as R. H. Tawney (a keen fisherman) famously put it: 'Freedom for the pike is death to the minnows.'[7]

J. S. Mill articulated the 'harm principle' in his essay *On Liberty* (1859), whereby individual liberty can only exist within the stricture that it does not harm others. He wrote:

> That the only purpose for which power can be rightfully exercised over any member of a civilized community, against his will, is to prevent harm to others. His own good, either physical or moral, is not sufficient warrant. He cannot rightfully be compelled to do or forbear because it will be better for him to do so, because it will make him happier, because, in the opinion of others, to do so would be wise, or even right . . . The only part of the conduct of anyone, for which he is amenable to society, is that which concerns others. In the part which merely concerns himself, his independence is, of right, absolute. Over himself, over his own body and mind, the individual is sovereign.

This is the case for classical liberty. It was radical in its time because the state forbade Catholics and nonconformists the full exercise of citizenship. Each president of the Liberal Democrats is presented with a copy of Mill's essay.

But freedom from constraint, from arbitrary imprisonment, from attack or injury, is only one, albeit vital, component. For socialists the question then arises: what is the point of liberty if it is only theoretical, bound up in a constitutional right or recurrent in political leaders' rhetoric, but unable to be exercised in everyday life? It is what R. H. Tawney meant when he said that rights must not be merely formal 'like the right of all who can afford it to dine at the Ritz.'[8]

The practical ability to enjoy liberty, to be able to do something as well have the freedom to do it, is what social justice is all about. It is the principle behind laws to give people with disabilities rights to work, goods and services, to ensure that no pub or hotel can refuse to serve gay people, and to guarantee black people the right to go about their business free from signs saying 'Whites Only'.

The New Labour governments elected in 1997, 2001 and 2005 were caricatured as being authoritarian and unconcerned with civil liberties. The government elected in 2010 has gone about removing many measures introduced by the Labour Party, for example scrapping ID cards and decommissioning CCTV cameras. Yet an ID card does not remove the civil liberties or individual freedoms of a citizen. It is merely an expression of citizenship. By making it harder for terrorists or other criminals to take lives or smuggle drugs, guns and people, a system of ID cards can enhance and increase liberty. Not having ID cards does not add to the sum of freedom. CCTV cameras restrict the liberty of those who want to commit crimes or conduct anti-social behaviour; they enhance the liberty of those wanting to walk down the street free from assault or robbery. As one politician put it: 'In many communities across the UK, particularly in our most deprived communities, high levels of crime are today a far greater threat to liberty than the over-zealous activities of home secretaries.'

The author of those words is the former Liberal Democrat Cabinet minister David Laws, writing in *The Orange Book*. For New Labour, liberty had a strong class component. On many deprived estates people were not free. They were not able to exercise basic liberties such as going out after dark, being able to park their car without it being vandalised, and knowing their house wouldn't be burgled if they went on holiday. But worse in some ways was the absence of positive freedoms: freedom to receive a decent education and go to university, freedom to experience a range of cultures, freedom to travel.

There are young people living on estates for whom their estate is the world, and their city the universe. They have never been to a restaurant (the Ritz or anywhere else), never been abroad, never visited a museum or art gallery, never been to a concert, and never been to another city. Many have never been to work, know no-one in work, or live in a house with no-one in work. New Labour made no apologies for seeking to widen the horizons and extend the opportunities for people whose economic and personal circumstances reduced their liberty.

When freedom is dependent on the economic means to purchase it, it is not genuine freedom, but a chimera. Similarly, when freedom is related to power, to an individual's place within a regimented or restricted society, then it is not genuine freedom. Liberty must not only include freedom of expression, thought and belief, freedom to be who you are and do what you want to do; it must also be freedom to grow, to learn, to expand your horizons, to enjoy the best of what life has to offer, and to develop to the full extent of your aptitudes.

This realisation that liberty is sterile without the means to exercise it does two things in the mind of the socialist: first, it creates a distinct break with the conservative or liberal concept of liberty (and allows a theoretical disentangling to take place); and second, it demands a practical remedy. That leads up to the second of Labour's trinity of values, equality.

Summary

The aim of socialism is liberty. The means to achieve it is greater equality. For socialists, freedom does not mean freedom to do what you like, regardless of the cost to other people, your community or the environment. It is not a narrow economic concept – not the conservative and liberal idea of laissez-faire, or the absence of restraint, regulations and rules. Nor is freedom simply a fig-leaf for a smaller state, as the Thatcher/Reagan conservatives would have us believe.

Liberty means an unlocking of human talent and expression, freedom from constraints such as a lack on ambition or narrow horizons, and also freedom to experience life to the full by providing springboards for people to transcend poverty and disadvantage. Freedom of the individual must always be balanced against freedom for the whole community. Where individual liberties clash with those of the community (for example the liberty to litter the streets, keep unruly pets or play loud music), socialists should side with the community.

7. Equality

> 'Socialism is the imaginative belief that all men, however unequal they may be in powers of mind and body, are in a really significant sense equal, not merely before the law but one with another.'
>
> G. D. H. Cole, *The Simple Case for Socialism* (1935)

On the Sunday before he died, at the age of fifty-nine, Tony Crosland took a stroll in the gardens of Dorneywood, the grace-and-favour home which came with his job as foreign secretary. It was his only visit. His interlocutor was Roy Hattersley, then forty-five, and in discussing political philosophy, Crosland constructed a neat one-line definition of what was meant by socialism: 'The pursuit of equality and the protection of freedom – in the knowledge that until we are truly equal we will not be truly free.'[1]

Until we are truly equal, we will not be truly free. Equality, then, is not an end in itself, but a means to an end. It is easy to confuse it with the ends, because of socialists' horror at the manifestations at home and abroad of inequality. Part of the socialist psyche includes a revulsion towards poverty, homelessness and starvation, which is counterpoised with the super-rich: the have-nots and the have-yachts. It found its expression in the early demands of the trade union movement, the Fabian Society (which published *Why Are the Many Poor?* by George Bernard Shaw), and the Labour Party itself.

One of New Labour's most important measures was the introduction in 1999 of a national minimum wage, which tackled inequality at the bottom end of the income spectrum. Conservatives in the UK opposed the idea of a minimum wage because they claimed it would have the perverse effect of creating greater unemployment amongst low-paid workers. In this they were supported by the work of the US economist George Stigler and other free-market economists at the Chicago School of Economics, who made the classic case against national minimum wages, namely that they restrict access to labour markets for the poorest and most unskilled workers, stifle entrepreneurialism and hamper small businesses, and create unemployment.

After a decade, the national minimum wage is an established part of the UK economy and accepted across the political spectrum. The prime minister, David Cameron, has overcome his initial scepticism and now supports it. In London, Conservative mayor Boris Johnson supports a 'living wage' for staff working for the Greater London Authority. A living wage is assessed on what an individual needs in terms of accommodation, food, clothing etc., based on the cost of goods and services.

What the national minimum wage showed was New Labour's early determination, along with measures to tackle rough sleeping, extra tax credits for poor families, and so on, to tackle inequality by reducing poverty at the lowest end of the spectrum, rather than levelling down from the top. There was no national maximum wage.

Does equality equal uniformity?

Equality should not mean 'equality of outcome'.

A concept of equality which ignored the infinite variety of humankind, our different talents and aptitudes, would be eccentric and perverse. George Bernard Shaw made the case for strict equality of income at a lecture delivered at the National Liberal Club on May Day 1913: 'When I speak of the case for equality I mean human equality; and that, of course, can only mean one thing: it means equality of income.'[2] He railed against the idea of equality of opportunity, which he called a 'ghastly mockery': 'How are you going to give everyone in this room equal opportunities with me of writing plays?'

Shaw's idea that an arithmetic levelling of all incomes would create an equal society was wrong, and attempts at levelling societies, in China, Cambodia, Russia and elsewhere, in the twentieth century delivered systems of repression, murder, hierarchy and privilege which are as far from the socialist ideal as is possible. Strict economic redistributionists also ignore the fact that power exists in forms other than spending power. Equality, to mean anything, must mean an egalitarian distribution of political, social, cultural and economic power, throughout society. That's what social justice must mean.

Where once socialists saw the route to an equal society in terms of redistribution of wealth, through taxation, today we should see it in terms of redistribution of democratic power. The contribution to socialism of the rights movements for women, lesbians and gays, disabled people and other minorities has been to see social justice in terms other than purely economic. For example, Section 28 of the Local Government Act in 1988, which forbade the 'promotion of homosexuality' by local authorities, had nothing to do with economic rights. It was a right-wing government pandering to anti-gay prejudice, and shoring up its social conservative base. The campaign that arose in opposition to Section 28 brought together people from all kinds of backgrounds, with all kinds of politics. The campaign's legacy was the 'mainstreaming' of lesbian and gay rights into democratic socialism, in a way which socialists up to the 1970s, who saw wealth distribution as central, would not have considered.

Labour's useful idiots

It is easy to blame the Tories or right-wing media, think-tanks or academics for creating this caricature of the socialist ideal of equality. Through reasoned argument and vicious satire, the right has successfully painted equality as a great levelling-down, a uniformity of mediocrity and misery, a terrifying dystopia. When the London Residuary Body moved into County Hall after the abolition of the GLC, a rumour went round that hundreds of Chinese Communist uniforms had been found in the basement: a superb example of black propaganda.

But the greatest culprits for this perversion of socialism have been socialists. There have always been those on the left who have either deliberately, or through muddle-headedness, confused equality with uniformity. Within the Labour Party there were those who were vocal supporters of the USSR.

Beatrice and Sidney Webb visited the Soviet Union in 1932, and in 1935 published *Soviet Communism: A New Civilisation?*. In later editions, the question mark disappeared, such was their lack of doubt. On the thorny question of whether or not Stalin was a dictator, they wrote:

> We have given particular attention to this point, collecting all the available evidence, and noting carefully the inferences to be drawn from the experience of the past eight years (1926–1934). We do not think that the Party is governed by the will of a single person or that Stalin is the sort of person to claim or desire such a position. He has himself very explicitly denied any such personal dictatorship in terms which, whether or not he is credited with sincerity, certainly accord with our own impression of the facts.

The Webbs, then, at a time when the outline of Stalin's terror was well known, if not the full extent of the horror, were happy to take him at his word that he was not a dictator. A lesser-known work, *The Truth about Soviet Russia*, appeared in 1942, which again gave full backing to the USSR (albeit by then a wartime ally). There is no excuse for this. George Orwell wrote his allegory of Soviet repression and the betrayal of socialist ideals the following year. A couple of years after that came *Nineteen Eighty-four*, the most effective warning against dictatorship in the English language. From the time *Animal Farm* was published, in 1945, until 1989, it and *Nineteen Eighty-four* were banned in the 'new civilisation' of which the Webbs so approved.

D. N. Pritt was MP for Hammersmith North between 1935 and 1940. After a fact-finding mission to Russia in 1932 as part of the New Fabian Research Bureau, he enthusiastically supported the Soviet Union under Stalin, and was awarded the International Stalin Peace Prize in 1954. Pritt, along with a small group of other Labour MPs, formed the Labour Independent Group to cheerlead for the murderous, blood-soaked Stalinist regime. Within the Parliamentary Labour Party, the trade unions and the constituency Labour parties, there have always been Communist fellow-travellers, sympathisers and apologists for repressive regimes, from Serbia to Iraq, Cambodia to Albania. These are the 'useful idiots' described by Lenin, whose particular brand of idiocy allows Labour's enemies to paint all socialists as communists or apologists for the gulag or the killing fields.

An egalitarian society

If the socialist value of equality does not mean uniformity, what does it mean?

No socialist should mistake equality for sameness. It is an *egalitarian* impulse that drives socialists onwards, not a desire to see everyone living the same life, living in the same-sized house, doing the same kind of work, and earning the same amount of money. Keir Hardie wrote: 'Socialism implies the inherent equality of all human beings. It does not assume they are all alike, but only that all are equal.'[3] And as Bernard Crick wrote in an essay on the eve of Tony Blair's landslide in 1997: 'Surely the long-term aim is towards a more egalitarian society. Not an equal, but an egalitarian society is our aim.'[4]

Crick goes on to say that an egalitarian society would have as a prerequisite 'radically more democratic, decentralised and civic, participative institutions' making the important link between greater equality and a more equal distribution of power. He also calls for incoming Labour ministers to eschew their ministerial perks, privileges, cars and first-class travel, in order to 'live by our values now, and every day'. Unfortunately, this was not advice taken at the time by Labour ministers, or subsequently. There is no doubt that the trappings of office, and scenes of John Prescott playing croquet on the lawn at Dorneywood, contributed to the strong sense that Labour ministers were 'out of touch'. Because of the constituency system, which keeps ministers' feet on the ground through regular exposure to their constituents' concerns (unlike in other countries), the charge of being out of touch was mostly unfair and unfounded. But by 2010, that was the strong and widespread perception amongst the voters.

Egalitarianism is about more than equal opportunities, because equality of opportunity is meaningless without the power to take up the opportunity. 'Equality of opportunity' is an idea that anyone, including conservatives, can sign up to. In a society with theoretical equality of opportunity, failure to fulfil opportunities can be blamed on individual weakness, ignorance, fecklessness or laziness. It is impossible to measure, assess or even for the individual to be aware of. Perversely, 'equal opportunities' became associated in some minds with giving women, disabled people and people from ethnic minorities special treatment and favouritism in the distribution of benefits, social services and employment.

Tony Crosland, looking back over his own philosophical journey, wrote:

Socialism, in our view, was basically about equality. By equality, we meant more than a meritocratic society of equal opportunities in which the greatest rewards would go to those with the most fortunate genetic endowment and family background; we adopted the 'strong' definition of equality – what Rawls has subsequently called the 'democratic' as opposed to the 'liberal' conception. We also mean more than a simple redistribution of income. We wanted a wider social equality embracing the distribution of property, the education system, social-class relationships, power and privilege in industry – indeed all that was enshrined in the age-old socialist dream of a more 'classless society'.[5]

Note that the 'meritocratic society' that Crosland refers to is, for him, a negative idea, in the sense intended by Michael Young.

Amartya Sen, the Indian-born Harvard academic, has sought to offer a modern definition of equality which is proving much more useful. In *The Idea of Justice* (2009) Sen argues that whilst philosophers such as John Rawls have offered a vision of a perfect system of social justice, what is needed is a practical definition, taking into account the 'real world'. The key idea is that the 'capabilities' of individuals to fulfil their aptitudes and live full lives need to be taken into account when judging welfare and social systems. This idea of 'equal capabilities' has animated Labour figures such as James Purnell to launch a debate on a modern notion of equality (and led to a fantastic ding-dong on BBC *Newsnight* between Purnell and the old Croslandite Roy Hattersley). Sen's work takes us in a more helpful direction than a fixation on either arithmetic equality (which takes no account of human diversity), or wealth redistribution (which takes no account of either political realities or other forms of inequality).

A socialism that seeks to impose a standard of life on everyone, through a national system of housing, education, healthcare and social services, would remove individual freedom of choice, and crush individual ambition, talent and imagination. This was the inbuilt danger with systems of council housing, comprehensive education, or social services which failed to recognise individual needs, personal tastes and lifestyles, and failed to recognise that we are all different and that society changes. Aspects of the post-war welfare state were imbued with a drive for 'equality' – but the result was an equal distribution of alienation, frustration, poor standards and quality, and powerlessness for the recipient.

Overall, the Labour governments failed to create equal life chances for everyone in Britain. At the tail end of the last Labour government, Gordon Brown asked the former Cabinet minister Alan Milburn to chair a panel looking into fair access to the professions. Its report, *Unleashing Aspiration*,[6] showed that Britain had become *less* socially mobile than in the 1950s and 1960s, when a combination of grammar schools, new universities and a growth in the professions with more 'room at the top' meant that talented working-class children could become doctors, lawyers, architects, civil servants, journalists and academics.

Stark differences in income remain, but so do differences in power, opportunity and chances for social mobility. Britain, after a decade or more of Labour government, is in many ways more class ridden, socially static, and unfair. The poorest people have seen their living standards improve. But the poorest children on the toughest estates have no more chance of becoming engineers, surgeons or lawyers than the poorest children in Victorian times.

Summary

Equality is easily parodied as a great levelling-down in society, making everyone equally miserable, impoverished and downtrodden. *Nineteen Eighty-four* vividly described a society where everyone was theoretically equal, yet political elites could exercise god-like power over others. Conservatives have used this parody of equality, and pointed to countries such as Cambodia or Albania, as a way of destroying notions of equality and turning egalitarianism into a dirty word. Yet for the socialist, equality does not mean arithmetic identity between individuals. Even George Orwell's list of socialist demands only included 'limitation of incomes, on such a scale that the highest tax-free income in Britain does not exceed the lowest by more than ten to one'.[7]

A modern definition of equality means both the capability for individuals, as equal citizens, to lead a rich fulfilling life, within the context of a strong community, and the narrowing of the chasm between rich and poor, high and low, within society. This latter imperative is more than a romantic nod in the direction of the utopian dreamers such as William Morris; it is demonstrably the route to a healthier, happier population, making fewer, less expensive demands on the welfare state. It does not mean soaking the rich, but raising the poor. But more than simply tackling the worst excesses of a free-market society, it means bringing in a more egalitarian way of living.

Essential to Labour's revival is a robust national debate about the nature of equality, what an egalitarian society would look like, and the practical measures (in the spirit of the national minimum wage) that would take us there.

8. Community

> 'When one came straight from England the aspect of Barcelona was something startling and overwhelming. It was the first time that I had ever been in a town where the working class was in the saddle.'
>
> George Orwell, *Homage to Catalonia* (1938)

I was first introduced to the idea of *ubuntu* by listening to a speech by Bill Clinton at the Labour Party conference in 2006. *Ubuntu* is an African philosophical concept which can be very loosely translated as 'togetherness' or 'affinity' with one another. It speaks to the interconnectedness of the human family, the connections between the living and the dead, and in political terms the need for co-operation and solidarity. It rests on the simple idea that you can't be human all by yourself.

This idea of togetherness, expressed as 'fellowship', 'solidarity', 'fraternity', 'brother-/sisterhood' or 'community', has been central to socialism. It describes the feelings of affinity within the socialist movement (where people still call each other 'comrade', 'brother' and 'sister', not always with irony) and also the internationalist spirit, which says that our connections with one another extend beyond nationality, race and creed. In the global age, this is literally true for the first time in human history.

It speaks to a concept of human behaviour and nature which is instinctively collaborative and generous, but which the social environment and economic system distorts into a spirit of competition and Darwinian survival of the fittest. Community (my preferred term) is about more than the social good that kindness, neighbourliness and social interaction releases. It suggests something about the sense of fulfilment that community can realise in the individual. As one of Tony Blair's favourite philosophers, John Macmurray, wrote: 'We need one another to be ourselves.' Macmurray placed community within a Christian framework, with fellowship imagined as *communion*.

But it exists within the secular socialist tradition too. When I worked, briefly, at Walthamstow Town Hall I was greeted each morning with the inscription above the door 'Fellowship is life, lack of fellowship is death'. The Walthamstow resident who expressed that thought, William Morris, saw fellowship as the ideal state of what he called 'communism', meaning the absence of private property, class, money and government. In *News from Nowhere*, Morris describes humans living in harmony with one another and the natural environment, taking pleasure in work and craftsmanship, and having no need for coercive laws or restrictions. The House of Commons has become, in Morris's socialist utopia, a store for horse dung.[1] It was Morris whose socialist writings inspired G. D. H. Cole to become a socialist.

In the age of globalisation, with a reduction in state spending, community becomes more, not less, important. Anthony Crosland and the other revisionists had little to say about community, because until the 1950s and 1960s, working-class communities existed in a reasonably stable form, with the ties of kinship, family and geographical identity well established.

In 1962, Peter Willmott and Michael Young produced their famous study of community life in Bethnal Green, in the East End of London, which they contrasted with the new council estate in Debden in Essex to which many East End families were forcibly moved after the war. Their book *Family and Kinship in East London* (known in the trade as 'Fakinel') could describe the scene in Bethnal Green in the early 1960s as being like a village:

Established residents claimed to 'know everyone'. They could do so because most people were connected by kinship ties to a network of other families, and through them to a host of friends and acquaintances. Ties of blood and marriage were local ties . . . This was rather different from the popular view of what a modern metropolis is like. Bethnal Green is not so much a crowd of individuals – restless, lonely, rootless – as an orderly community based on family and neighbourhood groupings.

For much of Labour's century in existence, the idea of 'community' could refer to actual communities like Bethnal Green, based on streets and neighbourhoods, shared experiences of employment and patterns of work, and common social norms. The idea of people looking out for one another, looking after one another's children, rallying round in times of personal adversity, and being in and out of one another's houses is not fanciful; it describes the reality of millions of people's lives until a few decades ago.

It was well described (some would say romanticised) in George Orwell's *The Road to Wigan Pier*, and in his other political writings. Orwell's biographer Bernard Crick suggests:

Orwell genuinely believed, no mere platitude or rhetoric this, in the innate decency (the word he is fond of) of ordinary people. True values are not to be created nor old values 'transfigured' by the revolution, or in a new revolutionary consciousness; they exist already in the decency, fraternity, mutual aid, sociability, tolerance and scepticism towards authority of the working class – values which have survived the competitive individualism and reduction of everything to money values, engendered by capitalism, which has almost swallowed the middle classes . . . Decency is not an empty word, but is part of the moral values of socialism that are embedded in working class culture.[2]

Even today, despite all the forces which atomise our society, the human desire to coalesce can overcome great barriers. In times of national emergency, or local tragedy, people come together in great common causes. When a neighbour is in trouble, in most places in the country, people will look out for them. When an international tragedy strikes – a tsunami, earthquake or volcano – Britons will donate millions of pounds to disaster relief charities. British people are capable of great acts of selflessness, as well as self-interest, collaboration as well as competition, altruism as well as personal ambition.

Britain is a country of volunteers. As well as the army of people caring for others in their own family, every community has charity shop volunteers, hospital visitors, magistrates, school governors, special constables and a wide range of other volunteers providing services to others.

The social scientist Richard Titmuss wrote in his last book, *The Gift Relationship* (1970), about the differences between the UK and US systems of blood donation. In the US blood is a commercial product, sold by donors to make money; in the UK it is given free by donors who believe they will help others (and expect to be helped by others if they need blood themselves). Titmuss makes the point that people are naturally altruistic, and will help others without financial reward, as a mark of their common bonds of humanity. To introduce payment into the transaction drives people apart. His work helped to reform blood donation services in the US.

People attend music festivals, sporting occasions, demonstrations and marches, in order to share in a collective experience with others. Through social networking, individuals can meet strangers at a moment's notice. Crowds can be created in so-called flashmobs. In April 2006, thousands of strangers congregated at Victoria station in London and took part in a 'silent disco' – dancing to music through headphones. In March 2008, in more than twenty-five cities, an international flash mob met to hold a mass pillow fight.

Through social media, new forms of community are created,

with their own vernacular, etiquette and modes of behaviour. Some remain online, but what is significant is that people are using social media in order to meet up, arrange social activities and do politics.

The rise of individualism

Richard Crossman called R. H. Tawney's *The Acquisitive Society* (1921) his 'socialist bible'. Tawney, in his first significant book, argues that modern capitalism drives people apart, makes them view their fellow as a competitor, and makes them behave in mean-spirited ways. This was an ethical socialist (in Tawney's case Christian socialist) analysis of the alienation and atomisation caused by capitalist relations between worker and worker, and between worker and employer. This has remained the core argument in British politics – the role of the individual entrepreneur, pioneer, risk-taker, dissident and leader, versus the role of the collective. For the socialist, the answer lies in a combination of the two: great men and women emerge from the crowd, because the crowd lifts them up. Only through a strong society can individual talents be nurtured. The problem with a purely individualistic society is that only a tiny number of individuals can prosper; most do not.

In Autumn 1987, Margaret Thatcher gave an interview to *Woman's Own* magazine, which gave rise to one of her most famous quotations. In context, the quotation reads:

> I think we've been through a period where too many people
> have been given to understand that if they have a problem,
> it's the government's job to cope with it. 'I have a problem, I'll
> get a grant.' 'I'm homeless, the government must house me.'
> They're casting their problem on society. And, you know,
> there is no such thing as society. There are individual men
> and women, and there are families. And no government can
> do anything except through people, and people must look

to themselves first. It's our duty to look after ourselves and then, also to look after our neighbour. People have got the entitlements too much in mind, without the obligations.

When viewed in context, Thatcher's remark loses some of the potency of the stark assertion 'there is no such thing as society'. But her essential message for the readers of *Woman's Own* was that if you find yourself in any kind of trouble, or even without a home, you are basically on your own. The later remarks about reciprocity and obligations could have been uttered by Tony Blair.

Such is the nature of politics that Labour in opposition seized upon the remark, and turned it into the slogan of the anti-Thatcher resistance in the late 1980s. The leader of the opposition Neil Kinnock turned it into a riff for a speech:

'No such thing as society', she says. No obligation to the community. No sense of solidarity. No principles of sharing or caring.

'No such thing as society'. No sisterhood, no brotherhood. No neighbourhood. No honouring other people's mothers and fathers. No succouring other people's little children.

'No such thing as society'. No number other than one. No person other than me. No time other than now.

No such thing as society, just 'me' and 'now'. That is Margaret Thatcher's society.

Through the 1970s, 1980s and 1990s there was a real sense that society was fracturing. It was a time of great social upheaval, from the last slum clearances and rehousing of working-class families into estates and tower blocks, through the inner-city riots in London, Liverpool, Bristol and Birmingham, the miners' strike in 1984–5, recessions and deindustrialisation, to the poll tax riots in 1990. This was broken Britain: a society comprising communities with strong ties of kinship replaced by one which was suspicious, avaricious, apprehensive and sporadically unsafe. Many on the left have demonised the 1980s, although for a lot of people that period, like the so-called 'devil's decade' of the 1930s, was a time of personal prosperity and advancement.

The sociologist Robert Putnam has described the decline in communal activities in the USA, from attending political meetings to going bowling, in the second half of the twentieth century.[3] The phenomenon of 'bowling alone' exists in the UK too. Many of the communal activities which our grandparents enjoyed – the Boys' Brigade, church youth club, political parties – have been replaced in many parts of the country with insularity, a fear of strangers and a life centred around the private space, not the public one. It would be convenient to blame the rise in insularity, and decline of sociability, on the Conservative Party. But it is obvious that the breakdown in traditional social ties and collective forms of activity is a feature of most developed capitalist countries, not just the UK, and has been happening for thirty or forty years, when both Labour and Conservative parties have been in office. Although individualistic rhetoric exacerbates the problem, and government policies which create more crime and anti-social behaviour drive people off the streets and into their homes, there is something deeper at work.

A sense of community

As the Conservative-led government prepares its assault on the institutions, programmes and initiatives that provide 'glue' to many of our geographic communities (especially the most disadvantaged), the Labour Party needs to address head on what it means by community, and how a sense of community should inform the revival in its political fortunes.

A community is not inherently benevolent, and its members need not necessarily benefit from their affiliation with one another.

Members of religious cults, political sects or criminal gangs may enjoy temporary feelings of belonging and kinship (often in stark contrast to their previous lives) but the overall experience is destructive. The British National Party offers fellowship to its members, constructed on a myth of racial connectivity and shared history (going back to the end of the last Ice Age). So does the Socialist Workers' Party, which tells its recruits they are about to lead the entire working class into a revolution. Various religious sects offer eternity in the next life to new recruits, as well as 'love-bombing' in this life. In return for whatever benefits might be on offer, the member must sublimate their own personality and capacity for individual thought, and often divest themselves of their relationships and property.

Communities can be repressive, narrow, unimaginative and built on conformity. Individualism may be squeezed from within a community. This was the experience of gay men and women within many working-class communities, or the experience of Muslim women wanting to defy misogynist cultural traditions, or the experience of the member of a street gang wanting to leaving the gang. Fictional accounts of the Liverpool hairdresser Rita, who wanted to get educated, or Billy Elliot, who wanted to dance, or other similar tales of individuals who sought to transcend the boundaries of their communities show that community can be a stifling place.

Communities can be set against communities. In some parts of the country, settled white working-class communities are in competition for resources (real or imagined) with recently arrived immigrant communities. Each community is close knit, and rich in tradition, yet finds co-existence with other communities a daily struggle. Other communities, based on ethnicity, religion or both, can be in conflict with others with a different make-up. In our own times we have witnessed horrific violence between Hutu and Tutsi, Croat and Bosnian, Palestinian and Israeli, and Protestant and Catholic.

Bernard Crick makes the important point that 'fraternity without liberty is a nightmare, liberty without fraternity is competitive cruelty, but fraternity with liberty is humanity's greatest dream'.[4] Community is benevolent only if it is democratic, with differences of views and minority opinions heard and tolerated, and if it is egalitarian, with each member respected and valued. Within a community should be the platforms for self-expression and self-actualisation. A community should be powerful, and the members that compose it powerful within it.

This idea of community, as a centre of power and democracy, owes much to the co-operative ideal. It also reaches into Britain's history as a nation of friendly societies, mutual aid societies, welfare clubs, trade unions, women's organisations, charities and religious groups.

If Labour is to live out the value of community, the party needs to focus its efforts away from the large-scale institutions of the state, (especially unelected quangos and unaccountable government agencies), away from vast government departments, and towards the small and medium-sized voluntary and democratic community groups, which should deliver a larger share of the public and social services.

Labour should develop the idea of *democratic* communities, with local people taking decisions, running services and owning assets within the community. If we want to revitalise our democratic system, then tinkering with the system of voting, or reforming the second chamber, will not have the desired effect. You learn democracy by taking part in it, not by watching other people do it. Within the community people can learn the skills of collaboration, mediation and negotiation, and the basic tradecraft of democracy: forging coalitions of interest, canvassing for support, balancing priorities and options, and being subject to scrutiny and accountability.

J. S. Mill said:

> We do not learn to read or write, to ride or swim, by merely being told how to do it, but by doing it, so it is only by

practising popular government on a limited scale that the
people will ever learn how to exercise it on a larger one.[5]

G. D. H. Cole argued that it is through participation at the local
level and in local associations that people could learn the practice
of democracy: 'Over the vast mechanism of modern politics the
individual has no control, not because the state is too big, but
because he is given no chance of learning the rudiments of self-
government within a smaller unit.'[6]

It is at the level of the local community – the village,
neighbourhood or estate – that true democracy can be created
and real citizenship exercised. An incoming Labour government
should be prepared for a massive transfer of power from the
centre to the local, with proper safeguards to avoid inequities,
and support for people to take charge in a meaningful way. The
exact nature of the transfer of power from the professional,
administrative, managerial and political classes to working people
and their families should be the central theme of Labour's road
back to power. When David Cameron's 'Big Society' slogan has
been revealed as a fig-leaf for centrally imposed public spending
cuts, people will want an alternative approach to local democracy
and control over their lives.

Summary

Human beings are by nature collaborative and sociable animals.
The desire to live together, to help another and to be kind to each
other is innate in all of us. This sense of interconnectedness,
dubbed *ubuntu* in some African cultures or expressed as 'fraternity'
on the left, comprises the most important but most neglected of
socialism's trinity of values.

For much of Labour's 100-plus years, the idea of a community
was a settled notion, comprising the bonds of kinship, family and

shared interest of workers in the same industry or trade, within stable geographical areas. Labour leaders who came from mining or other industrial backgrounds knew 'community' as a living creed, not a theoretical construct. Aneurin Bevan, founder of the NHS, was more influenced by his experience of the Tredegar miners' health scheme, which they funded and ran themselves, than by the Beveridge report.

In a Britain rapidly changing through technology, economic shifts and immigration, the need to understand and support notions of community becomes even more important for the Labour Party. Despite some laudable initiatives, such as the New Deal for Communities programme, the Labour governments failed to create democratic communities, with real power to shape their neighbourhoods and the local environment. Democratic communities require the large-scale transfer of political power and assets from central and regional agencies to local people and bodies. At this level, by being given responsibility and resources, people will become full citizens and authors of their own destinies. It will put them, in Orwell's phrase 'in the saddle.' By building our democracy from the neighbourhood upwards, Britain can continue its journey towards being a fully fledged democracy.

9. The case for revisionism

> 'The means most suitable to one generation might be wholly irrelevant to the next'
>
> Tony Crosland, *The Future of Socialism* (1956)

Values must be applied to problems, and run through policies, if they are to have any worth.

The method of revising policies and programmes to reflect traditional values in a modern setting is called 'revisionism'. Many have made the point that values must not be confused with policies. The former are immutable, the latter are changeable. Policy changes as circumstances change. Labour's policy must be kept under constant review, because of the pace and scale of change. When Labour politicians have become fixated on one policy or another – nationalisation of the steel industry, unilateral nuclear disarmament, comprehensive schools or certain electoral systems – they can lose sight of values and turn individual policies into totems. When that happens within the Labour Party, the result is usually great schisms and divisive sectarianism. That's what happened in the 1950s, and again in the early 1980s.

In *New Labour's Old Roots* Patrick Diamond seeks to make clear the connection between New Labour and the revisionists throughout Labour's history, and the ethical, values-based socialism of people such as R. H. Tawney. Diamond offers a definition of revisionism: 'Revisionism can be better understood as a cast of mind. The revisionist account of one generation is the orthodoxy of the next.'

The revisionist cast of mind is what Labour needs so desperately now: not shibboleths or orthodoxies, nor arguments and blame. Labour needs to apply the revisionist method to modern problems and concerns, and shape a programme based on what needs to be done, not imagined problems or assumed concerns.

The first revisionist: Eduard Bernstein

The first socialist to be described as a revisionist was the German political writer Eduard Bernstein (1850–1932), who sought to update Marxism in line with modern democratic methods. In the 1890s Bernstein was exiled in London, and in contact with Friedrich Engels and the newly formed Fabian Society. He was executor to Engels's estate, and fulfilled his wish to have his ashes scattered at sea. Bernstein, Eleanor Marx and others hired a boat from Eastbourne beach (which Marx and Engels used to regularly visit), and took it past Beachy Head to dispose of Engels's remains.

He developed the theory of 'evolutionary socialism' in his 1899 book of the same name, whereby socialism would come about as the result of gradual, progressive and incremental reforms to the social and economic system. These changes would be brought about by trade unions and elected socialists in Parliament. Sidney Webb, and his Fabian belief in the 'inevitability of gradualness', was not a million miles away from this.

Bernstein made the point that socialism is more about the process of reform and change than a fixation about the end result. He distilled it into his famous aphorism: 'For me the goal is nothing; the movement is everything.' James Callaghan, some eighty years later, restated the case that 'you can march towards the New Jerusalem, but you can never arrive.' Bernstein's work was important because it established a methodology, whereas Marx and Engels had only supplied a theology.

The lost revisionist: Evan Durbin

Evan Durbin, Labour MP for Edmonton, had the potential to be one of Labour's brightest stars, even its leader. He died in 1948, at the age of forty-two, at Strangles Beach, in north Cornwall, drowning after rescuing his own daughter and another child from rough seas. His legacy is a great work of revisionism: *The Politics of Democratic Socialism* (1940). He was a close associate of R. H. Tawney, and a friend and contemporary of Hugh Gaitskell, both of whom read his book in draft. Gaitskell and Durbin started at New College, Oxford at the same time in 1924, and both fought, and lost, neighbouring Kent seats in 1935. In his foreword to the revised edition, Gaitskell says that various thinkers influenced Durbin's work, including Tawney, G. D. H. Cole, Hugh Dalton and J. M. Keynes. The value they all shared was 'social justice – but it was an ideal in no way inspired by class hatred. They were equally devoted to democracy and personal freedom. They believed in tolerance and they understood the need for compromise.'

Durbin decisively rejected Marxism, which he saw as alien to British values. He was equally harsh towards Labour Party members on the left of the party who shared the tenets of Marxism, and rejected the idea of a 'popular front' between the Labour and Communist parties to fight fascism. He was committed to parliamentary democracy, which he viewed as a necessary condition of socialism. He wrote: 'To betray democracy is to betray socialism.'

However, Durbin was wholly signed up to the prevalent view that socialism was the same as planning and state control. Although a revisionist, he was a centraliser and a corporate socialist, as was most of the Labour Party in the early 1940s. Planning was, according to Cole, Labour's 'professed creed'. Had he lived through the 1950s and 1960s, served in the Wilson Labour governments, and seen the failures of the state-run industries and welfare systems, perhaps his formidable intellect would have been directed at a new work of revisionism. If you find yourself on Strangles Beach, spare a thought for Evan Durbin, who saved two children but couldn't save himself.

The greatest revisionist: Tony Crosland

In June 2010, when asked by Jeremy Paxman who was greatest leader Labour never had, David Miliband replied without hesitation: Anthony Crosland. The high priest of Labour revisionism was born in 1918. Before the war, he got a second-class degree from Oxford in 'Mods'. Unhappy with his result, he returned after the war and got a first in PPE in just one year, and went on to teach, amongst others, Tony Benn. In the period between these bouts of study, Tony Crosland served in the Parachute Regiment. Several of his friends were killed at Arnhem.

Under Hugh Dalton's protective wing, Crosland was elected to Parliament for South Gloucestershire in 1950, but lost in 1955. What the people of South Gloucestershire achieved by ejecting their MP they will probably never know. For Crosland used the time away from Parliament to write a book, with the explicit aim of becoming 'the new Bernstein'.

I was given a hardback copy of Crosland's *The Future of Socialism* for my twenty-second birthday in 1989, as communism was collapsing and the Cold War coming to an end. I read great chunks of it on a long journey to Yorkshire during my Christmas holidays.

It has at its heart an argument for equality – not just of opportunity, but of assets and wealth. Equality for Crosland was the Holy Grail. Without it, there could be no social justice, no freedom, no personal development, no liberation from poverty and disadvantage.

He argued that state ownership of nationalised industries did not deliver greater personal freedom, or greater equality, or any other socialist objectives. His powerful disentanglement of socialist ends and means, of nationalisation from socialism, seemed to me to be as relevant in the late 1980s, at the tail end of Labour's Policy Review, as it was in the late 1950s. There was a plea for more levity and joy in public life, and a rejection of restrictions on abortion, homosexuality, divorce and civil liberties. In one of the most famous passages Crosland argues (with more than a hint of William Morris) for a modern public realm, where a modern citizenry can congregate amidst beautifully designed public buildings and spaces:

> We need not only higher exports and old-age pensions, but more open-air cafes, brighter and gayer streets at night, later closing hours for public houses, more local repertory theatres, better and more hospitable hoteliers and restaurateurs, brighter and cleaner eating houses, more riverside cafes, more pleasure gardens on the Battersea model, more murals and pictures in public places, better designs for furniture and pottery and women's clothes, statues in the centre of new housing estates, better-designed new street lamps and telephone kiosks and so on ad infinitum.

There was also a side-swipe at the Webbian Fabian tradition, with its tap-water, statistical analysis and airlessness: 'The time has come for a greater emphasis on private life, on freedom and dissent, on culture, beauty, leisure and even frivolity. Total abstinence and a good filing system are not now the right signposts for a socialist Utopia.'

Crosland's starting point was that each generation of socialists must decide how to apply the values of socialism in their own time and context. Crosland's driving motivation was equality. But he saw equality as an issue of assets, incomes and wealth, rather than, for example, an equal distribution of power between men and women. As part of the generation who lived through strong post-war economic growth, Crosland was as much a prisoner of his experience as anyone else. In *The Future of Socialism* in 1956 he was optimistic about growth in the economy. By the time he wrote *The Conservative Enemy* six years later, he was less so.

He had a reasonably settled view of Britain as a mature democracy, without much need for further reform. He was interested in participatory forms of democracy such as tenants' rights, but with the caveat that participatory democracy had limited uses in a complex industrial society.

He was dismissive too of the new single-issue groups such as Shelter and the Child Poverty Action Group which emerged in the 1960s as being too middle class, and not necessarily socialist. By 1970 he was alive to environmental issues, and wove them into his political speeches and writings. In a Fabian Society pamphlet in 1971, he added 'strict social control over the environment' to a more traditional list of socialist concerns, including protecting the countryside from more industry.[1]

Ultimately, Crosland failed to revise his own revisionism. He added a little, and subtracted a little, from his 1956 *magnum opus* over the years, but never applied his own revisionist instincts to the new world of the 1970s, with its oil price rises, terrorism (both Irish and Islamist), rampant inflation, mass unemployment and deindustrialisation. He defended the core arguments of *The Future of Socialism* over the next twenty years. In *Socialism Now* (1974) Crosland said: 'There is no need for revisionists to revise our definition of socialism.' David Lipsey wrote: 'Crosland had erected a towering castle. The rest of his life was devoted to defending it against all comers.'[2]

Crosland provides modern socialists with the compelling simplicity of the argument that greater equality leads to a more socialist society. By offering a values-based approach, he gives us a socialism which is not about nationalisation of private companies, or one policy or manifesto over another, but a broad direction in which to take society, and a standard by which to judge political action. He was never the leader of the party (in the Labour leadership election in 1976 he won only seventeen votes from his parliamentary colleagues. Even Roy Hattersley, his representative on earth, didn't vote for him). Yet he provided leadership to a generation of socialists by proving it is possible to be passionately moderate. He died in 1977, whilst serving as foreign secretary in the Callaghan government. The job he really wanted, chancellor of the exchequer, eluded him.

The Germans show the way: Bad Godesberg

By 1959, the German Social Democrat Party (SPD) had been defeated twice by Konrad Adenauer's Christian Democrats. To reflect the post-war changes in German society and the economy, German revisionists argued that the party must change its statement of aims and values, and reject the Marxist tone of its constitution. At a conference in November, at Bad Godesberg near Bonn, the SPD adopted a new programme, which began:

> Socialists aim to establish a society in which every individual can develop his personality and as a responsible member of the community, take part in the political, economic and cultural life of mankind. Freedom and justice are interdependent, since the dignity of man rests on his claim to individual responsibility just as much as on his acknowledgement of the right of others to develop their personality and, as equal partners, help shape society. Freedom, justice and solidarity, which are everyone's obligation towards his neighbours and spring from our common humanity, are the fundamental values of socialism. Democratic socialism, which in Europe is rooted in Christian ethics, humanism and classical philosophy, does not proclaim ultimate truths – not because of any lack of understanding of or indifference to philosophical or religious truths, but out of respect for the individual's choice in these matters of conscience in which neither the state nor any political party should be allowed to interfere.
>
> The Social Democratic Party is the party of freedom of thought. It is a community of men holding different beliefs and ideas. Their agreement is based on the moral principles and political aims they have in common. The Social Democratic Party strives for a way of life in accordance with

these principles. Socialism is a constant task – to fight for
freedom and justice, to preserve them and to live up to them.

The adoption of the Bad Godesberg programme is a famous part of
the history of revisionism, but not until researching this book did I
ever read what it says. Despite being a translation from the German,
it's rather inspiring, and remarkably modern in its tone. It has stood
the test of time well.

The failed revisionist: Hugh Gaitskell

As a revisionist, Hugh Gaitskell (1906–63) believed that state control
did not equal socialism. As leader of the party, he attempted to
revise Clause IV in a British Bad Godesberg. It was an abject failure
because Gaitskell failed to prepare the ground – he announced it in
a speech at the 1959 party conference; he had no 'machine' within
the party to win over the trade unions and constituency parties;
and the forces ranged against revision of Clause IV, led by Aneurin
Bevan, were too strong.

Gaitskell was right; those opposed to him were wrong. Not only
was the 1918 text not a reflection of what socialism was, it also cost
Labour millions of votes by being open to Tory parody. Following
Labour's defeat in 1959, Gaitskell received evidence from the national
secretary, Morgan Phillips, that the policy of nationalisation had
cost the party support. Phillips told Gaitskell: 'Nationalisation. This
was far and away the most frequently mentioned liability.'[3]

In his speech to the 1959 conference Gaitskell said: 'I disagree . . .
that public ownership is the be-all and end-all, the ultimate first
principle and aim of socialism, and in particular a misunderstanding
about ends and means.'[4]

Gaitskell provoked a backlash, and was left isolated and damaged.
The NEC decided to leave Clause IV alone, and to draft a new
declaration to update, but not replace, the old wording. The new

declaration (the 'New Testament'), adopted by the party conference (and since mostly forgotten), started out by saying: 'The British Labour Party is a democratic socialist party. Its central ideal is the brotherhood of man.' It went on to commit the party

- to reject discrimination on grounds of race, colour or creed;
- to state that no country should rule over another;
- to support world peace and disarmament;
- to affirm the duty of rich nations to assist poor ones;
- to stand for social justice, with wealth shared fairly, and equal opportunities;
- to abolish classes;
- to have full employment, rising production and stable prices;
- for democracy in industry;
- for varying forms of common ownership;
- for happiness and freedom of the individual against the 'glorification of the state';
- and to uphold political freedom and free democratic institutions.[5]

It lacks the poetry of the Webb version, but also the revisionist backbone of the Blair version. As an attempt to 'clarify' Clause IV, it fails. As the product of several hands, and brains, with differing interpretations of socialism, it reads as what it is: the work of a committee.

Hugh Gaitskell was a great revisionist. His closest relationships were with Hugh Dalton, Anthony Crosland and Evan Durbin. As a young man at Oxford he volunteered for G. D. H. and Margaret Cole, driving them to and from meetings and providing research support. He knew R. H. Tawney well. He had a long-standing affair with Anne Fleming, wife of the James Bond novelist Ian Fleming. He loved to roll up the carpet, put a record on and dance the night away. Gaitskell was the kind of politician who would not have survived in the modern media age. He caused a stink when he advised people to stop taking baths during the fuel crisis in 1947, adding, 'Personally, I have not had a great many baths myself.'[6] But whatever his foibles, his death at the age of fifty-six – like those of Durbin, Crosland and later John Smith and Robin Cook – robbed the Labour Party and the country of a great talent at too young an age.

The reluctant revisionist: Neil Kinnock

Neil Kinnock's revisionist impulses were motivated by electoral necessity, not convictions about their veracity. His political career was constructed as a man of the left; his hero, although he never met him, was Aneurin Bevan, and he emulated his rhetorical style. At the Sheffield rally in 1992 an ageing Barbara Castle mixed up their names by mistake. Kinnock backed CND and Clause IV, and was devoted to Michael Foot. He boycotted the Queen's Speech, along with Dennis Skinner, by sitting in the Commons, as a protest against monarchy. Yet from the clay of this Tribunite socialist was fashioned, through bitter experience, one of Labour's greatest revisionists.

Kinnock became leader of the Labour Party following the heavy defeat of 1983. Labour won just 32.2 per cent of the popular vote, and lost fifty-one seats. It was a defeat only just worse than Labour's result in 2010. The first months of his leadership were dominated by the miners' strike, during which his instinctive support for the miners was tempered by his opposition to Arthur Scargill's leadership of the National Union of Mineworkers. His attack on the revolutionary socialist group Militant in 1985 was courageous and allowed Labour to construct some ideological walls at the edge of the party's view of socialism, beyond which it would not step. By bringing in Peter Mandelson in 1985 to head up the party's communications and campaigns, the party's 1987 election campaign was professional and slick. But in 1987, Labour lost seats in the south to the Tories, and gained only twenty seats overall. There was a post-defeat debate, as in 1959 when Douglas Jay had suggested changing the party's name, about whether Labour would ever form a government again, and whether to do a deal with the Liberals.

It was obvious that Labour's failure was not one of presentation but of policy. The suspicion that Labour was a party of the poor, of welfare recipients and of minorities, that it was dominated by left-wing trade unions, and that it had extreme policies on defence and nationalisation weighed heavily in the minds of the voters. There was an issue too about Kinnock's personal presentational style and his nationality.

Kinnock decided that a thorough review of policy was needed, underpinned by a political mission to reconnect Labour with the people. In 1985 he had given a Fabian lecture where he established socialism as a system of values. In 1987 he charged his deputy, Roy Hattersley, with drafting a new statement of aims and values. Hattersley, devotee of Crosland and author of *Choose Freedom* (1987), came up with a statement which provided the backcloth to the subsequent policy review. *Democratic Socialist Aims and Values* was published with the new Labour red rose logo on a background of light brown (critics called it 'fudge'). It was said that if you stared long and hard enough at the centre of the red rose, you could see Lenin's face. I remember box-loads of them in the basement of Walworth Road, awaiting dispatch, attractively priced at just 75p.

It echoed Hattersley's recent book, but also reached back to a much older tradition of ethical socialism. Parts are pure Tawney: 'Our concern as socialists is with individual liberty. But this is not the doctrine of callous individualism. A society based on ruthless social and economic competition entrenches the privileges of a minority whilst restricting the rights of the rest of society.'

The document called for 'a greater sector of the economy to be socially owned' and renationalisation of the public utilities. In calling for a mixed economy, *Aims and Values* advocated more municipal and co-operative enterprises, as well as 'new forms of organisation and ownership in which private and public ownership can be combined', perhaps a precursor to the Private Finance Initiative (PFI).

In opposition, parties have little else to do other than review and rewrite their own policy documents, and hold meetings to discuss them. Someone else is running the country. The period 1988–90 was dominated by the policy review. The party's shadow Cabinet – Hattersley, Jack Cunningham, David Blunkett, Bryan Gould, Gerald Kaufman, John Smith, Robin Cook and others – led seven policy review groups into defence, the economy, tax and public spending. The process is described in detail in Patrick Wintour and Colin Hughes's book, *Labour Rebuilt: The New Model Party*. The result, after much editing, was *Meet the Challenge, Make the Change: A New Agenda for Britain*, passed by the party conference in 1989. It reversed the albatross of unilateral nuclear disarmament, was pro-European, and, crucially, revised traditional Clause IV socialism. It stated:

> We must learn the lessons from our experience of Morrisonian state corporations. Where public ownership is the right answer, it must be more sensitive to the consumer and more attuned to the national interest. It need not take the form of one hundred per cent state ownership or of one national institution; we shall look favourably on forms, which are more flexible and decentralised.

This was the real Clause IV moment. The problem was that the voters either didn't notice, or didn't believe it. At the 1992 election the swing from the Tories to Labour was just 2.2 per cent. The party lost for the fourth time in a row, despite gaining forty-two seats. Outside Walworth Road, car-loads of Young Conservatives drove up and down singing 'four-nil, four-nil, four-nil'. A week later Kinnock and Hattersley resigned.

Revisionism triumphant: Tony Blair

After the 1992 defeat, the debate about whether or not to revise Clause IV, Part 4 was given new impetus by two leading figures. Neil Kinnock made a television programme in which he not only advocated a new Clause IV, but also wrote one. In 1993 Jack Straw, with members of Blackburn Labour Party, produced a pamphlet, *Policy and Ideology*, which argued for a new form of words. The leader, John Smith, had refused to countenance such a move.

Following Smith's death, and Tony Blair's election as leader, the debate increased. When Blair announced in his conference speech in 1994 that he and his deputy, John Prescott, would look again at Labour's constitution, it only dawned slowly that he meant a revision of Clause IV. The copies of the speech handed to journalists in advance did not have that section attached. I was standing at the back of the Winter Gardens, Blackpool when he made the announcement, having been tipped off a little earlier by someone close to Blair that he was going to 'abolish Clause IV'. It was an incredibly exciting moment.

There was a debate about fundamentals, held in local Labour parties and trade unions, and with Blair himself on tour, that ran until a special conference the following April, held at Methodist Central Hall in Westminster (the venue that saw the Labour conference which approved the original Clause IV in 1918).

The special conference saw modernisers pitted against traditionalists. Stephen Twigg took on Arthur Scargill. Young people railed against the old order. The motion was passed, and Blair came onto the stage with a cheeky joke: 'The name of our party. . .' he said, then paused. 'It stays the same.'

The irony of that little joke was that by the conference in autumn 1994, the party had been rebranded as 'New Labour' (lifted straight from Bill Clinton's 'New Democrats') and in effect had been renamed. David Lipsey had argued in a Fabian pamphlet[7] in 1992 that Labour should change its name. ('The word "new" would do no harm,' he wrote.) But no leader had ever dared to do it. Even Blair didn't overtly rename the Labour Party; he did it by stealth.

The new Clause IV, mostly drafted by Tony Blair himself, reads as follows:

> 1. The Labour Party is a democratic socialist party. It believes that by the strength of our common endeavour, we achieve more than we achieve alone so as to create for each of us the means to realise our true potential and for all of us a community in which power, wealth and opportunity are in the hands of the many not the few, where the rights we enjoy reflect the duties we owe, and where we live together, freely, in a spirit of solidarity, tolerance and respect.
>
> 2. To these ends we work for:
>
> - a dynamic economy, serving the public interest, in which the enterprise of the market and the rigour of competition are joined with the forces of partnership and co-operation to produce the wealth the nation needs and the opportunity for all to work and prosper, with a thriving public sector and high quality services, where those undertakings essential to the common good are either owned by the public or accountable to them;
>
> - a just society, which judges its strength by the condition of the weak as much as the strong, provides security against fear, and justice at work; which nurtures families, promotes equality of opportunity and delivers people from the tyranny of poverty, prejudice and the abuse of power;
>
> - an open democracy, in which government is held to account by the people; decisions are taken as far as practicable by the communities they affect; and where fundamental human rights are guaranteed;

- a healthy environment, which we protect, enhance and hold in trust for future generations.

3. Labour is committed to the defence and security of the British people, and to co-operating in European institutions, the United Nations, the Commonwealth and other international bodies to secure peace, freedom, democracy, economic security and environmental protection for all.

4. Labour will work in pursuit of these aims with trade unions, co-operative societies and other affiliated organisations, and also with voluntary organisations, consumer groups and other representative bodies.

5. On the basis of these principles, Labour seeks the trust of the people to govern.

It's a clever piece of work. It makes the clear statement of a belief in markets and the 'forces of competition' as the method to create growth and wealth, thus ending the age-old arguments about nationalisation. But it also uses the word 'socialist', which the Sidney Webb version did not. Part 1 contains the kernel of the socialist argument: that we achieve more together than we do alone. This is Blair's conviction in the need for a strong society and supportive communities. Part 2 contains the oft-overlooked phrase that 'decisions are taken as far as practicable by the communities they affect', which supports the case for decentralisation, devolution and localism (which this book is seeking to make).

Nearly forty years after Bad Godesberg, and Hugh Gaitskell's humiliation, in 1995 Labour finally joined the family of revisionist socialist parties.

When revisionism fails: a warning

There are many examples from Labour's history of what happens when its revisionist instinct fails, and policy and principle become entangled. There is a salutary lesson from Labour's opposition to the sale of council houses.

The only lasting measure to emerge from Labour's short-lived first administration in 1924 was the Wheatley Act, promoted by Red Clydeside MP John Wheatley. This was a housing act which enabled local councils to build and run homes with affordable rents for workers. By the 1930s, nearly half a million new homes had been built. In the post-war housing boom, most parts of Britain were changed by new estates of council houses, both low-rise houses with gardens, and tower-blocks. This was seen as a manifestation of modern socialism: planned communities, with public spaces and decently proportioned homes, replacing the jerry-built, privately owned slums and their indifferent landlords.

The Thatcher government, following the example set by the Conservative-controlled GLC in the late 1970s, introduced the 1980 Housing Act, which included the famous 'right to buy'. This was perhaps Margaret Thatcher's most cunning act. By publicly handing sets of keys to young couples who had bought their council house, she appeared a tribune of the people, the great liberator. It was the near-perfect alignment of the grand theories of Hayek and Keith Joseph, with a practical policy which everyone could understand. It wrong-footed the Labour front bench, none of whom had much experience of living in a council flat, who opposed people's aspiration to own their own home, mow their own lawn, paint their own front door and put their own shelves up. Alan Milburn, later a Labour Cabinet minister, could remember the resentment caused by state control of people's homes:

> I grew up on a council housing estate in the middle of County Durham, and it isn't a very nice thing when you come home from school and find your door, which was red in the morning, has been painted yellow. My mum had not agreed for it to be painted yellow, someone from the council did.[8]

Hundreds of thousands of families who had the council as their landlord exercised their 'right to buy', sparking a boom in DIY and ending the uniformity of much of British social housing. The Conservatives in their 1983 manifesto could make the case to the electorate that the right to buy

> is the biggest single step towards a home-owning democracy ever taken. It is also the largest transfer of property from the State to the individual. No less than half a million council houses and flats were sold in the last Parliament to the people who live in them. By our encouragement of private house building and our new range of schemes to help first-time buyers, there are a million more owner-occupiers today than four years ago.
>
> The Labour Party has met these proposals with vicious and prolonged resistance and is still fighting a rearguard action against wider home ownership. A Labour government would take away the tenant's right to buy his council house, would prevent councils selling even voluntarily at a discount, and would force any former tenant who wanted to sell his house to sell it back to the council.

It was another nail in Labour's coffin in the 1983 election, as thousands of C2 voters on former council estates, the first generation in their families to own their own homes, voted Conservative for the first time.

An interesting historical footnote to the right-to-buy story is that a similar scheme was actively discussed in the previous Labour government. Joe Haines (Harold Wilson's press secretary), who had been born in an East End slum, rehoused in a council house, and by the 1970s owned his own home, put forward a proposal for council tenants to buy their properties. The Number 10 policy unit worked up a detailed plan, which was systematically undermined, then destroyed, by Labour ministers worried about the reaction from their local councillors and the Labour NEC, and by civil servants for whom the idea was too 'novel'. In 1977, when Britain still had six million council houses and flats, Haines, with great prescience, wrote that his idea 'was systematically killed off. If Labour loses council housing votes in future, they will know who to blame.'[9]

This example of Labour's failure to be on the side of the public against the state, and on the side of reform versus the status quo, serves as a useful cautionary tale for future Labour governments.

The future of revisionism

The scale of Labour's defeat in 2010 should be the accelerator, not the brake, on a new phase of revisionism. Labour must apply the methodology of revisionism, just as Bernstein, Durbin, Crosland, Kinnock and Blair did in their times and circumstances. The values of socialism, though timeless, must be reinvigorated. Labour's machinery and organisation is in great need of refreshment, but a debate about the relationship between the unions and the party, or about the size and composition of the National Executive, or the voting power at conference is a distraction if the fundamentals are not in place.

Now is not the time for displacement activity. When Blair revised Clause IV, there was a significant debate in the party. Heavyweights such as Robin Cook weighed in with their contributions. Local Labour members got to hear the arguments and make their views known. It strengthened the party organisationally as well as theoretically.

The new Labour Party leader should spark the same level of debate. It may be that Clause IV needs another look. It is a product of its time, just as surely as the 1918 version was. It is far from perfect. It was never intended to become holy writ. David Miliband has suggested he wants to see Clause IV enacted, not redrafted. This is a laudable ambition, but unrealisable without winning an election.

Labour can't win unless it can show it can apply its values to the modern age in new and bold ways, without a retreat into its own comfort zone.

10. Democracy and decentralisation

'It is impossible to be a socialist without being a democrat, or a sincere democrat without being a socialist.'

Douglas Jay, *The Socialist Case* (1937)

Labour and the democratic tradition

There are so many false prophets and nightmarish political systems which have claimed the name 'socialist' that for much of the Labour Party's history it was felt the need for a prefix to qualify what kind of socialism it meant. During the existence of the USSR, Labour attached the prefix 'democratic' to 'socialism' to distinguish it from Soviet communism. It was felt necessary, not least because Labour's enemies made constant efforts to paint the party as communists, or in sympathy with the Soviet Union, from the Zinoviev letter forgery in 1924, to the Conservative Party poster in 1983 'Like Your Manifesto, Comrade', which claimed similarities between the Labour and Communist Party election manifestos. As students in the 1980s, we found the term 'democratic socialism' useful to distinguish ourselves from the undemocratic Socialist Workers' Party, Militant Tendency, Socialist Organiser, and the other small revolutionary sects which seemed to exist only within higher education and have memberships purely composed of the sons and daughters of the affluent.

You can't have socialism without democracy. There are different forms of democracy, of course. A pure participatory democracy, with all citizens taking part as equals, as in ancient Athens, would be egalitarian and socialistic. A pure representative democracy, without proper systems of recall and accountability, can be an entirely unequal society (this is closer to what we have now). But democratic impulses should run through socialist assumptions like electricity. Aside from the great struggles for votes for women in the early years of Labour's existence (Keir Hardie was a prominent supporter), and the devolution to Wales and Scotland eighty years later, the period of the Labour Party's activity did not see seismic changes to Britain's system of parliamentary democracy. Many, from Tony Benn to Aneurin Bevan, were romantically attached to Parliament as an institution. That has meant that development of democracy as an ideal and practice has been largely neglected within socialist thought. Labour's revival will depend on a new focus on the institutions of democracy, and new forms of democracy being introduced alongside our traditional model of voting for others, then blaming them when things go badly.

Rediscovering the decentralist tradition

Labour must become the party of decentralisation and devolution. Rather than redistributing power amongst political elites, Labour must pass power to the people, from central state to local state, and from local state to communities and citizens. This is what David Miliband has called 'double devolution'. This must be a matter of principle, done not grudgingly or timidly, but confidently in ways which are impossible to reverse.

Socialism in the twentieth century was dominated by theories of the state. Our governing ethos was how the state could be used to help people. The nineteenth-century tradition of self-help, co-operation and self-government within British socialism was subjugated to the statist tradition of centralised organisations and 'Whitehall knows best'. The irony was, as historian A. H. Halsey pointed out, that 'the movement which had invented the social forms of modern participatory democracy and practised them in union branch and co-op meeting, thereby laying a Tocquevillian foundation for democracy, was ironically fated to develop through its political party the threats of a bureaucratic state'.[1]

The Labour movement was founded by people imbued with the ethos of the local co-op, the trade union branch, the socialist society and nonconformist religion. G. D. H. Cole, the great proponent of decentralised socialism, could declare in the 1950s: 'I am neither a communist nor a social democrat because I regard both as creeds of centralisation and bureaucracy.'[2] The party itself was a federation of local groups, building from the bottom up towards representation in Parliament. The statement of socialist aims in Clause IV, Part 4, with its call for common ownership of the means of production, distribution and exchange, was considered at the time a loose definition, encompassing municipal ownership and co-operative ownership, as well as state ownership.

Between the wars, during the global depression, Labour's interpretation of common ownership hardened into a conviction that the central state must own and direct enough of the economy to be able to make a difference. The Second World War, with state direction of every aspect of British life, cemented the equation of socialism equalling nationalisation. Labour's 1945 manifesto set out its pledges for nationalising the Bank of England, railways, iron and steel, coal, and the social services. Socialists' distrust of the state was replaced with a view of the state as the essential vehicle for social change, and then by the substitution of any radical instincts or fresh thought with a shopping list of industries that should be state controlled.

Following the Attlee government, a critique emerged – not from the right, but from the left – that argued the state was too big, its institutions too remote, and citizens had too little power within either the economy or public services like the NHS, the comprehensive school system, council houses, or care for children, disabled people or the elderly.

By the 1950s, it was obvious that state ownership of nationalised industries such as the National Coal Board (NCB) had done little to liberate the workers. R. H. S. Crossman, later a famous Cabinet diarist, told the Fabian Society in 1955 that

> vast, bureaucratic public corporations . . . failed to fulfil the two essential requirements for socialism, namely, that a state-owned industry should be fully responsible to Parliament and give a share of management to its workers . . . the growth of a vast, centralised state bureaucracy constitutes a grave potential threat to social democracy.[3]

In 1963, the academic Brian Abel-Smith, who went on to be a special adviser to Labour Cabinet ministers Barbara Castle, Richard Crossman and David Ennals, wrote a Fabian pamphlet, *Freedom in the Welfare State*, which argued that 'Britain's public services are now a bad advertisement for socialism'. He lambasted the 'queues and rationing', the 'atmosphere of wartime austerity' and a system where the user of social services must 'wait your turn and are told what you will have'. In 1980 Tony Benn wrote in *Arguments for Socialism* that 'nationalisation plus Lord Robens [the moderate erstwhile chairman of the NCB] does not add up to socialism'.

Evan Luard, in *Socialism without the State* (1979), charts the usurpation of socialism, historically mistrusting of the state and built on local models of mutualism, by state socialism, a system of nationalised agencies, companies and industries. Writing at a time of state control throughout the USSR and China, and before the Thatcherite programme of privatisation in the UK, Luard advocated an entirely contrary approach to socialism. It should be local, the optimum level being the neighbourhood, and based on locally owned and democratically controlled institutions.

> The jointly run neighbourhood laundry, the neighbourhood bakery, the neighbourhood hairdresser, run not for

private profit but for the equal benefit of all who live in
the neighbourhood, might give some genuine sense of
participation, of sharing, such as has not been provided by
most public undertakings until now.

There was a revived interest in the 1970s and 1980s in non-statist
socialism. Peter Hain called it 'libertarian socialism'. David Blunkett
and Geoff Green wrote a Fabian pamphlet in 1985, *Building from
the Bottom: The Sheffield Experience*, which saw local socialism as a
centre of resistance to the Tory government. In 1984 Anthony Wright
could declare in a Fabian pamphlet: 'We are all decentralisers now,
at least in the sense in which a century ago Lord Harcourt could
declare that we were then all socialists . . . what "participation" was
to the 1960s, "decentralisation" looks like becoming for the 1980s.'[4]

New Labour and decentralisation

Within New Labour, the decentralist tradition was crushed by those
who believed central government (i.e. themselves) could determine
what was best for local communities. Failure to pass power to
the people, preferring to redistribute it amongst politicians and
bureaucrats, is one of New Labour's great disappointments. We
allowed democracy to ossify, and also created a space for the Tories
to masquerade as the party of devolution and local control. You can
see the argument being played out in the debate about 'free schools',
which sounds to the voters as though the Tories are on the side of
the parents, and Labour is on the side of the council. Phil Collins
defined the paradigm in an article in *The Spectator* as 'between Alan
Milburn's anger that the council chose the colour of his door and Ed
Balls's centrally issued guidelines for rhubarb crumble'.

As we have seen, Labour's burst of revisionism in the late 1980s and
early 1990s equipped the party with a commitment to (some would
argue over-reliance on) markets. The argument about wholesale

nationalisation was settled; calls for state control of industry, even of the public utilities such as water and gas, became more muted. No wholesale attempts to renationalise British Telecom, British Gas, water companies or rail companies were made by successive Labour ministers.

However, whilst Labour had finally rid itself of its obsession with nationalisation, it continued to view the central state as the primary agency of social reform. As previous generations had fixed on nationalisation as the panacea, so some (but not all) Labour ministers fixed on increased public expenditure and expanding government activity as the solution to social ills. As with nationalisation, Labour runs the risk of confusing ends and means. Increasing public spending, and growing the size of the state, are not ends in themselves. In many cases, for example increased welfare payments, they are a symbol of policy failure. They may be a means to achieving a goal, in line with Labour's values. Or they may end up creating pointless quangos, regiments of officials, vanity projects, and counter-productive initiatives which bear little connection to Labour's values.

What are the limits of the state?

In 1945 the writer Arthur Koestler, pacifist Bertrand Russell, publisher Victor Gollancz and George Orwell attempted to establish a 'League for the Dignity and Rights of Man'. They failed, although some of the ideas surfaced twenty years later with the foundation of Amnesty International. Orwell, a brilliant writer but shambolic organiser, drafted a manifesto for the new league. He wrote that the main functions of the state should be:

1. To guarantee the newborn citizen his equality of chance.
2. To protect him against economic exploitation by individuals or groups.

3. To protect him against the fettering or misappropriation of his creative faculties and achievements.

4. To fulfil these tasks with maximum efficiency and a minimum of interference.[5]

This provides as good a definition as any of the state in a socialist society. It is not the overarching state, but the enabling state, helping the individual to get on in life, to be creative and fulfilled, but with the maximum of efficiency and minimum of interference.

The mortal danger for Labour in 2010 was that it looked like the party of higher taxes, bigger debts and profligate spending, without winning, or attempting to win, the arguments about why public spending was a good idea. It ended up defending big-budget regional development agencies and quangos, without explaining why. On this terrain, Labour cannot win popular support, because the British are not natural supporters of a large state.

The scale of the cuts being enacted, and the types of body being targeted, by the government suggests that there is hidden ideological wiring running through it. Conservatives favour a small state, lower taxes and fewer government schemes. So do some of the classical liberals within the Liberal Democrats. Behind the talk of a 'Big Society', the Liberal Democrats are providing the Tories with political cover for what is essentially an agenda of which Margaret Thatcher would approve. But Labour must not dismiss the 'Big Society' out of hand. It should support initiatives which give the citizen real power and control.

Labour must make a different kind of argument about the state: for a state which may be smaller, but which is fully democratic, decentralised and egalitarian, and which enables the individual to prosper. Labour must kill off any lingering attachment to the central state as the primary means for social progress. It may be a hard habit to kick, but whatever the great questions of the age, state socialism is not going to be the answer.

Whatever the precise mechanism, Labour desperately needs

to take a long, hard look at itself, its values and the policies that express those values. To merely defend the record of a government decisively defeated risks further defeats. Imagine the folly of Labour defending this policy or that, whilst the Tory-led government makes strides forward. Labour would become locked in the past. The defeat in 2010 would be the first in a series, not a one-off event.

Part Three

11. Preparing the ground

> 'Socialism cannot come overnight, as the product of a weekend revolution. The members of the Labour Party, like the British people, are practical-minded men and women.'
>
> *Let Us Face the Future* (1945)

Labour's revival depends on a fresh assessment of the core values of democratic socialism, and their application, in the spirit of revisionism, to the modern world. Tomorrow's Labour Party must learn the lessons from its mistakes, especially the last period of Labour government, but can also draw on its own traditions and histories for inspiration and a recovery of self-belief.

This fundamental reappraisal is the first duty of a new leader. Without it, the party will rush headlong into displacement activity: election campaigns, parliamentary oppositionalism and internal policy wrangles, for example over whether first past the post or the alternative vote system is better for elections to the House of Commons. Such internalised conversations leave the voters cold, even if conducted in a placid and polite fashion, which the Labour Party usually finds hard to manage.

There are three broad areas of concern to which Labour must address its attention in the coming months, and on which it must create a platform for a coming general election. More importantly, Labour must be ready with a broad approach to these areas, which will inform specific policy ideas and activity in government. The three areas are:

- Creating a democratic politics
- Creating a fairer society
- Creating a mutual economy.

Each reinforces the others; none can be tackled in isolation. A true democracy creates by definition a fairer society. A fairer society means that the economy works for the benefit of all. Each aspect of the programme feeds into the others. Running through a democratic politics, a fairer society and a mutual economy is the imperative to tackle the greatest issues of the age: environmental protection, equality for women, trade justice, and preventing the spread of ideologies of hate, from the BNP to Islamist extremism.

These three areas give Labour a canvas on which to paint. When the time comes for manifestos, there needs to be an overarching 'narrative' or story which the party can sell to the electorate. The narrative comes first, then the policy detail. One of the problems with Labour's 2010 manifesto was that it contained a wealth of policy, some of it imaginative and courageous, but no clear story about what kind of society Labour wanted. Creating a democratic politics, a fairer society and a mutual economy gives Labour a story to tell about the kind of society we want, and the values of individual freedom, equality between people and a strong society to live in, which will guide us in government.

The first great challenge, then, is creating a democratic politics.

12. Creating a democratic politics

'In a British election it is agreed that most of the electors do not attend meetings at all, and, of those who do, the vast majority attend meetings of the candidates they have already decided to support. Little election literature is valid that is either long or involved; to attain its end, it needs to be suspiciously general, full of wide promises, passionately critical of the other side, built on some tremendous slogan that will stay in the electoral memory at least until polling day. The new techniques of wireless and movietone have still further complicated methodology. With both, a beautiful voice counts enormously; with the second, the actor's technique is fundamental.'

Harold Laski, *Democracy in Crisis* (1933)

Harold Laski, the socialist academic, made his complaint in 1933, but it is a cry echoed in every generation: voter apathy is destroying politics, the parties are to blame by dumbing down, and it's all about spin, not substance. There was no golden age. For every Chartist, there were a hundred working men who stayed at home; for every suffragette, a hundred women who wanted a respectable family life; for every party activist, a thousand citizens who thought them crazy.

Richard Tawney saw democracy as 'not only a form of government, but a type of society.'[1] Others, such as G. D. H. Cole, saw democracy as the route to liberty and equality, and offered a description of a free, equal society which by any other name would be socialism. The Levellers were prepared to die for democracy, not as a system of electing a parliament, but as a way of living in harmony with others. Britain has never been a full democracy on this model. We have a democratic system, but not a democratic society. The fundamental truth is that until we are truly democratic, we won't be truly free. Labour must cease to be the party of constitutional tinkering, with each policy the product of careful calibration and assessment of narrow party advantage. Instead, Labour must be the party that people believe will give them sovereignty over the decisions they care about.

In Britain our 'democracy' consists of voting for others, then complaining that they don't do what we want. The representative model of democracy – we elect our representatives, and they act on our behalf – has many flaws. These flaws include the electoral system, the types of people who stand for office, and the expectations we place on them once elected.

The system we use to elect our representatives in the House of Commons – 'first past the post' – is imperfect and has many critics. The number of seats a party wins in the Commons does not reflect the numbers of votes cast. Most MPs are elected with a minority of votes within the constituency. Across huge areas of the country, people are 'represented' by people they did not vote for and whose political views they disagree with. At a local authority level, the situation is even worse, with turnouts in the teens, and the vast majority of us unable to name a single one of our local councillors.

In 1994 David Miliband wrote that

> politics in the advanced capitalist world has rarely been held in lower esteem. Whether measured by opinion polls or by the rise of protest parties, the formal institutions of politics, and the politicians who populate them, are held in low regard. At best, they seem as impotent in the face of

economic complexity and social change; at worst, they are part of a conspiracy to defraud the general public.[2]

New Labour failed to revive the political system, despite important reforms such as the devolved assemblies and elected mayors. And this was before the expenses scandal, which confirmed in most people's minds that politicians are literally part of a conspiracy to defraud the public.

The triumph of the political class

In 2010, Labour's leadership contest was fought between five candidates, all of whom had been to either Oxford or Cambridge universities, and two of whom had been to Harvard as well. Four out of the five were white men who had worked as special advisers before being elected to Parliament. None was a manual worker, or a skilled worker, or could be considered 'working class'. Two out of the five went to the same school, grew up in the same areas, and shared the same parents. The prime minister, David Cameron, was a former Conservative Party researcher (along with George Osborne, the chancellor, and Andrew Lansley, the health secretary) and special adviser. Vince Cable was a special adviser. Nick Clegg, a former MEP, is a fully paid-up member of the political class.

Of the 2010 intake of new MPs, very few were from non-political backgrounds. They were overwhelmingly university educated, middle class, and had done jobs in politics, from being a councillor, to working in Parliament, to being a special adviser, to working for Gordon Brown. One, Ian Lavery, had been a coal-miner.

Our representatives are becoming less representative. The long-hours culture, and the need to be away from family life during the week, means that most people with children are put off becoming an MP. MPs are drawn from a shrinking talent pool, and start to look and sound like each other. Where would the Ernest Bevins, the Jennie Lees or even the Keir Hardies of yesteryear fit into today's Parliamentary Labour Party? The system of selection, and the requirements of the 24-hour media, militate against 'characters' being selected or elected.

The revelations of the expenses scandal created an impression that MPs were lazy, over-paid parasites. It is an impression that will take decades to repair. But any member of the public, spending any time with an MP or a minister, would see an entirely different side of the story. After sharing a day in the life of an MP, most people would not willingly swap places. There's the endless travelling to and from London – perhaps ten or more hours a week on trains and planes. There's work every single weekend. There's endless scrutiny, opposition and insults.

There are queues of people at every surgery, often with desperate cases which need solving, but no practical power or means to help. We should decide whether we want our MPs to be legislators or social workers. If the latter, they should be funded and trained to provide social work and advice services, and not be expected to attend Parliament so often.

There's no privacy, with tabloid newspapers ready to go through your bins if there's a story in it. Ministers have it even worse – they are constituency MPs, as well as taking life-and-death decisions every day, working into the small hours on the red boxes every night, and all of it in the knowledge their government career will, in all probability, end in tears.

The parties need to address the issue of the social background of their candidates. The Liberal Democrats, for example, have no black or minority ethnic MPs at all. If their MPs represented the make-up of the general population, they should have at least five. It suggests that the Liberal Democrat system of parliamentary candidate selection is institutionally racist. The Labour Party, always an amalgam of working-class and middle-class people, has swung so far towards the latter, and away from the former, that the name 'labour' could be challenged under the Trades Descriptions

Act. The Tories remain the party of millionaires, landowners, the upper-middle class and the products of the public schools. Their modernising rhetoric has not been matched by a change in their culture or composition.

The vast majority of electors, scanning the benches of the House of Commons, would struggle to find someone who looks or sounds like them, or shares the same background. Many MPs have huge sympathy with their constituents; most genuinely want to help. But very few have lived on benefits, struggled to pay the bills, or waited until the end of the day to buy cheap bread in the supermarket. We have created a political class, distinct and separate from mainstream society, huddling together for comfort behind Pugin's neo-Gothic walls and colonnades.

Mr Pugin's Palace of Fun

Labour's programme of democratic renewal should start with the Houses of Parliament. The only thing to understand about the Houses of Parliament is that they are a fake. Built in the 1840s to replace the ones that burnt to the ground, they were designed by Augustus Pugin, along with Charles Barry, to look and feel like a medieval cathedral. Pugin, Anglican, workaholic and syphilitic, wanted Parliament to look like it had been there since the Dark Ages. Part of the structure, around Westminster Hall, really is medieval. But the main part of the building, with its neo-Gothic towers and cloisters, its iconography and brasswork, is early Victorian.

Aneurin Bevan, who arrived for the first time in 1929, wrote a wonderful passage in *In Place of Fear* to describe the atmosphere in the House of Commons:

> His [the new MP's] first impression is that he is in church. The vaulted roofs and stained-glass windows, the rows of statues of great statesmen of the past, the echoing halls,

the soft-footed attendants and the whispered conversation, contrast depressingly with the crowded meetings and the clang and clash of hot opinions he has just left behind in his election campaign. Here he is, a tribune of the people, coming to make his voice heard in the seats of power. Instead, it seems he is expected to worship; and the most conservative of all religions – ancestor worship.

The first thing he should bear in mind is that these were not his ancestors. His forebears had no part in the past, the accumulated dust of which now muffles his own footfalls. His forefathers were tending sheep or ploughing the land, or serving the statesmen whose names he sees written on the walls around him, or whose portraits look down upon him in the long corridors. It is not the past of his people that extends in colourful pageantry before his eyes. They were shut out from all this; were forbidden to take part in the dramatic scenes depicted in these frescoes.

The Commons chamber itself is even more fake – not 1840s, but 1940s. The chamber was twice fire-bombed by the Luftwaffe. Given the choice between preserving the chamber, or saving Westminster Hall, Winston Churchill directed the fire crews to save the real, not the pretend. The destruction of the chamber of the House of Commons was hushed up during the war.

It was faithfully reconstructed after the war with its chapel atmosphere and too few seats for all the MPs, on Churchill's orders, and thanks to donations from Commonwealth countries. If you look closely at the Speaker's chair, or the dispatch box, you can see little signs showing which country donated the wood. The 1945 parliament met in the chamber of the House of Lords whilst the construction work was being undertaken. During the war, Parliament met down the road in Church House, the headquarters of the Church of England.

The Labour Party has a fixation with the Houses of Parliament, as though the impressive nature of the architecture and design has moulded the party's entire approach to democracy. The earliest Labour MPs (without previous experience of Oxbridge colleges or the cloisters of, say, Fettes) must have found it intimidating, awe-inspiring and ultimately seductive. Generation after generation of Labour MPs have become 'parliamentarians', using the Palace as a club and, eventually, rest-home. Ralph Miliband, who was once famous as a Marxist academic rather than as the father of David and Ed, wrote:

> Of political parties claiming socialism to be their aim, the Labour Party has always been one of the most dogmatic – not about socialism, but about the parliamentary system. Empirical and flexible about all else, its leaders have always made devotion to that system their fixed point of reference and the conditioning factor of their political behaviour.[3]

That last telling point, that Labour leaders have had their political behaviour 'conditioned' by the parliamentary system, helps to explain why Labour in office has been so timid in unleashing democratic forms of governance over other areas of the state, and why ideas such as social enterprises, mutuals and co-operatives have had such half-hearted support. It goes some way to explain too why the party has been so fearful of extra-parliamentary campaigns, protests, direct action and experiments in democracy, from the rent strikes of Red Clydeside in the 1920s, to the squatters' movement in the 1940s and the student demonstrations of the 1960s.

Labour must break out of its parliamentarianism. Social change comes from below, not on high. The demands of the people are articulated through a variety of means, but parliamentary democracy is not the only one. The party should view Parliament in its proper context – one important institution of democracy, but not the only one that exists in a devolved UK which is part of the EU, and not the only that *should* exist in the future if power is to be devolved as locally as possible. Labour should bring democracy to bear wherever power is exercised.

Making 'representative' democracy representative

A colleague pointed out to me during the expenses scandal that people across politics had the answer to the problem – and it was whatever constitutional reform they had been championing before the expenses scandal. The harsh fact is that there is no single, simple solution to the breakdown in trust in politicians and authority of Parliament. Labour's quick-fix solution put forward at the 2010 election, the alternative vote (AV) for parliamentary seats, was simply the 'least worst' option for reform that the party managers could come up with, without provoking a split in a party which has as many passionate supporters for change as it does adherents to the status quo. The reality is that representative democracy needs a radical overall, across the full range of its institutions and cultures. A change of oil won't do the job when a new engine is needed.

Labour points proudly to its record in office on constitutional change. It's a familiar litany: the Scottish Parliament, the Welsh Assembly, the London Assembly, and abolition of the bulk of hereditary members of the House of Lords. Each is to be welcomed. It was an agenda developed by Labour in opposition, after much consultation and deliberation, much of it under Kinnock and Smith. There was a huge head of steam behind the devolved assemblies, and they were delivered in Labour's first flush of reforming zeal. In the second and third terms, Labour's radicalism on the constitution came to a juddering halt. Partly this was because of the failure to win referendums on English regional assemblies, partly because House of Lords reform came to resemble the Eton Wall Game – much grunting and shoving, but no obvious rules, and an outcome nobody understands. In the end, Labour ran out of ideas and radicalism.

How should the new Labour leadership proceed?

Reforming the electoral system

Labour has been debated alternatives to first-past-the-post for as long as it has existed. The 1929 Labour government introduced a bill to bring in AV, but it fell, along with the government, in 1931. In the 1990s, Raymond Plant chaired a commission into electoral reform for the party (I spoke in favour of the commission at the Labour Party conference in 1990). John Smith promised a referendum on reform in the first term of a Labour government. The 1997 manifesto promised a commission, and a referendum, and Tony Blair asked Roy Jenkins to chair the commission.

Reporting in 1998, the Jenkins commission ruled out AV, because it is not a proportional system and represented too timid a change. 'AV-plus' was the system the commission favoured, which elected all seats on AV, so that every MP had a majority of support within the constituency, and also topped up Parliament with MPs elected to reflect the overall number of votes cast. This system would give more stable governments, retain the important links between a representative and the place they represent, and reflect the numbers of votes cast in a much fairer way.

It is almost beyond belief that in their coalition negotiations Nick Clegg and the Liberal Democrats failed to win the promise for a referendum on proportional representation. This issue, above all else, is the one which animates Liberal Democrats. Yet their party's leadership was prepared to ditch it in return for seats in the Cabinet, a decision which will come to haunt them.

If there's a referendum on a switch to AV, then the Tory Party will campaign against it. Labour's position should be to support a 'yes' vote, but promise to go much further when returned to office. Liberal Democrat supporters of electoral reform should know that neither the Conservatives nor, it seems, the 'orange book' Liberal Democrat leadership can deliver a proportional system; only Labour is the party of real electoral reform.

More representative representatives

Labour should worry that its candidates are being drawn from a narrowing talent base. This is not to criticise any individuals. Most Labour MPs are talented and energetic. But if we establish what Hazel Blears has called a 'transmission belt' from Oxford, to MPs' researcher, to special adviser, to safe seat, to minister, to the Cabinet, perhaps by way of Harvard and the Institute for Public Policy Research, then we should not be surprised if our Labour governments become homogenised. The party works best when it draws on a wide variety of skills, from the trade union movement as well as Oxbridge. Harold Wilson's government may have had eight Oxford firsts, but it also had a good share of men and women who had held manual jobs and worked their way up without contacts and patronage. It is important that politicians with 'real life' experience such as Alan Johnson, John Prescott and Bob Ainsworth should not be the Last of the Proletarians in a Labour Cabinet.

A friend was joking that we need to start a new pressure group, 'C2s for Labour'. It is only when tested against 'real life' experience that policy questions can be satisfactorily settled. Since the 1980s the Labour Party has had to contract out the voice of the C2s to focus groups run by pollsters such as Philip Gould and Deborah Mattinson. Market research methods will always have a role in political communications, but far better is to have political leaders who 'get it' in the first place. Ernest Bevin didn't need a focus group to tell what the workers were thinking; he instinctively knew.

Labour needs to look again at its selection processes, and provide points of access for people from a range of backgrounds. Length of party service and positions held should be balanced with personal values, attitudes and aptitudes. A foundation should be established, along the lines of Emily's List (which sought to encourage women candidates) and Dorothy's List (which seeks to encourage lesbians and gay men) to support working-class candidates as they navigate the selection process. A Labour-friendly trade union – USDAW or Community perhaps – might want to take up the challenge.

House of Lords reform

Labour must finish off the job of reforming the House of Lords. In government Labour's Lords reform programme became a joke, with no single solution finding enough supporters, the result being a system that no-one favours. In 2007 Labour published a white paper on House of Lords reform. The Commons voted overwhelmingly for a fully elected House of Lords. The peers voted for a fully appointed House of Lords. In July 2008 Jack Straw introduced a further white paper setting out how a wholly or mostly elected second chamber might work, with the Commons retaining its primacy. No reform took place leading up to the election. The Conservative-led government is pledged to establish a committee to look at reform along democratic lines. Labour's inertia on Lords reform was a major disappointment, especially after a promising start.

The way forward is simple: Labour should campaign for a wholly elected second chamber, elected on proportional representation from each region and nation of the UK. There should be no appointments. The role of the second chamber – scrutinising and revising legislation – should be spelled out clearly, and the primacy of the House of Commons made obvious. Members of this new 'Senate' should have seven-year terms of office, funding for staff and an office, and a salary. There should be no more than 200 members of the Senate, and each should operate under a system of 'recall' should they breach the public's trust.

The argument for appointments of peers is that it allows the House of Lords to be a depository of the nation's wisdom, with former prime ministers debating with former police commissioners, university vice-chancellors, bishops and scientists. Whilst there are some great and good individuals in the Lords, there are also a lot of people sent there for less noble reasons: the repayment of services rendered, and also lots of superannuated politicians who treat the place like a retirement home.

If we are worried about losing the rich seam of talent and sagacity that the current Lords contains, there are should be a new advisory body established, along the lines of the Privy Council (which should be abolished). The peers could co-opt members of the advisory council, and ask them to produce specific notes of guidance to help the Senate in its duties.

Recall of MPs and other representatives

Once elected, there is nothing any of us can do to get rid of our representatives, no matter what they do and say, in between elections. Labour should embrace and campaign on a new system of 'recall' for all elected representatives, from councillors to members of the new Senate. Recall mechanisms are a means whereby local people can trigger a by-election in their constituency between general elections if enough of them demand it by signing a petition. This, above all else, would reconnect the people with their democratic system. Recall mechanisms exist in Switzerland and fifteen of the United States of America. It was a recall mechanism that brought Arnold Schwarzenegger into office in California, following the recall of governor Gray Davis in 2003. The only time it has happened in the USA before that was in 1921.

There would have to be robust safeguards. For example the bar should be set high enough so that a by-election is only triggered if it truly reflects the views of local people, not just the politically active minority. Only one by-election should be triggered against a sitting MP or other representative. There should be a short period of time in which to collect the signatures on the petition, so it cannot be a rolling petition.

In 2008, before the expenses scandal, recall mechanisms were discussed within the Labour government as part of the formulation of the *Communities in Control* white paper. Officials at the Department for Communities and Local Government worked up options for a system which would fit into a British context. The original text of the white paper read:

> We will introduce a new right of local electorates to trigger a by-election in a parliamentary or council seat if they can raise a petition of two-thirds of the total number of voters in the previous election. This powerful mechanism would be used, as in the USA, in extremis, where the trust between an elected representative and their electorate had broken down, for example because of new information coming to light about the elected candidate, because of a criminal conviction between elections, or because of the politician changing their political allegiance mid-term. The candidate elected would be entitled to stand again in the by-election, and if elected would continue to serve their term of office. Only one petition-triggered by-election would be allowed in each council or parliamentary term. The right to trigger a by-election would cover local councillors, MPs, members of devolved assemblies, and elected Mayors.

The idea of recall mechanisms was ruled out at this time by the prime minister, Gordon Brown. After the expenses scandal, it was rediscovered and formed part of Labour's election manifesto, but only after it had been announced as policy for the Conservative Party.

It is a fundamental principle in a democracy that democratic power is given on loan to a representative. The means to take it away should rest with the same people who grant the power in the first place. All representatives should know, in the back of their mind, and at all times, that their position in a parliament or assembly is temporary and contingent on them carrying out the wishes of the people.

Direct democracy and participatory democracy

Representative democracy is only one kind of democracy, and the least 'democratic' kind. It involves casting a vote for people for a four- or five-year period, with little accountability or sanction if you don't like what they've done. By its nature it creates a semi-permanent class of politicians, distinct from the rest of us. The other kinds we haven't even tried in this country with any seriousness.

Participatory democracy is a form of democratic engagement which comes much closer to the ideas of egalitarianism and citizenship which should be at the heart of Labour's agenda. It describes systems whereby citizens are engaged in a particular decision or policy, and given enough time to negotiate, mediate and cogitate on the answer. Citizens' Juries enjoyed a vogue, and then dropped down the government's agenda; they should once again be used across the public services, especially when decided how to allocate shrinking resources.

The allocation of resources, with competing priorities, lends itself to a form of participatory democracy called participatory budgeting. Porto Alegre in the south of Brazil is the centre of one of the most famous examples of participatory budgeting in the world. For over twenty years residents have engaged with the allocation of resources for their city. Around 50,000 people, out of 1.5 million residents, take part in budgeting each year. Delegates are elected from neighbourhoods specifically to discuss the budget. Many of the neighbourhoods in and around Porto Alegre are slums, and the annual budget debates engage some of the poorest, most disadvantaged people in the world. The World Bank suggests that the system of democracy itself has enabled a significant improvement in public services, including schools and sewerage. Around 140 Brazilian municipalities have adopted the same system as Porto Alegre, as well as councils and cities across the globe.

The Labour government encouraged the spread of participatory budgeting by establishing a unit, run by Church Action on Poverty in Manchester. Schemes have been run in Cornwall, Leicester, Wigan, Walsall, Newcastle, Sunderland, Salford and Sunderland. These schemes barely scratch the surface, most people in the UK are unaware of them, and most public money is spent without public engagement. Participatory budgeting should become the norm within public authorities and agencies, and we should aim for over half of public agency budgets to be subject to participatory budgeting.

Referendums

Referendums are a form of direct democracy, with citizens usually offered a simple 'yes' or 'no' to a policy or constitutional change (although in Australia in 1977, a referendum offered a choice of four different national anthems). In Switzerland, they form a central part of democratic life, where there have been more than 500 national referendums since the 1850s, and operate at the canton and local level.

They have been a regular feature in the USA since the reforms of the 'Progressive Era', which ran from the 1890s to the 1920s, designed to break up the power of party machines. President Theodore Roosevelt said in 1912: 'I believe in the Initiative and Referendum, which should be used not to destroy representative government, but to correct it whenever it becomes misrepresentative.'[4]

The last time the entire population of the United Kingdom went to the polls in a referendum was in 1975, to vote for or against Britain's continuing membership of the European Economic Community. The 1975 referendum avoided a split in the Labour Cabinet by allowing Cabinet ministers to campaign on either side of the question. Harold Wilson, James Callaghan, Denis Healey, and Roy Jenkins joined the 'yes' campaign (along with Margaret Thatcher). Tony Benn, Barbara Castle, Michael Foot and the TUC joined the 'no' campaign.

Since then there have been nine referendums in parts of the UK: in London to establish a mayor and assembly, in Northern Ireland, Scotland and Wales to establish devolved assemblies, in the north-east to vote for a regional assembly, and in various towns and boroughs to establish elected mayors. The referendum promised in 1997 on electoral reform for the Commons failed to materialise, and the one on the new EU constitution failed to take place after 2004.

The Conservative-led government will hold a national referendum on a move to AV for elections to the House of Commons. As in 1975, Cabinet ministers will not be bound by collective responsibility, and will join both sides of the debate. Deputy prime minister Nick Clegg will find himself campaigning against the majority of his Cabinet colleagues, although David Cameron may decide to sit it out, or even join the 'yes' campaign.

Referendums should be an important part of the redrawing of the British democratic map. The Labour Party should commit to using the tool of referendums on major pieces of legislation, perhaps one or two a year.

But Labour should go further. Each of the constituent assemblies and local authorities of the UK should be empowered to hold referendums on contentious issues. Importantly, local people should be able to raise a petition to trigger a referendum. A shift towards a Swiss-style system of referendums should be supported by electronic voting.

Petitions

Petitions are a form of democratic expression which pre-date the extension of the franchise in the UK. The campaign against the slave trade in the late eighteenth and early nineteenth centuries was conducted through hundreds of petitions to Parliament calling for abolition. The first Chartist petition in 1839, demanding democratic reforms, contained over a million signatures. Later ones were bigger, although undermined by opponents of reform by pointing out obvious forgeries like 'the Duke of Wellington'. Parliament today receives hundreds of petitions. The Number 10 website established a system of e-petitions.

The problem with our system of petitions is that they do not have power. They are essentially the act of a supplicant, humbly requesting attention from the powerful. Originally they were used by subjects to seek clemency from the King. The current culture reflects this master–servant relationship. They are not binding; they can be safely ignored.

A new range of petitions should be introduced, including the power to force a debate on an issue onto the agenda of any of the UK representative assemblies; the power to force a public inquiry on an issue (for example deaths at Stafford Hospital, or Deepcut Barracks); and the power to trigger a by-election in a parliamentary, council, mayoral or assembly seat.

Through this tapestry of representative, participatory and direct methods of democracy, power can be diffused and passed downwards and outwards throughout society. Britain, for so long proud to be the mother of parliaments, can try something new: democracy.

Citizenship as a way of life

If the Labour Party, in partnership with the British people, were to introduce the multi-layered democracy outlined above, we would go a long way towards answering one of the great unanswered questions in British political life: are we subjects or citizens? It goes beyond whether we are merely subjects of the monarch (although there are plenty of people who would like that to be the case); it extends to whether we are subjects of the governing class, whether our collective mind-set is one of subjugation or citizenship. Because Britain, unlike France or the USA, has never had a political revolution where citizenship was emphatically established, it remains an unsettled and unsettling question.

Citizenship has within its meaning the central idea of egalitarianism: that we are all equal before the law, we all have equal rights to join others in society, and everyone is a someone, no matter what they earn or where they live. It reeks of the French Revolution's Declaration of the Rights of Man and of the Citizen in 1789, or the United States' Declaration of Independence in 1776. Behind citizenship is the driving force of the Enlightenment, and the idea that reason, not superstition or tradition, should mould our lives. Citizenship is an exciting word. It lends itself to parody too. *Citizen Smith*, the television comedy about a bedsit revolutionary and leader of the Tooting Popular Front, comes to mind.

Citizenship contains the implication of activity: that being a citizen is an active state and carries duties, responsibilities and liabilities towards the common good. This is the citizenship of the ancient Greek world, where to be a citizen was to be a fully active member of the *polis* or city-state (and where we get the word 'politics' from). In *poleis* such as Athens, every male citizen was both ruler and ruled, participating in the running of the city and the making of its laws. Today, the idea of the jury, randomly selected from citizens who are compelled to take part, exists within our system to echo the Greek city states. Citizens came together in the *agora*, or central meeting place, to conduct their commerce, politics and socializing. To refuse to take part – to be *agoraphobic* – was the ultimate act of anti-social behaviour. Aristotle said: 'To take no part in the running of the community's affairs is to be either a beast or a god.'

But whilst the Ancients saw citizenship as a public activity, the Moderns have created a citizenship which is about private life, rights rather than responsibilities, and a retreat from the public sphere. Citizenship is seen as a list of entitlements rather than an imperative for social action.

In 1999, the Labour education secretary, David Blunkett, invited his old politics tutor (and co-author of the pamphlet I mentioned in the preface), Bernard Crick, to chair a panel on teaching citizenship in British schools. The Crick report ambitiously stated:

> We aim at no less than a change in the political culture of this country both nationally and locally: for people to think of themselves as active citizens, willing, able and equipped to have an influence on public life and with the critical capacities to weigh evidence before speaking and acting; to build on and to extend radically to young people the best in existing traditions of community involvement and public service, and to make them individually confident in finding new forms of involvement and action among themselves.[5]

Nearly a decade later citizenship teaching forms part of the school experience of hundreds of thousands of children, which is a step forward, but we have not reached the goal. Partly this has been a failure of the quality of teaching – when teachers, through no fault of their own, have no sense of citizenship, how can they imbue others with civic virtue? Partly it is because giving children a taste of citizenship in school is not enough. If it were, we would be turning out proficient mathematicians, scientists, authors and sportsmen and women, and all the other disciplines in the curriculum, at a much higher rate.

Labour should take the principles of the Crick report – that citizenship can be taught as well as experienced – and apply them across society. Every public servant – teachers, prison officers, civil servants, members of the armed services, the police, nurses, immigration officers, and all the rest – should be trained in citizenship as part of their job. Millions of people are employed directly by the state; part of the arrangement should be training in citizenship so that everyone, from the person that answers the phone at your council, to the hospital porter, to the school janitor, has the ethos of Athenian democracy flowing through their veins. But it shouldn't end there. No student should be able to graduate without studying citizenship as a compulsory component of their course, and no foreign national should be granted citizenship without passing the course.

Of course, you can't teach citizenship as an abstract theory if it is divorced from everyday life. As Labour dismantles the central state, and the functions of the state are taken over by more and more mutually owned groups, and as democratic principles are applied to state institutions such as the NHS, then there will be more practical opportunities for active citizenship. The link between what is taught in the classroom and what is going on in the street will be made clearer.

The standard argument at this point from the political class, or at least those short-sighted members of it who want to hoard power for themselves, is that the majority of people are too busy, lazy, prejudiced or uneducated to want to become active citizens. Anthony Crosland made this point when he argued that the people of Grimsby had little desire to live in an Athenian state of democracy:

> Experience shows that only a small minority wish to participate in this way. I repeat what I have often said: the majority prefer to lead a full family life and cultivate their gardens. And a good thing too, for if we believe in socialism as a means of increasing personal freedom and the range of choice, we do not necessarily want a busy bustling society in which everyone is politically active and fussing around in an interfering and responsible manner, and herding us all into participating groups.[6]

Beatrice Webb let her egalitarian mask slip and revealed a rather ugly face of elitism, when she remarked: 'Democracy is not the multiplication of ignorant opinions.' A charitable view might be that she was making a plea for adult education; more likely she was making a plea to leave it to the enlightened, educated, altruistic administrative classes, for whom she was the patron saint, and her husband the archbishop.

There is no compelling reason why the people of Grimsby, or any other part of the United Kingdom, should be any more lazy and useless than the slum dwellers of Porto Alegre, the cantons of Switzerland or the *poleis* of ancient Greece. For politicians to deny people the opportunity to be fully grown citizens is purely selfish, and ultimately self-defeating. Just as, in a consumer society, we are weighing up options, testing evidence and discussing with peers the consumer choices we make, so in a democracy we will spend an equal amount of time taking part in acts of citizenship. It will, as Crick suggested, become 'normal'.

Reform of the civil service

We need to reform Whitehall. The problem is not the individuals, but the system. I don't believe that civil servants deliberately block or sabotage government legislation. But the system stifles creativity and generates so much pointless activity that ministers have little time to develop their leadership skills.

One of the biggest issues is the 'fast-stream' system, developed to expose the young, bright leaders of tomorrow to different areas of work within the civil service on twelve- or eighteen-month placements. It allows them to experience a range of different policy areas, agencies and departments before they are thirty. As a career development tool for civil servants, it is undoubtedly effective. However, ministers' timescales are a little different. It might take two or three years for a policy to grow from manifesto to green paper, white paper, legislation and eventually statute. It may then take many more months, or even years, to implement the policy, and perhaps decades to assess its efficacy. This means that whoever is at the start of the policy production line will not be there at the end. And those at the end were not there at the beginning. In effect, no-one 'owns' a policy, or feels any great sense of attachment to it, or feels responsible for its impact. If it goes wrong, its originators can blame its inheritors, and vice versa.

The same is true of ministers and advisers. By the time I arrived at the Department of Health in 2005, there was a sense that many aspects of the NHS reform programme had been devised by people who were no longer there. We spent a lot of time wondering what it was they had in mind, and what they wanted to achieve. In some meetings, I had the feeling that the only person with a clear comprehension of why we were reforming the NHS was Tony Blair. When he went in 2007, the NHS reform programme was like a car without a driver.

There must be a way of making civil servants feel ownership over policy from start to finish, and feel that their own career development will depend on the successful delivery of the government's wishes. In the US system, the entire top end of the administration is appointed by the president and his team in the weeks between election in November and inauguration in January. In the UK, the equivalent would be for the entire civil service, grade three and above, to be appointed by the prime minister and sacked when the government fell. It is hard to see how such a system would work in the UK context.

But another way might be possible. An incoming Labour government could establish a 'cabinet' system for ministers, which means that departments would have key functions directed by small teams appointed by the minister, working alongside the permanent civil service. This was the system that Neil Kinnock would have introduced if elected in 1992.

An accommodation would have to be reached about the degree to which 'political appointments' could give management instructions to civil servants. Under Blair, only two people had such a power (Alastair Campbell and Jonathan Powell). Gordon Brown revoked these powers on coming into Number 10. Another model might be the one already in place in the Treasury, which has a Council of Economic Advisers, modelled on the White House equivalent, which under Brown comprised eleven experts in aspects of economic policy.

The civil service is not a single organisation. Government departments are like Swiss cantons, with distinct cultures, structures and processes. Policy wonks, always on the lookout for a barbarous phrase, call this 'silo-isation' – everyone doing their own thing.

This competition between departments leads to pointless turf wars. In the current climate of cuts, the main concern of senior civil servants is to protect their budgets, numbers of staff and areas of policy. Ministers often collaborate with this attitude, because they too believe status comes with size of department. John Prescott and Michael Heseltine, with their vast offices and gigantic departments, leap to mind.

Ministers are treated very well when they're in office. They are flattered. Everyone laughs at their jokes and listens to their stories. Once they are gone they are instantly expunged, like the 'unpersons' in *Nineteen Eighty-four*. David Laws left the government in 2010, and the waters closed over his head with ruthless efficiency. The name on his office door was changed within minutes of his resignation.

Tony Benn, who left ministerial office in 1979, outlined the main ways the civil service exercised real power:

1. By briefing ministers
2. By setting the framework of policy
3. By the control of information
4. By the mobilisation of external pressure
5. By the use of expertise
6. By the use of the Central Policy Review Staff (at Number 10)
7. By the use of patronage.[7]

Even Benn would admit that he never really found a way to work with his officials, whom he viewed with a suspicion and distrust that was mostly reciprocated. During the student uprising in 1968, he was warned by his officials that the anarchists might try to storm the department and take control. His reply was: 'I've been trying to do that for months.'

The powers Benn identified thirty years ago are a broadly accurate description of the power of the civil service today, regardless of who is in office. It is true that ministers lead lives shaped by the civil service: the private office, the diary secretary, the press office and the official driver. But an effective minister soon learns to run the department, not the other way round. Ministers need to be open to a range of influences: the ways policies work in their own constituencies, their local party activists, the people in their surgeries, the advice from their special advisers, and ideas from think-tanks.

A sensible reform would be to appoint more special advisers: more for secretaries of state, and new ones for ministers of state and other junior ministers. In a coalition arrangement with more than one party in government, this becomes more necessary. As part of a radical approach to the state, and to power, a revived Labour Party cannot ignore the power of the civil service and leave it untouched as part of a bigger settlement.

The monarchy

In a truly egalitarian society, there would be no monarchy. The idea that a hereditary institution, the product of invasion, war, murder and plots, should have a central role in our unwritten constitution and our culture is anathema to any sense of socialism. Yet the monarchy retains high levels of public support. It would be hard to imagine a reforming government attempting to abolish the monarchy, but should the institution be left untouched?

For the Labour Party, the monarchy has been a great taboo. It hasn't been discussed at the party conference since the 1920s. Harold Wilson, James Callaghan and Tony Blair co-opted the monarchy into their governments' PR drives. Wilson carried a picture of himself and the Queen in his wallet until it fell to bits. Blair used the Queen and Prince Philip's golden wedding celebrations to project his own image as the new prime minister. No Labour government has tried to lead a process of reform of the monarchy.

A government genuinely committed to reform should look at the following areas: the finances of the royal family, including the civil list and tax; the honours system; access for the public to royal art collections, palaces and land; the role of the 'royal prerogative' in Parliament; and a clear distinction between working and non-working members of the royal family, with contracts of employment.

The monarchy itself is more open to change than the Labour government has understood. The only genuine royal tradition is change. All else is invention and reinvention to suit changing times and tastes, in pursuit of self-preservation. The 'way ahead' group of senior royals plans and plots the future of the 'firm'. Labour ministers should engage with these discussions, and lead a debate about how a fundamentally undemocratic and elitist institution can sit amidst a modern, egalitarian society, as happens in Sweden.

The role of political parties

To function, democratic systems require a plurality of political parties. Political parties serve to aggregate views, put forward candidates, run elections and shape political conversations. That is why 'independent' candidates, such as Esther Rantzen, who lost her deposit in 2010 in Luton, tend to perform so poorly in elections to Westminster. Voters tend to vote for party political candidates on the basis of values and flagship policies, not on the basis of the personal attributes and characteristics of the candidates.

Once elected, members of the same party can coalesce to form blocs within assemblies, organising whips and 'making sense' of democracy. The alternative, representatives each voting any which way on every issue, would result in chaos. As Private Willis sings in *Iolanthe*:

> But then the prospect of a lot
> Of dull MPs in close proximity,
> All thinking for themselves, is what
> No man can face with equanimity.

If we value our political parties, we should be prepared to pay for them through an enhanced system of state funding. We already have limited state funding in the UK. Opposition parties are granted 'Short money', named after the Labour minister who introduced the scheme in 1979, to fund research and central office functions. Under the last Labour government Short money trebled, making the Conservatives and Liberal Democrats beneficiaries of the taxpayers' unwitting largesse.

State funding is the only answer to the problems of reform of the party funding system. A system of grants for specific types of party activity, for example community campaigning or political education, would allow taxpayers' money to be seen as an investment in democracy, not cash for political propaganda and posters. Grants could be allocated on the basis of numbers of members, or innovative campaigning.

The Conservative-led government is threatening an entirely partisan approach to party funding, which would prevent thousands of trade unionists, through their subscriptions, donating small amounts to the Labour Party. Like the Schleswig-Holstein Question, which Palmerston suggested had been understood by only three people, 'the Prince Consort, who is dead; a German professor, who has gone mad; and I, who have forgotten all about it', party funding is a hard debate to understand. Sir Haydon Phillips, former permanent secretary and chairman of the National Theatre, the Salisbury Cathedral Fabric Advisory Committee and the Marlborough College Council, was asked to investigate party funding and came away unable to slice the Gordian knot. The Conservatives want to cap donations at a fixed amount, say £50,000, because they know it will damage the Labour Party. Labour has been resistant to any reforms which undermine the ties between the trade unions and the party. Both parties approach the discussion with partisan interests foremost in their minds, and on that basis, no acceptable reform will be possible.

Political parties have fallen out of fashion. Even some Labour MPs boast that their local campaigns are boosted by non-party members. Within Labour there are those who advocate systems of non-member 'supporters' clubs', or 'primaries' of local residents to choose parliamentary candidates. The problem with reliance on community volunteers is that they may decide to support another candidate. Primaries could form part of local experiments in new forms of engagement. But it is vital that being a member of the Labour Party, or any party, affords the individual rights, powers and duties; otherwise, why would anyone bother to join a party? These rights should include rights to select candidates, hold representatives to account and develop policy.

The main problem with the local Labour parties is cultural. They tend to be inward-looking, administrative and focused, rightly, on elections. As Labour wins more council seats in coming years, as usually happens when the party is in opposition at Westminster, the job of selecting and electing candidates becomes even more important. Some of the better constituency Labour parties are campaigning organisations, with links throughout the local civic society.

But the missing ingredient in the life of the local Labour Party is social entrepreneurship. Few, if any, local Labour parties consider part of their role to be social change. Yet they comprise individuals with all kinds of skills, talents and experiences. Often there are local premises and other assets which could be the hub of social enterprises in a neighbourhood. Community crèches, cafés, bicycle repair workshops, translation services, IT training, recycling schemes, allotments, drop-in centres, transport for elderly people, youth clubs and study circles could all be run by Labour parties. Imagine if the spirit of Michael Young could be inculcated into the life of the local Labour Party. As the epicentre of local change, the party would be an attractive place for new members, thousands of whom have joined since the general election.

As more power is passed to community groups, more assets transferred to local groups, and as local community life becomes more egalitarian and democratic, the Labour Party at the local level should be a lead agency for social change. It will require a massive switch away from the 'next business' culture which prevails at the moment, but it will ensure that party membership does not further decline, and local parties do not ossify.

Summary

Britain has a half-grown, adolescent democracy, over-reliant on one form of democratic governance and under-developed in all the other forms of democracy. It is the absence of a mature, flourishing democracy that helps to explain so many of our society's ills, from wasteful public expenditure to distrust in the political system.

Labour must champion new forms of direct democracy, including referendums and petitions, and be prepared to pass real power to the citizen, even though that means less power for politicians.

Institutions such as the civil service and monarchy should be modernised within a modern democracy. The Labour Party itself should re-engineer its local processes and activities, and turn outwards to social entrepreneurship.

13. Creating a fairer society

'It is indeed our intention to: (a) Bring about a fundamental and irreversible shift in the balance of power and wealth in favour of working people and their families (b) Eliminate poverty wherever it exists in Britain, and commit ourselves to a substantial increase in our contribution to fight poverty abroad (c) Make power in industry genuinely accountable to the workers and the community at large (d) Achieve far greater economic equality – in income, wealth and living standards (e) Increase social equality by giving far greater importance to full employment, housing, education and social benefits (f) Improve the environment in which our people live and work and spend their leisure.'

Labour Party manifesto (1974)

New Labour failed to make the argument for greater equality. There was a sense that talk of redistribution, tackling poverty, even equal opportunities was too redolent of the old Labour Party that had been so electorally disastrous in the 1970s and 1980s. The kind of language used in the February 1974 election manifesto at the start of this chapter, with its stridency and confidence, was gone by the 1990s. The experience of the Thatcher government proved to a generation of socialists that nothing was 'irreversible'. The loss of so many elections made Labour understandably cautious about anything that might smack of red revolution.

'Equality' gave way to 'fairness' in public pronouncements, seeking to connect Labour's measures with the innate British sense of fair play. The redistribution of wealth through the national minimum wage and the tax and benefits system was based on growth in the economy. It was classic Crosland. Yet it was Crosland locked in the attic, like an embarrassing relative. It was egalitarianism by stealth. Labour stemmed the tide of inequality, but did not make Britain more equal. After more than a decade in office, Labour's legacy was a more unequal society – not because Labour's policies to create an equal society failed, but because none was truly attempted.

Although elements of New Labour's assault on inequality seem well established, such as the national minimum wage (although even this is precarious), others, such as the child trust fund, do not. Without winning the argument about greater equality, and by sublimating its egalitarian urges, Labour today in opposition is faced with a Conservative-led government which has no compunction about making Britain more unequal. As part of Labour's revival, the conversation with the public about greater equality will have to be louder, and more convincing.

An egalitarian society is not only one where individuals can reach fulfilment, but also where society itself becomes stronger, decent and civilised. It becomes a virtuous circle: an egalitarian society leads to happier people, who in turn contribute to the well-being of their society. The dominant norm of society is co-operation, not competition. Margaret Thatcher understood the role of public policy in shaping human behaviour when she said in 1981: 'Economics are the method; the object is to change the soul.'

The unequal society

Our country remains a place where an person's advancement depends not on their individual talents and aspirations, but on a range of factors beyond their control: where they were born, what their parents did, what school they went to, which sex, race and religion they are, whether they have a disability or not, and their postcode. It is impossible to calculate how much human potential has been wasted over the centuries because of inequality in society, or much more advanced our society could be now, if every potential scientist, economist, novelist, designer or artist had been able to realise their talent instead of being held back by accident of birth.

In the final months of the Labour government, the party's deputy leader, Harriet Harman, commissioned a report into the state of economic inequality in Britain. The report, *An Anatomy of Economic Inequality in the UK: Report of the National Equality Panel*, appeared in the febrile pre-election period, and was immediately denounced as a new phase in the 'class war' by the right-wing newspapers. For example, on 21 January 2010 the *Daily Mail* had the headline 'Harriet Harman revives class war with equality bible', whilst on the same day the *Daily Telegraph* offered 'Harriet Harman reopens class war with speech on inequality'.

The panel's main conclusion was that Britain is an unequal country, more so than many other industrial countries and more so than a generation ago. Amongst the wealth of findings were the following highlights:

- When three-year-olds are assessed on a measure of their 'school readiness', those from the poorest 20 per cent of the population on average score only half as well as those from the richest 20 per cent.
- Children who are eligible for free school meals do significantly less well at school at every stage. At Key Stage 4, only 27 per cent of them got good GCSE passes last year, compared with 54 per cent of those who were not eligible for free meals.
- Only 4 per cent of children receiving free school meals at age fifteen went on to higher education, compared with 33 per cent of those who were not eligible.

- Average life expectancy in the most affluent areas of the country is around thirteen years longer than in the poorest areas.
- Men in the richest 20 per cent of the population are four times more likely to be members of an occupational pension scheme, with the financial security that goes with it, than those from the poorest 20 per cent.

The report argued that

> wide inequalities erode the bonds of common citizenship and recognition of human dignity across economic divides . . . systematic differences between groups – for instance, by gender, ethnicity or religion – unrelated to experience or qualifications, constitute what would be seen by some as being the most central issue, violating fundamental principles of social justice, rooted in recognition of equal worth and respect.

This is surely the point. No-one, not even the fiercest egalitarian, would argue that everyone should earn the same, live in the same-sized house and drive the same car. Yet even the strongest proponents of inequality, those at the top with the most to lose, could argue that it is right to hold people back, so that no matter how hard they try and what motivations they may have, they never make it. All of us, from childhood, have a developed sense of fairness. It is plainly not fair for some to prosper and others to wallow in poverty, based on factors that have nothing to do with the individuals. Unfairness is locked in at an early age, with life chances determined at birth.

The report went on to make the point that

> even if such differences were eliminated completely so that, for instance, men and women enjoyed equal incomes, but there remained large gaps between low and high income men and low and high income women respectively, many

would still not regard the resulting distribution as fair, as society as a whole would remain more unequal than they thought was just. This is, in part, because a crucial test of whether inequalities in outcomes are seen as fair or unfair will depend on whether they reflect choices made against a background where the opportunities open to people were equal to start with, or whether they stem from aspects of their lives over which they have manifestly little control.'

The problem with New Labour's approach – tackling poverty, not inequality – is that it provides temporary relief, not a permanent solution. The public policy objective of getting homeless people off the streets was morally just and effective. But it was temporary. A new government might simply reverse the measures that reduced the numbers of rough sleepers, and they would rise again. The national minimum wage was a huge step forward a decade ago. But a Conservative government, whilst recognising that to abolish it outright would be politically unacceptable, could simply fail to increase it year on year, so that its relative value decreases over time. The temporary relief of poverty is the work of charity. The work of a Labour government is to change the relationships in society so that poverty is eradicated. G. D. H. Cole said the primary problem in his times was not poverty but 'slavery', by which he meant the absence of democratic control by people over their own lives.

There is growing evidence that socialists' traditional egalitarian impulses are more than philosophical. They are about more than 'fairness', they are about economic efficiency and national success. An important book, *The Spirit Level: Why More Equal Societies Almost Always Do Better* by Richard Wilkinson and Kate Pickett, appeared in 2007. The authors sought to show that countries that are more equal, in terms of distribution of wealth and opportunities, are more advanced across a range of factors, including mental illness, obesity, drug use, teenage pregnancy, homicide, imprisonment, literacy, infant mortality and life expectancy.

On a graph showing health and social problems against income inequality within countries, Japan, Norway, Finland, Sweden, the Netherlands, Belgium, Denmark and Switzerland are the most equal, having societies with the fewest social problems. The United Kingdom, Portugal, and the USA are the most unequal, and most beset with social problems. The United States, the 'richest' and 'freest' country, is almost off the scale. Wilkinson and Pickett write: 'The evidence shows that even small decreases in inequality, already a reality in some rich market democracies, make a very important difference to the quality of life.'

The authors have established the Equality Trust, which suggests that if the UK halved the level of inequality, then murder rates would halve, mental illness would reduce by two-thirds, obesity would halve, imprisonment would reduce by 80 per cent, and teen births would reduce by 80 per cent.[1]

The epidemiologist Michael Marmot wrote a book in 2004, based on a study of British civil servants, called *The Status Syndrome: How Social Standing Affects Our Health and Longevity*. It showed that an individual's health, well-being and life expectancy are directly related to their status (not just income and assets) within society. The degree to which an individual can control their life, and take meaningful decisions, has a direct impact on their chances of stroke, depression, heart disease, cancer and suicide.

Professor Richard Layard's book *Happiness: Lessons from a New Science* (2005) suggests that increases in income do not make the individual any happier, if there are still inequalities in income distribution. In short, people chase greater income by working harder, but will never catch up with those even richer, and so greater income makes people unhappier still.

The Sheffield academic Danny Dorling suggests: 'If you had to choose one word to characterize the nature of human society as it is currently arranged worldwide, there is no better word than "injustice".'[2] He presents the 'five tenets of injustice', which he holds to be the underpinning of social inequality today: elitism is efficient, exclusion is necessary, prejudice is natural, greed is good and despair is inevitable. One by one, Dorling demolishes each of these false ideas.

The growing canon of works on inequality in our society, and the benefits to our length of life, health and well-being of a more equal, egalitarian society, add up to a stronger, more urgent argument. It is not an argument which has been successfully translated into the lexicon of electoral politics yet. But that doesn't make it any less compelling.

What these studies show is that greater equality is more than a romantic notion, or an ignoble expression of envy, class hatred or misguided leftism. It is an essential prerequisite for a better society, with a freer people living longer, happier lives. Labour's egalitarian instincts, driven by the value of equality, have a growing base of evidence on which to build an argument and a story about how it wants to recast society.

The marriage of equality and aspiration

There is an obvious series of political bear-traps. The first is that if Labour talks about 'equality' without context or explanation, we risk deliberate obfuscation by our opponents, who will paint 'equality' as drab uniformity and sameness. Council estates, comprehensive schools, take-it-or-leave-it social services – Labour must never fall into the trap of becoming associated with the failed policies of previous generations. Indeed Labour has a duty to expose the failings of systems and policies for which it is responsible. If there's even a whiff that Labour's vision of equality is a council house, a job in a factory, a mediocre local school and hospital and a vote every five years, then the modern electorate will reject us out of hand. Equality must be expressed in new and attractive ways.

The second trap is that Labour's calls for equality look hypocritical if its leading lights behave in ways that look elitist. The more Labour politicians shout about equality, the closer the scrutiny becomes on their choices of schools for their children, the number of properties they own, the cars they drive, the expenses they claim, and the golf clubs they belong to. This is not a plea for a new Puritanism. It is a plea for equality to be properly explained, especially by those who seek to advocate it. Consider the public row that Labour MP Diane Abbott created when she sent her child to a fee-paying school, made worse by the suggestion it was what any 'West Indian mother' would do.

Thirdly, for Labour to talk about equality is to open the party up to accusations of class war. The British people have shown that they have no objections to being governed by people that went to public school, whether it was Clement Attlee, Tony Blair, Boris Johnson or David Cameron. Labour's attempts to paint Tories as 'toffs', for example during the Crewe & Nantwich by-election, were mostly counter-productive. It ended up sounding chippy and unpleasant. Most people recognise that Cameron didn't choose which school to go to, and shouldn't be attacked for the choices of his parents. Even the famous Bullingdon Club photograph, with Cameron in his white tie and tails, did as much damage as the photo of Tony Blair in a straw boater, which was none. If there is any sense amongst the public that the taxation system is being used by Labour to 'punish' the rich, or to make 'the pips squeak' as Denis Healey once promised, then even moderate earners will make common cause with high earners and even the super-rich. This is not because middle England earns enough to necessarily be affected personally by punitive tax rates, but because they consider and hope that one day they might be. People look up, not down.

A fourth danger is that the phraseology of equality becomes mistranslated. All too often when some Labour politicians talked about 'fairness' they meant that there should be more women high court judges, or black bankers. When great chunks of the electorate talked about 'fairness' they meant that no-one should be allowed to live on benefits whilst their neighbours struggled to work and pay taxes, or that their son or daughter should be able to buy or rent a home nearby as a higher priority than a family of Somalis or Afghanis. If ever there was a disconnect between politicians and people it is over notions of what's 'fair'.

Labour must be upfront – an egalitarian society means that everyone can try to fulfil their aspirations. An individualistic society is one that holds people back. Labour must be the party that comprehends, appreciates, values, nurtures and supports individual aspiration. This is the way to win back the recalcitrant C2 voters, especially in the south of England, who deserted Labour between 2007 and 2010. C2s work hard, earn their qualifications, start businesses, take on risk, and want the best for their children. They want a government which helps them in all these things, and if it can't help, they want it to get out of the way.

Aspiration is a trait which runs through people of all social classes, but the higher up the income ladder, the more it becomes a sense of entitlement, and the higher the bar of aspiration is set. Lower down, the horizons are lower, the support less, and to reach even a low bar becomes a greater struggle. The greatest ladder whereby working-class or lower-middle-class children could aspire to the professions was the grammar school system, which was dramatically reduced in the 1960s and 1970s. Today, academy schools can provide an aspirational environment, without the divisive selection examinations at eleven or twelve.

To create a framework of aspiration, Labour must see how people on higher incomes use their position to lock in the future for their children, and replicate it for the children of middle and low incomes. The children of high-income earners receive a good education, whether from the state or privately. They have parental support, and rooms full of encyclopedias and educational games. The talk from an early age is of 'which university to go to', not 'whether to go to university'. School holidays and weekends are packed with stimulating visits and trips. Social life revolves partly around conversation with adults. Holiday jobs, internships and gap years can be found in Parliament, law firms, publishers or newspaper offices. And at the back of the mind of the young person is usually the knowledge that their parents will provide the ultimate safety net if a risk fails or a job falls through.

Children from middle- or low-income families have very few of these advantages. They may have loving, supportive parents, excellent teachers and personal drive, but the absence of networks, easily grasped opportunities and raised horizons will hold them back.

The state can never replace the family. But the family can be given practical help by the state, especially a decentralised, democratic state.

Labour should explore ways in which parents, local authorities, schools, businesses and especially the third sector can give children from middle- and low-income families the same kind of support that upper-middle-class children get within their own stratum of society. This should not be targeted at children at risk of criminal behaviour, or already within the criminal justice system, who require a different kind of support. Many families feel that only kids who get into trouble are rewarded with sports schemes and day trips. Labour should provide a network of support including mentoring, university summer schools, trips to the theatre, opera and ballet, and access to quality internships within the professions.

Alan Milburn, the former Labour Cabinet minister, chaired an inquiry into fair access to the professions in 2009, which concluded that there was less, not more, social mobility since the expansion of the universities and the professions in the 1960s. In the post-war period, the egalitarianism of the war effort, when bright talented people were promoted into the right jobs, was still driving society. The reaction against 'Colonel Blimp' was still there. A bright grammar school boy could go to Oxford, join the professions and end up at the top of the tree, despite poor parents.

I think of my own father: born during the great depression, brought up in a single-parent family, left school at fourteen, worked hard, joined the RAF, commissioned as an officer after serving in the ranks, left the services and went straight into air traffic control, at a time of booming international travel, bought a house in the late 1960s, earned his degree from the Open University in his forties, retired on a decent pension, and died knowing that his son had been firmly planted in the middle classes. It is hard to see how a child born today in similar circumstances would have the same opportunities for social mobility, despite whatever drive and ambition they may possess.

The Milburn report pointed to a 'not for the likes of me' syndrome, which held the children of non-professionals back: one in two children with parents who are professionals want to pursue a professional career. Only one in six children from average family income backgrounds want to do the same. For the very poorest children the aspiration to become a doctor or lawyer is as likely as becoming a pop star or professional footballer.

The report recommended a range of policies designed to break down the barriers and increase social mobility, including a national network of mentors, a school alumni database, an overhaul of the work experience programme in schools, each profession to recruit youth ambassadors to reach out to other young people, more apprenticeships, more professional experiences within university courses, and a transparent and fair system of internships.

As one of the Labour Party's champions of decentralisation, Milburn also makes the important point that social mobility depends on the diffusion of power, as well as assets and wealth:

> Social mobility will not advance if we think it is only wealth that is unevenly distributed in our society. We make proposals that are about redistributing power. If Britain is to get moving again socially, people need to be able not just to get a job or training or childcare but also to enjoy greater control and to have a bigger say in how they lead their lives. Unlocking our country so that it is open to aspiration and

> effort requires a new drive to fundamentally change how
> power is distributed in our society.

There was a moment in the 1960s when it felt like aspiration could be realised, when working-class children could reach the top by hard work and talent, and in the knowledge of a benevolent welfare state, a growing NHS, new universities and increasingly social liberalism. That moment turned sour. In the 1960s, the Beatles could sing about becoming a 'paperback writer'. By the 1970s, the Clash were singing with savage irony about career opportunities to make tea at the BBC or to be a ticket inspector. By the 1980s, bands sang about ghost towns, dole queues and urban riots, and even Wham! could get 'DHSS' into a song lyric. The moment has passed.

Creating a society where talents can flourish and young people can look around and see only opportunities is Labour's goal. It's the way the next generation of Labour politicians can sell an egalitarian society to a sceptical electorate, hooked on the idea that inequality is natural, that society depends on there being unequal social classes, and that greater equality means less individual freedom, when the opposite is the case.

An equal right to life

Take a walk around the graveyards of Barnsley, Glasgow, Doncaster or Liverpool, and then repeat the exercise in Guildford, Chichester or Winchester, and you will see the impact of 'health inequalities' in modern British society. People who are poorer live shorter, more unhealthy lives. Men in Blackpool now live on average for 73.2 years, 10.5 less than their counterparts in Kensington & Chelsea. Women in Hartlepool have the lowest female life expectancy at 78.1 years, around 9.6 years less than in a central London borough. Life expectancy drops by a year for every stop on the London Underground between Westminster and Canning Town. This is the greatest scandal of our unequal society – that how long you have to live is determined by your place in the social order.

On 16 December 1976, a remarkable letter appeared in *New Society* magazine, addressed to the Labour health secretary, David Ennals, from Richard G. Wilkinson (thirty years on, one of the authors of *The Spirit Level*). It challenged the Labour minister in no uncertain terms:

> You have the misfortune to be confronted by the largest social class differences in death rates since accurate figures were first collected in the 1920s and 1930s. Almost all the major causes of death including heart disease, stroke, lung cancer, stomach cancer, cervical cancer, pneumonia and bronchitis, are two or three times more common among unskilled manual workers and their families (social class V) than among senior professional and managerial families (social class I) . . . the overall death rate is now 50 per cent higher in social classes IV and V combined (the bottom quarter of the population) than it is in social classes I and II combined (the top quarter of the population).
>
> No matter whether one looks at the relative or absolute size of the gap between the death rates of upper and lower social classes it is two or three times as large now as it was in the early 1930s. It widened slightly during the 1930s and 1940s; it widened dramatically during the 1950s (in spite of the NHS); and it has continued to widen since then.

What Wilkinson's analysis showed is that despite thirty years of the NHS, poor people were dying younger, from mainly preventable causes, than rich people. He detailed their diets and showed that poorer people were eating more fat, salt and sugar, and less fibre, vitamins and fruit and vegetables. They were smoking more. With the end of food rationing in the late 1940s, the diet of poor people became unhealthier.

The letter concludes:

> If the government is to have even moderate success in
> bringing down the death rates of the lower social classes –
> death rates which have not fallen significantly during the
> last quarter of a century – we know that health will need
> to become a major consideration across a wide area of food
> and agricultural policy where it has been conspicuously
> absent since the Second World War. Unless effective action
> is taken we can only expect the differences in death rates and
> life expectancy between rich and poor to grow during your
> period in office as Secretary of State just as they did under
> your predecessors.

Ennals's response to the letter in *New Society* was to establish
a commission, under Sir Douglas Black, to investigate health
inequalities. The Black report was a major piece of work. It
corroborated what Wilkinson had said and went further, looking
at the health of children, disabled people and women across the
social spectrum. It showed a clear link between social class and
health, with health getting worse with every pound drop in income.
Significantly, it also showed that the NHS was failing to provide an
equal service to all citizens in every part of the country. The poorest
people got the poorest standards of care from the 'national' health
service. Dr Julian Tudor Hart, in an article in *The Lancet* in 1971, had
identified this as the 'inverse care law' – those that needed care the
most got the least, and vice versa. The historian of the NHS, Charles
Webster, wrote that

> the NHS . . . tended to mirror and perpetuate the
> accumulated idiosyncrasies and inequalities in health care
> provision contained in the inherited system, and which in
> the main reflected deep-seated patterns in the distribution
> of wealth, which had determined that those sections of the

community experiencing the greatest problems of ill-health were provided with the worst health services.[3]

The Black report made thirty-seven recommendations for action, including improved child safety, surveys into diets, a shift away from hospital and towards community-based care, fair distribution of GP surgeries, including poorer areas, free milk for children, more day nurseries, care for people in their own homes for as long as possible, home helps for disabled people, a ban on tobacco advertising, counselling for smokers trying to quit, no-smoking areas in public places, a ten-year plan for cigarette manufacturers to phase out cigarettes, an increase in child benefit, universal free school meals, and repairs to sub-standard housing. It could have formed the core of a Labour manifesto. Indeed many of the proposals led to initiatives such as Sure Start, health action zones and the smoking ban, which the Labour government elected in 1997 introduced.

Although commissioned under a Labour government, the Black report was published – 'suppressed' may be more accurate – under a Conservative government. It was published in 1980 by the then DHSS, and limited to a run of 260 copies issued on a Bank Holiday Monday. Under the Tories health inequalities were ignored, and the link between socio-economic status and ill health not recognised.

In 1998 the newly elected Labour government commissioned a new report into health inequalities from Sir Donald Acheson. The Acheson report identified poverty as the key determinant of health, and called for increased benefits for mothers, better diets, and action on smoking and drinking.

Twelve years later, in 2010, Sir Michael Marmot again identified the link between poverty and ill health. His report estimated that up to 202,000 early deaths could be avoided, if everyone in the population enjoyed the same health as university graduates. The report suggested that inequality in illness accounts for £33 billion of lost productivity every year. Marmot called for an increase in the national minimum wage as a sure way to increase public health.

About 4 per cent of the NHS budget is spent on preventative health and public health initiatives. One of the first acts of the Conservative-led government was to scrap public information campaigns about drugs, smoking and teen pregnancies. It seems unlikely that the government will even attempt to reduce health inequalities, but without rigorous action from government, health inequalities don't stay the same, they get worse.

Any Labour secretary of state for health, including the one I worked for, is under enormous pressure to deliver an NHS which works well, avoids winter bed crises, can handle peaks of demand and doesn't become a major political issue. Under the last phase of Blair, health secretaries were under instruction to deliver reforms to the NHS to bring waiting lists down, to restructure the financial arrangements of the NHS, and to secure a world-beating service. The longer-term imperative to equalise public health and reduce inequalities in life expectancy came a poor second to the immediacy of the NHS. The Department of Health often felt more like a department for the NHS. The smoking ban will stand out as a landmark contribution to public health; in time it will be shown to have saved lives. But the underlying inequalities in health in Britain remain largely untackled.

All governments since 1997 have proclaimed their commitment to public health. The next Labour government will have to do better than talk.

The first challenge is the demographic time bomb. In 2011, the number of over-65s exceeds the number of under-16s in Britain for the first time. By 2033, the over-65s will comprise over a fifth of the population. The number of over-85s will double in the same period. Centenarians will become commonplace. The centrepiece of Labour's 2010 manifesto was a 'national care service' with free personal care for the most vulnerable people. Public health policy and the NHS will have to take account of older people as never before. The NHS, and the welfare state in general, were not designed to cope with the number and needs of Britain's older people. It was beyond the imagination of Beveridge or Bevan. It must be a priority for the next Labour government.

The NHS was designed to deal with industrial diseases such as emphysema, children's conditions caused by poor diet and malnutrition, industrial accidents in the mines and factories, and a vast unmet need in dentistry, poor eyesight and other chronic conditions. Aneurin Bevan believed that as the backlog of medical treatment was dealt with, and as treatment became free at the point of need, demands on the service would fall. Instead, advances in medicine and technology, and a population living longer, meant that demand has increased every year since the NHS's foundation. The pioneers of the NHS also had faith that it would become truly 'national' because it was established as a single entity, with a uniform system. As we have seen, health inequalities persisted, and became worse under the NHS. As the Fabian academic Brian Abel-Smith said in the 1980s: 'If socialists believed forty years ago that all that was needed to equalise health status between social classes was to remove the money barriers to access to health care, they were seriously mistaken.'[4]

The new challenges for the NHS are children who are so overweight they will die before their parents, the persistence of smoking in society, widespread drug use, so-called 'binge drinking' and other patterns of alcohol abuse. Huge numbers of people are suffering from different forms of mental illness: one in four of the adult population, one in ten children, two out of every five older people living in a care home, and nine out of ten in the prison population. The NHS was not designed to deal with needs on this scale, and cannot deliver an effective service.

Labour will need to recast the NHS and establish a wider network of organisations to tackle health inequalities. GPs will have to be contractually compelled to establish practices on estates and poor neighbourhoods which they've traditionally avoided. The voluntary sector will have to be given the support it needs to provide training in nutrition and cooking. Food co-ops can provide fruit and vegetables in 'food deserts' where the only food available is processed and deadly. A new assault on smoking must be launched, including increased taxes, action to tackle smuggling and the black market, more warnings on packaging, stiffer penalties for vendors selling to children, and a ban on smoking outside public buildings. The Department for Health must become a department for public health, not a department to administer the NHS. The NHS is a tool in public health, not an end in itself. Most of all, a new Labour government must plough resources into mental health services, 'talking therapies' counselling and other services.

There is no worse manifestation of inequality in Britain than the obvious fact that the poor live shorter, unhappier, unhealthier lives than the rich. An egalitarian society, with a fair distribution of work, income and wealth, would end this injustice within a generation, and this must be Labour's goal.

Personalisation in the public services

One of the ways in which Labour's opponents managed to sell the argument that egalitarianism meant a uniform, monochrome, lifeless society was Labour's attachment to social services and institutions which seemed to reinforce conformity and mediocrity. The challenge for Labour's new leadership is to craft public services which are not uniform and mediocre, but which serve individual needs with ever-improving standards of service. To create public services which are equally good for everyone, they have to be different for everyone, not the same. This counter-intuitive insight is what drove much of the New Labour agenda between 1997 and 2007, and a combination of investment and reform meant that standards improved. It was hard going for some in the Labour Party, who saw reforms which increased diversity as somehow against equality.

As ever R. H. Tawney is our guide:

> But equality of provision is not identity of provision. It is
> to be achieved, not by treating different needs the same
> way, but by devoting equal care to ensuring they are met
> in the different ways most appropriate to them, as is done
> by a doctor who prescribes different regimens for different
> constitutions, or a teacher who develops different types of
> intelligence by different curricula.[5]

As Tawney suggests, to achieve greater equality, social services and
welfare systems have to treat people differently, not the same. Two
methods to achieve this are either to involve people in the design
and delivery of services, or to allow people to do it for themselves
through co-operatives and mutuals, by giving away power and
resources from the central state.

New Labour went some of the way towards this goal, with the
'personalisation' of social services. Schemes such as the Expert
Patients Programme empowered people with chronic conditions
to take more control over their treatment within the NHS. But the
main mechanism New Labour adopted was to involve a plurality
of suppliers, including the private sector, to supply a degree of
'contestability' within services, and to give the user a degree of choice.

In the NHS, waiting times for knee operations and cataract
removals dwindled to next to nothing thanks to the introduction
of independent sector treatment centres. Many within the health
service expressed great disquiet about the use of the private sector.
But very few of the patients who received fast, efficient treatment
were heard complaining.

Labour used a regime of targets within the public services to
measure how services were performing, and therefore how and
where to direct resources to improve them. The targets were essential
in delivering better services. They meant that, for example, waiting
times in Accident & Emergency or for heart operations fell to their

lowest since the NHS began. But Labour lost the argument to the Tories, who said that targets were 'interference' in the running of local services, and that 'the professionals' should be allowed to make the decisions. Their spokespeople, and now their ministers, talked of 'targets culture' and achieved their goal of imbuing it with negative connotations. One of the first acts of the Conservative-led government was to scrap targets for time spent in A&E and waits for hospital treatment and NHS operations. Scrapping the target means that waiting lists will go up.

Labour never got the credit for smaller class sizes in primary schools or shortened waits for NHS treatment because people don't make a comparison with their standard of service today, with their standard of service ten years ago when it was much worse. The reason is simple – anyone with children in primary school today didn't have them in primary school a decade ago, and few people undergoing operations in the NHS today had the same operation ten years ago either.

In the coming years Labour needs to show that it has cast off the shadow of its 'one size fits all' attitude to public services, and finally kill off the last vestiges of Fabian paternalism or Soviet centralism.

Academy schools

An important demonstration of how a non-uniform approach to public services can tackle inequality is the academy schools programme, established in 2000 by Tony Blair and driven onwards by Lord Adonis as schools minister. Academies are funded directly from government, but are cut free from local authority control and allowed to attract sponsors from the business or voluntary sector. The early indications from the first eleven schools, which had been failing comprehensives, were high levels of parent satisfaction, improvements in attendance and discipline, and steady improvement in academic performance. The schools were heavily over-subscribed. The academies programme was accelerated under Labour, and is now seen widely as the way forward for secondary education in the state sector.

As with the move to foundation trust status for NHS hospitals, the shift to academies and away from local authority-controlled comprehensives was bitterly opposed by those who confused 'equality' with 'uniformity', even if the schools were uniformly bad at educating children. There was a titanic struggle to get the legislation through Parliament. Neil Kinnock publicly attacked Labour government policy for the first time. The teaching unions were opposed. When Blair talked about the 'scars on his back' in 1999 resulting from attempts to reform public services, he was foreseeing the battle to establish academies.

What many of the opponents of academies ignore is that we have a two-tier system of education in Britain. The affluent can afford to move house to be near good state schools, or they can pay for private education. Affluence buys you a better education for your children within, as well as without, the state sector. What academy schools do is lever up the standard of education for the poorer pupils (as well as possibly persuading middle-class parents to stay with the state sector) and create greater equality between pupils of different social classes. Innovation, personalisation, diversity and choice, within a plural state system, are the ways to improve the life chances of the poorest people. Uniform services aimed at the lowest common denominator fail the poor, and fail the test of equality.

The new guilds: locally elected boards

Labour's policy must demonstrate a clear commitment to local control over services, as a sure way to match local needs. If the possibility arises for locally elected NHS boards, perhaps at the level of what is now the primary care trust, Labour should warmly embrace the opportunity and prepare candidates to stand for every NHS board. The idea of a NHS board with one-third local councillors, one-third healthcare professionals and one-third directly elected citizens was put forward within the Labour government in 2008, but was ruled out by Number 10. The same idea then appeared in the Coalition Agreement document in June 2010. Yet again Labour's centralising tendency allowed the party to be outflanked by the opposition.

Local boards could be elected on similar lines to run local police services, aspects of the criminal justice system, social care services, schools, colleges and universities, and other unaccountable public services. Rather than be sidelined by locally elected boards, local councillors would become involved in new ways in the running of services. When the Labour government's New Deal for Communities programme was at its height, many of the local boards allocating grants and directing services were elected, or partially elected. Election turnouts were often higher than for the council in the same area, and a range of 'non-traditional' candidates came forward to stand for office, disproving the naysayers who perennially suggest that people are too apathetic to take control of local services.

This tapestry of local accountability and democracy, working alongside local councils, would enrich local democracy and aid the aim of creating more active citizens. Coupled with the transfer of assets such as buildings and land, owned through trusts or mutuals, local income generation could be ensured, with an end to the over-reliance on the benevolence of ministers. It would be the start of a genuine redistribution of power and opportunity, which, as we have seen, is the necessary precursor to a more equal society. There is evidence too, for example from New Zealand, which moved to a system of elected health boards, that services improve if they are directed locally.

This is the modern version of guild socialism: democratic, decentralised power; active citizens with equal access to decision-making; the end of the overarching, we-know-best central state; and socialism returned to its ethical roots.

Revisionism and the problem of inequality

The goal of equality is always shifting. The fundamental inequalities between rich and poor have been long described and understood, and have been the animating force behind most of British socialism. Under a welfare state, whilst no-one is so poor they die in the street, the manifestations of poverty are different, and sometimes less easy to spot or tackle. The evidence is that life chances are pre-determined by social class, which is closely related to economic status. Even here new challenges emerge. Why are Bangladeshi and Pakistani workers in the UK more disadvantaged than other Asian workers, with almost half living in poverty? Black African and black Caribbean boys fall well behind the average for educational attainment at sixteen, making them more likely to be low-income earners. The education system spectacularly fails children from gypsy and traveller families.

Certain places and neighbourhoods suffer inequality. In 2001 the Labour government launched a huge strategy designed to ensure 'that within ten to twenty years no-one would be seriously disadvantaged by where they live'.[6] Thirty-nine areas were identified, including in Bradford, Brighton, Bristol, Hartlepool, Hull, Middlesbrough, Newham, Rochdale and Southampton. They received £2 billion between them to tackle the underlying causes of deprivation, and to bring their neighbourhoods up to the level of the rest. Great improvements were made, but overall the strategy has not ensured that no-one is disadvantaged by where they live. Many places in Britain remain blighted by crime, gangs, anti-social behaviour, noise and litter. The decent families living in those places are not equally free to walk down the street or go out after dark as people living in more stable neighbourhoods. Labour must address inequality between neighbourhoods with renewed energy.

In applying the revisionist method to inequality, the next generation of socialists must be alive to further forms of inequality beyond the purely economic: the inequality between men and women, between people of different physical and mental abilities, between lesbians, gays, bisexuals and transgendered people, between people of different races and faiths. Bernstein, Durbin, Crosland and the great socialist revisionists had little to say about the struggle for gay liberation. Today it forms a central part of Labour's policy programme, and measures such as civil partnerships are a widely accepted part of modern life. Even the Conservative Party, which introduced the reviled Section 28 of the Local Government Act in 1988, which forbade councils from 'promoting homosexuality', has apologised and accepted civil partnerships.

New forms of inequality will arise as society changes, and will exist in even the most egalitarian of societies. The nature of socialism is that it never arrives; what matters is the journey towards it.

Summary

Britain is a deeply divided society, with great differences in wealth, power and opportunity between social groups. Society is not 'broken', but it is desperately unfair, with individual talent being squandered because of barriers which are beyond the individual's control. Without a greater degree of equality, defined as the capability to get on in life, our economy will not prosper, and our democracy will not function properly. An incoming Labour government should be clearly committed to an egalitarian society, where the barriers to personal advancement and success are broken down. Labour must avoid class war rhetoric or punitive tax systems which will create a 'tax avoidance industry' and a mass exodus of the rich. Instead, Labour should marry the traditional concern for equality with the British sense of aspiration, showing that in an egalitarian society people can get on and do well for themselves, whereas in an individualistic society advancement depends on factors beyond your control, such as social class and postcode.

14. Creating a mutual economy

> 'Society may be formed so as to exist without crime, without poverty, with health greatly improved, with little, if any misery, and with intelligence and happiness increased a hundredfold.'
>
> Robert Owen
> *An Address to the Inhabitants of New Lanark* (1816)

Human beings are capable of both great kindness and great cruelty. When a community comes together after tragedy, when people help their neighbours in times of personal hardship, or when a nation unites in the face of common adversity, the collaborative instinct comes to the fore. Through a million random acts of kindness to strangers, we ensure that what Robert Kennedy called 'the same short moment of life' is ameliorated and made tolerable. With the right social conditions, humans perform great acts of heroism, sacrifice and altruism. The opposite is true. Throughout history, humans have performed acts of great barbarism, cruelty and murder. The National Health Service and the Holocaust were created on the same continent in the same decade.

Humans are both competitive and collaborative. A system which rewards avarice and greed will make people avaricious and greedy. A system which elevates co-operation into the supreme virtue will make people co-operative. Within society, the more co-operative and mutual organisations there are, the more co-operative and mutually minded people there will be. Most societies form their own rules of conduct: forming a queue for the bus, relinquishing a seat for a pregnant woman, helping to look for a lost child, helping to push a stalled car, coming to the aid of an elderly person. These rules of behaviour are not supported by laws; they come naturally, and are reinforced by instruction and example. They form what R. H. Tawney called 'the elementary decencies' of life.[1]

If we want a society of rats, then we must stick with the rat-race. If we seek a higher form of social organisation, then we need an economy and society based on the principles of co-operation.

More than nineteen million Britons are members of a mutual organisation. Employee-owned firms, such as the John Lewis Partnership, now account for a sector with a £25 billion annual turnover. There are 4,990 independent co-operatives in the UK employing 237,800 people. This includes 716 credit unions, 55 building societies, agricultural co-ops with a turnover of £4.9 billion, 241 community shops (like the one in *The Archers*), community pubs like the Star Inn in Salford, football club supporters' trusts, and co-operative wind farms.

Robert Owen, the Rochdale Pioneers and the early co-operators provide us with an ideal and a set of principles, including democratic ownership and control, enterprise not for profit, and fair shares of surpluses. Today, those principles need to be applied across the economy and public services, so that companies and institutions serve the consumer and the citizen, not private profit. Despite the good intentions, co-operatives still make up a small proportion of the economy and public services. Most people in the UK do not yet belong to a co-op. Co-operatives are still a minority pursuit, not the 'normal' way of doing business. To create the fairer, greener, democratic society that socialism demands there must be a transformation in the role and scope of the co-operative movement.

More help for co-operative businesses

The Labour Party manifesto in 2010 promised 'a step change in the role of employee-owned companies in the economy, recognising that many entrepreneurs would like to see their companies in the hands of their employees when they retire. We will review any outstanding barriers to the formation of more employee companies like the John Lewis Partnership.'[2] This enthusiasm should be replicated for other forms of mutual ownership. For example, the government should make more capital investment available through an investment fund. It should encourage the banks, especially the ones it owns, to make loans available for start-ups.

One practical step a government can take is to make mutually owned organisations 'preferred suppliers' when government departments buy goods and services. Each government department spends a small fortune on office supplies, bottled water, toilet paper, sandwiches and IT equipment. Nearly all of that money goes into the hands of private companies. The central state should use its massive spending power to create a new market for co-operatively produced goods and services. New co-operatives would form to enter the market. Existing ones would develop and grow to meet the increased demand. Within months, a Labour government could massively increase the co-op and mutual sector in the UK, without changing a single law.

Labour should look at utility companies, especially in the water and sewerage sector, with a view to mutualisation. It's already been done in Wales with the creation of Glas Cymru. Glas Cymru is a single-purpose company formed to own, finance and manage Welsh Water. It was brought into customer ownership through raising £1.9 billion on the bond markets. It is a 'company limited by guarantee' and because it has no shareholders, any financial surpluses are invested to benefit Welsh Water's customers.

Railtrack, the company that owns the tracks, tunnels and bridges on British railways, has been a state-owned enterprise since 2001, when Labour minister Stephen Byers nationalised it following safety failures and under-performance. Today it sits within the state's portfolio of assets for no good reason other than inertia. It should form the basis of a new mutually owned enterprise, or series of smaller enterprises, leasing infrastructure to the rail companies.

Similarly, British Waterways should become a co-operative. The canal network was nationalised by Labour in 1948, along with the railways. When Labour's transport minister Barbara Castle toured the waterways in 1967, she was the first minister to do so for thirty years. Thanks to the Labour government elected in 1966, and the vision in Barbara Castle's 1968 Transport Act, the canals were reinvented as places for leisure and environmental conservation. In March 2010, the Labour government made a pledge to turn British Waterways into a mutually owned and run organisation, with safeguards to protect the land and buildings in perpetuity, and avoid a future government privatising its assets. This pledge should be honoured.

Across the public sector there are all kinds of institutions which might be more effective in the mutual sector, from the BBC, to the Post Office, to doctors' surgeries, to government laboratories. Labour should be bold about increasing the size of the mutual sector, by mutualising state-owned bodies and by creating new mutuals to compete in the private sector. It should be doubled over the length of a parliament. Far more firms should be employee owned. At the moment only 2 per cent of companies are owned by the people who work for them. There should be a dramatic shift in favour of employee ownership, and incentives for workforces to buy their companies.

The financial crisis

If ever the interconnectedness and fragility of the global economic system was in doubt, the global financial crisis which started in

2007 proves the point. Millions of Americans were encouraged to buy houses in the belief that the favourable terms on which they borrowed the money would remain, and that the value of their property would go up over time. Millions more were enticed with easy credit to spend money they did not have and would never earn. When interest rates went up, and property prices went down, tens of thousands lost their homes. Investment banks and hedge funds (the so-called 'shadow banking system') were operating without the regulation of the commercial banks. Paul Krugman called this 'malign neglect', and their subsequent exposure was the core of the crisis.

In the UK, the Northern Rock bank suffered a run, the first for 150 years in the UK, with patient investors queuing to get their money. In February 2008, the Labour government nationalised Northern Rock. As the crisis spread around the world, the British government spent £500 million trying to bail out the banks. The Royal Bank of Scotland and HBOS-Lloyds TSB were brought into state control to prevent their collapse in October 2008.

On 15 September 2008 Lehman Brothers in New York filed for bankruptcy, and its ex-employees filed out of 745 Seventh Avenue clutching box files and souvenirs. The *Washington Post* reported in May 2010 that the estate of Lehman Brothers Holdings was suing JPMorgan Chase, alleging that the firm forced Lehman Brothers into bankruptcy by making it give up cash reserves it could have spent on staying afloat.

The financial crisis, and the recession it triggered, are consequences of the failure of the free, unregulated market. It also reveals the degree to which Western economies are built on air: bubbles of credit and debt without reference to assets or manufacturing.

Rahm Emanuel, the White House chief of staff, said you should never let a crisis go to waste. There has been a global reaction against the unfettered financial markets and the misery they have caused. There is renewed interest in sustainable, ethical and mutual forms of economic organisation. Labour should do more than debate financial regulation; it should shift Britain towards a mutual economy, built on principles of co-operation, long-term environmental sustainability and ethical investment.

The mutualisation of the financial services industry

In the 1980s and 1990s a wave of building societies, including the Abbey National, Cheltenham & Gloucester and Alliance & Leicester, moved from mutual ownership to private ownership, with members bribed to vote for demutualisation with the promise of a cheque in the post. Of the former building societies which demutualised, none remains as an independent institution trading on the stock market.

Northern Rock, currently owned by the state, should be mutualised. Of the remaining banks which have majority state ownership, the investment and retail arms should be disentangled, and the retail banks turned into mutuals. This would have been unthinkable a few years ago, but the fact that the state has invested so heavily, and that public opinion was unfazed by the nationalisation of the banks, suggests that people would welcome a further shift in ownership. It would create a healthy 'market' in mutually owned banks on the high street, and provide an ethical, stable, and customer-led sector within financial services.

Asset transfer

The Labour government dipped its toe into the business of transferring assets such as swimming pools, markets, and disused land and buildings from the state to local communities, following the publication in 2003 of a Fabian pamphlet by Hazel Blears called *Communities in Control*. When I was at the Department for Communities and Local Government we established an Asset Transfer Unit to catalyse the process. About 1,000 asset transfers have been completed, or are in train.

The current pace and scale is puny. Most councils, and each central government department, own assets which could be passed to local ownership. These need not be the run down, the disused and the unloved. It could be the jewels in the crown. Why does the government own the Queen Elizabeth II Conference Centre in the heart of Westminster? This could easily be made into a mutual, with links to the deprived wards which surround central Westminster. What about all the land and buildings owned by the NHS, or the Ministry of Defence? MoD land tends to be sold to the commercial sector for development. But the ownership of areas of land can also be transferred to create Land Trusts, owned by community groups, which generate income for local community schemes on a not-for-profit basis. Asset transfer can be accompanied by an 'asset lock', which prevents assets from being sold off for profit.

The idea of an asset transfer is to pass ownership of a physical asset such as buildings or land from the state to a local community group, operating as a mutual organisation. It is then owned and run by local people along democratic, not-for-profit lines. It can give a community a renewed energy and focus, bring different people together to work in concert, and unleash creativity and innovation. By organising as a co-op or mutual, local people can learn new skills and bolster local democracy. Asset transfers create new active citizens.

Co-operatives in the public services

Co-operatives and mutuals can operate within the state sector, providing services for example within the NHS and the education system. Before losing office, the Labour government announced that 100 schools would become 'co-operative schools'. These are schools which continue to operate within local authority control, but whose ownership passes to a trust comprising parents, teachers and governors. This is to be welcomed, but there are 17,000 primary schools in England alone. A hundred out of 17,000 is a drop in the ocean.

The foundation trust model of ownership in the NHS has been a success, with over half of hospital services now provided through such a trust. They are co-operatives within the NHS, and some have the Rochdale principles enshrined in their constitutions. They have a degree of autonomy from ministerial control, retain their surpluses for reinvestment in local health care and are accountable to the communities they serve through a local membership and an elected board. Foundation trusts were fiercely opposed by the British Medical Association, by Unison, by some Labour MPs and by the Gordon Brown when chancellor, who succeeded in partially curtailing their ability to borrow money.

Within the NHS, there are also smaller co-operatives. Central Surrey Health was established in 2007 by a nurse and a speech therapist to provide health services within the East Elmbridge and Mid Surrey Primary Care Trust. They met with bureaucratic opposition from the Department of Health, although not from ministers, and wrangles over their pension rights. But they are now firmly established and provide a model for other similar schemes across the NHS.

In housing too, there are co-operatives which are owned, managed and run by members and tenants. Some co-op housing schemes are aimed at 'key workers' such as nurses and police officers who are otherwise priced out of the housing market.

The original concept of Sure Starts was to provide children from disadvantaged backgrounds with childcare in centres owned and run by the community. The 200 original schemes, described by their inventor, Norman Glass, as 'anarcho-syndicalist', were an instrument of social justice, with local ownership of the buildings and land, and in-house services such as debt counselling for parents. Their expansion after 2005 left Sure Start as another arm of the state, in this case the Department for Children, Families and Schools. There are now 3,600 Sure Starts in England and Wales. The Conservative-led government has announced that Sure Starts can be transferred into the mutual and co-operative sector. This is a return to their roots, and Labour should be wary of opposing the move for opposition's sake, because it is what the Labour government intended them to be.

Wherever possible, Labour should apply the co-operative model to public services, across the range of education, health, criminal justice, social care and other services. The benefits are well established: greater employee satisfaction, more innovative service delivery, greater customer and client satisfaction, and assets which are owned by employees and local stakeholders, not the state, and therefore beyond the reach of ministerial interference.

The co-operative council

A glimpse of the future is provided by Lambeth council in south London, which is seeking to become the first 'co-operative council'. Since the Labour Party was elected to run Lambeth in 2006, it has engaged in a range of laudable initiatives which create mutuals and co-ops and put power in the hands of the community. Lambeth has transferred the site of the old Lilian Baylis School in Kennington to a community trust to run a sports and youth club – the UK's biggest asset transfer; it has established co-operatively managed housing estates; launched the biggest participatory budgeting scheme in the UK; devolved power to local communities to transform local public spaces and run 'green' initiatives; and personalised care budgets, giving control to care users. Lambeth is also home to Coin Street Community Builders on the South Bank, one of the country's biggest and most successful housing co-operatives, established at the height of Thatcherism with the help of the GLC.

Many of the most effective forms of public services were invented and enacted at a local level before a wider application. Finsbury council in London built the Finsbury Health Centre in 1938, providing healthcare free at the point of use, funded from the rates, and utilising the skills of Russian modernist designer Berthold Lubetkin. It provided the model for aspects the NHS. It might be that Lambeth council, if it can succeed in its aim of becoming a truly co-operative council, is a pathfinder for other local authorities.

Summary

Britain needs to rebalance its economy away from financial services and towards manufacturing, especially in the hi-tech and 'green' sectors. This requires a thriving private sector, with innovative firms and imaginative entrepreneurs. Britain needs wealth creators and risk takers. But there needs to be another shift – away from purely profit-driven firms, and towards enterprises run in the interests of the workforce, customers, communities and the environment.

The free market cannot ensure that each region and nation of the UK shares in economic growth. Last time the Tories were in power, the north–south divide grew into a chasm. Cities such as Liverpool, Manchester, Leeds and Newcastle suffered. In many parts of the country, from Bristol to Brixton, there were urban riots. By abolishing the regional development agencies (RDAs), the government has shown that it intends to repeat the same pattern. An important role for a government committed to equality is to ensure balance between north and south, and between different regions and nations within the UK.

People's assets are key to their future success. That's why the Labour government introduced the child trust fund, and why it is short sighted for the Conservative-led government to abolish it for the next generation. Raising incomes maintains or creates more consumption, but assets change the ways people behave, think and view their future. Labour must address the question of individual as well as community assets, and seek ways for the poorest people to build up assets over a generation.

Short-term profit-seeking is what created the financial crisis. Long-term mutualism is what will get us out of it and prevent it from happening again. The only way to move to a mutual economy is to take baby steps. Across each sector, in each industry, trade or service, in each locality, co-ops and mutuals must be allowed to establish themselves, grow and develop. There will be mistakes and failures. Public opinion must be marshalled onside at each stage. Nationalisation failed because the Labour Party imposed it for reasons of theology, when the public could see its practical limits had been reached. Aspects of privatisation have been successful and do not need to be reversed, such as telecoms. But by the time the Tories privatised the railways, they were driven by ideology, not common sense.

A radical Labour programme of mutualising the British economy – neither privatisation nor nationalisation but 'socialisation' – could start on a small scale and gain momentum. After all, it was only the experience gained within government that emboldened the Thatcherites. As Larry Elliott has written:

> There was little evidence that Mrs Thatcher quickly saw the possibilities of privatisation. The idea was not a feature of the 1979 Conservative manifesto, and the sell-offs between 1979 and 1983 were small-scale and tentative. The Thatcher government decided to offload companies such as Amersham International, which it saw no reason for the state to own, but in 1983 the structure of British industry was much the same as it had been in 1979.

Only if people have genuine ownership of, and a democratic stake in, the institutions and organisations that shape their lives, from schools to colleges, from hospitals to parks, from their homes to the companies they work for, can they be true citizens in a real democracy. If power lies in hands other than your own, you are not truly free.

Conclusion: Things can only get worse

'When the Labour Party loses power, the sequel is a rigorous, and in some quarters venomous, examination of the defects of the fallen government. There are accusations of missed opportunities, broken promises, decisions and policies that outraged the tenets of socialism, and in particular indifference to – or indeed defiance of – the opinions of the party rank and file and the resolutions of party conferences. Thus it was in 1951 and in 1970, and in 1979 it happened again.'

Mervyn Jones, *Michael Foot* (1994)

Since 1945, the Labour Party has left office four times: in 1951, 1970, 1979 and 2010.

In 1951 Clement Attlee went to the country just eighteen months after Labour had won a slender majority of five, in the expectation of increasing Labour's majority in Parliament. Instead, despite polling more votes than in 1950, and a quarter of a million more votes than the Conservatives, Labour lost the election. Labour did not win again until 1964, with the leader after the leader that replaced the leader that lost (Attlee resigned in 1955 and was replaced by Hugh Gaitskell, who died in 1960 and was replaced in turn by Harold Wilson). The 1950s were a decade characterised by Labour infighting between left and right, with nationalisation and nuclear disarmament as the main *casus belli*.

When Labour lost in 1970, after success in the 1964 and 1966 elections, it came as something of a shock. The opinion polls pointed to a Labour lead of over 10 points, but on the day Edward Heath's Conservatives won a majority of thirty-one seats. In retrospect, Labour should not have been so confident of victory. Sterling had been devalued in 1967. The government attempted to reform trade union laws, with Barbara Castle's *In Place of Strife*, but she was left isolated and forced into a retreat. Britain's application to join the EEC was vetoed. Wilson's backing for US intervention in Vietnam was opposed by many on the left. Young people over eighteen had the vote for the first time. Labour lost fifteen by-elections in a row from 1966 to 1970. It was not the firmest of foundations for electoral success. The party remained united, although on a leftward slide, after 1970, supporting Wilson to continue as leader. The party was re-elected four years later.

The defeat in 1979 was followed by a period of near-suicide, with factions fighting over the true meaning of socialism, ministers denounced as traitors, Trotskyists running amok inside the party and unions, and the party conference adopting increasingly left-wing policies. Tens of thousands of Labour voters deserted the party, especially in the south. Labour MPs deserted the party to join the Social Democratic Party. When the time came for the 1983 general election, Labour's behaviour since its defeat had so repulsed the voters that they rejected it with more force than in 1979. In 1983, Labour lost 9.5 per cent of its vote and 119 deposits (in one-fifth of the seats it contested). It came third in 292 seats. This, against the backcloth of four million people unemployed and industrial output down to a level last seen in 1967.

Austin Mitchell MP described it as 'four years in the death of the Labour Party' in a book of the same name. It is worth remembering that the Conservatives won the election despite cuts to public expenditure and rising unemployment. Labour would not win for another eighteen years, after three leaders had been and gone (Foot, Kinnock and Smith).

The lessons from history seem to be that if Labour can avoid fratricidal warfare or a lurch to the left, then periods in opposition can be short lived, as in 1970–74. If Labour decides to turn on itself, like an injured animal gnawing at its wounds, the result is a long period out of government.

Labour's first months in opposition after the defeat of 2010 suggested that it had learned the lessons from 1951 and 1979. The leadership election, whilst at times robust, avoided rancour. There was not the outpouring of anger towards the Labour Cabinet that had occurred in 1951 and 1979. Labour activists' anger, if there was any, was directed at the Conservatives and, with particular venom, at the Liberal Democrats for their role in the public sector cuts. Over 25,000 people joined the Labour Party in the first months after the election. Local Labour parties, many without a Labour MP for the first time in over a decade, hunkered down and prepared for council elections, elections in Scotland and Wales, and a general election, whenever it might come.

Becoming an effective opposition

The first pressing task for Labour was to become an effective opposition party, capable of exposing the weaknesses in the Conservative-led government, creating a counter-narrative to the one being spun by ministers and uniting the anti-government forces in the country. In the immediate aftermath of defeat, the Labour Party in Parliament organised around the old Cabinet, which formed shadow teams. Four of the five leadership contenders were shadow Cabinet ministers, which added impetus to their campaigning against the government. Elections were held for select committee positions and, under Labour Party rules, for the shadow Cabinet.

Opposition is a cruel, grinding, fatiguing business. If faced with a government with a working majority, it is soul-destroying for former ministers to watch their cherished legislation and achievements, carefully negotiated through Cabinet committees and won on the floor of the House, being demolished by their opponents. In the officials' box under the press gallery, as close to the chamber as you can get without being an MP, civil servants can see those former ministers they so recently worked for. They don't smile and wave.

In early July 2010, Labour MPs kept their Conservative and Liberal opponents up half the night debating the rise in VAT. If they were going to break their election promises, Labour MPs wanted the Liberal Democrats to suffer for it, if only from sleep deprivation. The terrible futility of their role in the coming years dawned on the newly elected Labour MPs. Parliamentary ambushes, clever amendments, a decent speech or two, close scrutiny and parliamentary questions designed to embarrass ministers.

For the Labour Party, the job of opposition becomes one of policy documents, statements from the National Executive Committee and national policy forum, and mini-manifestos. The focus becomes the paperwork, because there are no departments to run. I have a shelf-ful of policy documents produced by the Labour Party under Foot, Kinnock and Smith, none of which came close to being implemented. That's the reality of opposition: thankless, soulless and ultimately pointless unless it contributes to the return of your party to government.

Labour will need to learn quickly how to be an effective opposition. Effective Labour opposition politicians – such as Robin Cook – learned that the rapier is deadlier than the blunderbuss. Forensic dissection can strike harder than bombast. For all the shouting at Margaret Thatcher, she remained hegemonic, and nearly destroyed the Labour Party along the way. Keir Hardie once said that socialism does not come by shouting. It was a lesson that Labour in the 1980s took a while to learn.

This time, Labour will need to run an opposition in a manner that makes it look like an alternative, preferable government, not sore losers. A new leader must fashion a new team. Just as Neil

Kinnock nurtured Gordon Brown and Tony Blair, giving them important roles in the shadow Cabinet, so the new leader must identify the next generation and give them space to develop. He or she should not rely on the old guard. Senior ministers from the last government must be prepared to step aside and let a new generation come to the fore. Within the new parliament are the next generation of Labour Cabinet ministers and future prime ministers. Of the 2010 intake, any Labour leader must look at, for example, former Bank of England economist Rachel Reeves, Barrow & Furness MP John Woodcock, ex-lawyer Jonathan Reynolds, the former mayor of Waltham Forest, Stella Creasy, and 'retread' MP Stephen Twigg, and see potential Cabinet ministers. The balance will have to be struck between those elected in the shadow Cabinet elections and those appointed to their frontbench teams. There should be space too on the front bench for 'left' MPs such as John Cryer and Jon Cruddas.

There may be a temptation to oppose for opposition's sake. It should be avoided. If the Conservative government is proposing sensible measures, such as fixed-term parliaments (which Kinnock called for in 1992), then Labour should be seen to be putting the national interest above party politics. This is especially true on the conduct of the war in Afghanistan, and measures to combat Islamist terror plots. Labour's approach to opposition should be measured, with an eye on how it appears in the country, not in Parliament. Shrillness and hyperbole win no votes.

The period ahead

Making political predictions in print is always a tricky business. The Conservative-led coalition government has stated its aim as a five-year parliament. Will it run the course? Any government can survive Cabinet-level resignations. Gordon Brown survived several in a week. If Chris Huhne, Vince Cable and Danny Alexander decided to up sticks, the government could carry on. If Nick Clegg decided to take his party out of coalition, Cameron could survive at the head of a minority government. After the referendum on the alternative vote in May 2011, whichever way it goes, Clegg's own party may put pressure on to withdraw from the coalition. But if the Liberal Democrats can remain in a government which increases VAT and makes deep cuts in public spending, they seem likely to remain in office. They have the taste for ministerial life. It's hard to relinquish willingly.

It is entirely possible that the Liberal Democrats' reward for loyal service to the Conservative-led government will be to facilitate a Conservative victory at the election in 2015. The endgame for Cameron is a Conservative government with a working majority, not another five years of coalition.

If he wins, Cameron may offer one or two posts in a Conservative Cabinet to his former Liberal Democrat allies. But the Liberal Democrat party, already under strain, would see that as collaboration, not coalition. Clegg reminds me of Colonel Nicholson, the character played by Alec Guinness in *The Bridge on the River Kwai*. He sets his men, British prisoners of war, to work on the Burma railway for their Japanese captors. His desire to do a good job outweighs his duty to sabotage the Japanese war effort. Only at the end of the film does he realise the folly of his collaboration, and utters his final words: 'What have I done?' Looking around at the wreckage in five years' time, with Cameron back in Number 10 as prime minister of a majority Tory government, Clegg may well echo those words.

Uniting the centre-left

The Liberal Democrats are a complex party, gathering under their yellow banner a full spectrum of political opinion, from left-wing social democrats who used to be in the Labour Party, to radical Liberals in the Lloyd George mould, to economic liberals clustered around *The Orange Book*, published in 2004, which called for the end of the NHS as a tax-funded institution. The Liberal Democrats, as a party in full co-operation with the Conservatives, have vacated the centre and centre-left ground in politics. This presents Labour with a once-in-a-lifetime opportunity to camp itself firmly on the centre and centre-left of politics. On issues like constitutional reform, climate change, Europe, public service reform and international development, Labour can make the political weather and attract new support, not least from former Lib Dem supporters who feel betrayed and disgusted by their former party's actions in government. The person who daubed the word 'whores' on the windows of the Liberal Democrat offices in Putney in May 2010 spoke for thousands.

Labour must now work to win over those Liberal Democrat voters who feel politically homeless. Like the creatures in *Animal Farm*, they are pressed up against the glass, watching Liberal Democrats and Tories take assets from the poor and cut care for the vulnerable. They look from Liberal Democrat to Tory, and Tory to Liberal Democrat, and already it is hard to tell which is which. A third of Liberal Democrat seats – around nineteen – would be won by Labour if one in four people who voted Lib Dem last time vote Labour next time. Thirty Conservative seats would fall to Labour if just one in four Lib Dem voters switched to Labour in those constituencies. Fifty-five Conservative seats would fall to Labour if half of Lib Dem voters switched to Labour in those constituencies. Together with seats taken off the Lib Dems, this could be enough for Labour to win the next election.

There should be a deliberate, targeted outreach programme to Lib Dems, but not at the expense of the outreach programme to the five million people who voted Labour in 1997 and fell away in subsequent elections. Labour as a modern, centrist party, which looks and sounds like people from the communities it represents, with an agenda of giving people control over their own destinies, can win back the support it lost in 2005 and 2010.

Are the Conservatives the party of progress?

David Cameron has restyled his party. He has given it a new logo, new slogans, new policy 'aromas'. He has taken his tie off. He has ring-fenced the NHS and overseas aid. He has brought Modernity along to the party, introduced her to his stuffy friends, and set their hearts aflutter. Cameron has done to the Conservative Party what Sir Norman Foster did to the Reichstag: planted a contemporary design atop a traditional edifice.

A book by academic Tim Bale describes the journey the Conservatives have made since Margaret Thatcher was removed from office twenty years ago, through the Major government's inexorable decline and defeat, into the wilderness with William Hague in his baseball cap, the 'quiet man' Iain Duncan Smith and anti-immigrant Michael Howard, and successful recovery under David Cameron.[1] Bale shows that the Tories before 2005 did just about everything they could to avoid the burdens of office. They bled themselves white in Verdun-like battles over the European Union. They elected leaders that alienated the public. They engaged the kind of dog-whistle politics that might play in Australia but not in Hove. They blamed the voters for not voting Conservative, believing them to be either stupid or hoodwinked by Labour.

Bale describes the 'decontamination' strategy pursued by Cameron after his surprise win in the leadership contest of 2005. Cameron's whole approach is determined by applying commercial marketing methodology to politics. He sees the Conservative Party as a failing brand, and so after 2005 embarks on a PR strategy to rebuild market share. He does his market research to find out what the customers want. Bale writes that Cameron's moment of triumph at the 2005 Tory Party conference was because 'he understood, possibly because of his commercial PR experience, that his appearance had to be a pitch not a speech'. Cameron's leadership has been one long pitch.

There seemed to be a belief within Tory ranks that this is what Tony Blair, Peter Mandelson, Alastair Campbell and Philip Gould did with New Labour after 1994. They have failed to understand that New Labour was not just a marketing device, but an unearthing of the Labour Party's revisionist roots. It was a conscious disentangling of policies from ideology, and the application of timeless values to contemporary problems. New Labour could pray in aid socialist thinkers from Tony Crosland to Richard Tawney. Blair had John Macmurray to guide him (as well as his own Christian socialism).

The Tories have not gone through the same ideological rebirth, merely got a new website. There has been no Clause IV moment under Cameron, only endless recalibration and calculation. Former Conservative Cabinet minister Lord Fowler's book *A Political Suicide* serves as a timely warning to Labour about the dangers of self-indulgence and introspection as much as an account of the Tories' shortcomings. The Conservative Party was so keen to win an election that it was willing to try anything, except fundamental change. Bale quotes a member of a Conservative focus group who puts his finger on it, as only focus group participants can. He 'compared the Tories to a British telephone box, which looks appealing on the outside, but if you open the door it smells really bad'.

Forwards or backwards?

The next generation of socialists has one great advantage over its predecessors. For them, the prospect of a sustained period of Labour in office was an aspiration, but it had never been done. Labour in the twentieth century achieved great things: the welfare state, the NHS, the Open University, but lengthy periods of office always eluded them. From 1900 to 1997, Labour was in office for a total of twenty-one years, and in opposition for seventy-six years. Compared to the socialist parties of France, Germany or Sweden, the British Labour Party was fantastically unsuccessful.

The next generation of socialists does not have to suffer endless conferences debating 'Can Labour win?'. The experience of 1997,

2001 and 2005 shows that Labour can win parliamentary majorities and form governments which can last for a decade. The debate shifts from 'whether' to 'how' Labour should win, and how it should govern. Labour might be out of office for a matter of months; it might be for a decade or more. Either way, the task for the party now is to avoid the self-indulgence for which it won medals in the 1980s, and to focus on the needs of the country.

True to its values, inspired by its heroes, radical in its ambitions, the Labour Party can win again. Steeled by the experience of the last few years, it can be a government which avoids the mistakes of the past, and which transforms the opportunities for people in Britain.

In 1941, with German bombers overhead, and British military defeats all around, George Orwell wrote his personal socialist manifesto, *The Lion and the Unicorn*. I have a little hardback first edition of the book in front of me, bearing the stamp of Ruskin College Library, Oxford. The final lines are these:

> The heirs of Nelson and Cromwell are not in the House of Lords. They are in the fields and in the streets, in the factories and the armed forces, in the four-ale bar and the suburban back garden; and at present they are still kept under by a generation of ghosts. Compared to the task of bringing the real England to the surface, even the winning of the war, necessary though that it is, is secondary. By revolution we become more ourselves, not less. There is no question of stopping short, striking a compromise, salvaging 'democracy', standing still. Nothing ever stands still. We must add to our heritage or lose it, we must grow greater or grow less, we must go forward or go backward. I believe in England, and I believe that we shall go forward.

About the author

Paul Richards was born in 1967 in the East Riding of Yorkshire. He grew up in Buckinghamshire, and went to school in Amersham. In 1986, he became a student at Salford University, where he chaired the Labour Club. In 1990 he was elected chair of the National Organisation of Labour Students (NOLS).

In 1991 Paul was appointed researcher to the Rt Hon. Ann Taylor MP, then shadow Cabinet minister for environmental protection. After a short period as a Labour Party press officer, he worked for various bodies, including the Royal National Institute for Deaf People (RNID) and the Association of County Councils. Paul was an executive member of the Labour Co-ordinating Committee, a modernising pressure group. He is one of the founders of *Progress* magazine.

Paul was Labour's candidate for Billericay in 1997, and he stood in Lewes in 2001. He served for many years on the Fabian Society executive, and was national chair 2002–3. Paul was a special adviser at the Department of Health, the Cabinet Office and the Department for Communities and Local Government.

Paul's previous books are *Be Your Own Spin Doctor* (1998) and *How to Win an Election* (2001), and he edited *Tony Blair in His Own Words* (2004).

Paul Richards is married to Sarah, and they have two sons, Alexander and Oliver. They live in East Sussex by the sea.

Notes

Preface

1. Andrew Rawnsley, *The End of the Party* (2009).

Chapter 1: All the way for this?

1. 'Gordon Brown ditches respect agenda on youth crime', *The Times*, 11 January 2008.
2. Peter Watt, *Inside Out* (2010).
3. Polly Toynbee, *The Guardian*, 11 April 2008.
4. Gordon Brown, *The Times*, 2 June 2008.
5. *Next Left*, July 2009.

Chapter 2: The election campaign

1. Martin Kettle, Comment Is Free, Guardian website, 12 March 2008.
2. Douglas Alexander, interview in *The Guardian*, 19 February 2010.
3. Marina Hyde, *The Guardian,* 22 April 2010
4. Ed Balls
5. Caroline Badley, Labour List.
6. *Guardian*, 21 May 2010

Chapter 3: The election result

1. George Orwell, *The Lion and the Unicorn* (1941).
2. Liam Byrne MP, 'Why Did Labour Lose – and How Can We Win Again?', *Progress* 2010

Chapter 4: Voices and inspirations

1. E. P. Thompson, *The Making of the English Working Class* (1963).
2. Greg Rosen, *Serving the People* (2007).
3. William Morris, *How I Became a Socialist* (1896).
4. Ibid.
5. Karl Marx, *The German Question* (1846).
6. William Morris, *The Earthly Paradise* (1868).
7. Tony Benn, 'The Moral Basis of the Radical Left', Tawney Lecture, Christian Socialist Movement, 1988.
8. R. H. Tawney, *Equality* (1931).
9. Ross Terrill, *R. H. Tawney and His Times* (1974).
10. G. D. H. Cole, *A Century of Co-operation* (1944).
11. Margaret Cole, *Growing Up into Revolution* (1949).
12. Sonia Orwell and Ian Angus (eds), *The Collected Essays, Journalism and Letters of George Orwell, vol. 1: An Age like This, 1945–1950* (1968).
13. George Orwell, *The Road to Wigan Pier* (1937).
14. Equality and Public Service Speech to the British Association for the Advancement of Science, 11 September 2000.

Chapter 5: Labour's values

1. Bernard Crick *Low Cost Socialism* (1997).
2. Tony Blair, 'Socialism', Fabian Society lecture, 1994.
3. Quoted in Jack Straw, *Policy and Ideology* (1993).

Chapter 6: Liberty

1. Clement Attlee, *The Labour Party in Perspective* (1937).
2. Ronald Reagan, Farewell Address.
3. Quoted in Bernard Crick, *Socialism* (1987).
4. Margaret Thatcher, *The Path to Power* (1995).
5. John Ranelagh, *Thatcher's People* (1991).
6. Quoted in Greg Rosen, *Old Labour to New: The Dreams that Inspired, the Battles that Divided* (2005).
7. R. H. Tawney, *Equality* (1931).
8. R. H. Tawney, 'We Mean Freedom', in *'The Attack' and Other Papers* (1953).

Chapter 7: Equality

1. Quoted in Roy Hattersley, *Choose Freedom* (1987).
2. Quoted in Margaret Drabble, *Case for Equality* (1988).
3. *The Keir Hardie Calendar.*
4. Bernard Crick, *Low Cost Socialism* (1997).
5. Anthony Crosland, *Socialism Now* (1974).
6. Department for Business, Innovation and Skills, *Unleashing Aspiration: The Government Response to the Final Report of the Panel on Fair Access to the Professions* (2010)
7. George Orwell, *The Lion and the Unicorn* (1941).

Chapter 8: Community

1. William Morris, *News from Nowhere* (1891).
2. Bernard Crick, 'Introduction', in George Orwell, *The Lion and the Unicorn* ([1941] 1982).
3. Robert D. Putnam, *Bowling Alone* (2000).
4. Bernard Crick, *Socialist Values and Time* (1984).

5. J. S. Mill, quoted in Carole Pateman, *Participation and Democratic Theory* (1970).

6. G. D. H. Cole, quoted ibid.

Chapter 9: The case for revisionism

1. Anthony Crosland, *A Social-democratic Britain* (1971).

2. David Lipsey and Dick Leonard (eds), *The Socialist Agenda* (1981).

3. Quoted in Brian Brivati, *Hugh Gaitskell* (1996).

4. Quoted in Philip M. Williams, *Hugh Gaitskell* (1979).

5. Quoted in Harold Wilson, *The Relevance of British Socialism* (1964).

6. Quoted in Brivati, *Gaitskell*.

7. David Lipsey, *The Name of the Rose* (1992).

8. Profile of Alan Milburn in *The Guardian*, 12 June 2003.

9. Joe Haines, *The Politics of Power* (1977).

Chapter 10: Democracy and decentralisation

1. A. H. Halsey, *Change in British Society*, quoted in *Socialism and Decentralisation* (1984).

2. G. D. H. Cole, *A History of Socialist Thought*, 5 vols (1953–60).

3. Richard Crossman, *Socialism and the New Despotism* (1955).

4. *Socialism and Decentralisation* (1984).

5. Quoted in Bernard Crick, *George Orwell* (1980).

Chapter 12: Creating a democratic politics

1. Quoted in Ross Terrill, *R. H. Tawney and His Times: Socialism as Fellowship* (1973).

2. David Miliband, *Re-Inventing the Left* (1994).

3. Ralph Miliband, *Parliamentary Socialism* (1961).

4. Teddy Roosevelt, speech, Ohio.

5. Bernard Crick, *Education for Citizenship and the Teaching of Democracy in Schools* (1998).

6. Anthony Crosland, *Socialism Now* (1974).

7. Tony Benn, *Arguments for Socialism* (1981).

Chapter 13: Creating a fairer society

1. Equality Trust website.

2. Daniel Dorling, *Injustice* (2010).

3. Charles Webster, *The National Health Service* (1998).

4. Brian Abel-Smith, *Fabian Essays in Socialist Thought* (1984).

5. R. H. Tawney, quoted in Fabian Commission on Life Chances and Child Poverty, *Why Life Chances Matter* (2005).

6. Social Exclusion Unit, *A New Commitment to Neighbourhood Renewal* (2001).

Chapter 14: Creating a mutual economy

1. Quoted in David Blunkett and Bernard Crick, *The Labour Party's Aims and Values: An Unofficial Statement* (1988).

2. Labour Party, *A Future Fair for All* (2010).

Conclusion

1. Tim Bale, *The Conservative Party from Thatcher to Cameron* (2010).

Index